W.H. Auden

W.H. Auden has become one of the most influential writers of the twentieth century, famous for his political engagement as well as his distinctive style. Tony Sharpe's fresh and jargon-free readings will engage students new to Auden's work and those wishing to refresh their existing knowledge of this major poet.

This guide to Auden's poetry offers:

- an accessible introduction to the contexts and many interpretations of Auden's texts, from first publication to the present day
- an introduction to key critical texts and perspectives on Auden's life and work, situated in a broader critical history
- cross-references between sections of the guide, in order to suggest links between texts, contexts and criticism
- suggestions for further reading.

Part of the *Routledge Guides to Literature* series, this volume is essential reading for all those beginning detailed study of Auden and seeking not only a guide to his works but also a way through the wealth of contextual and critical material that surrounds them.

Tony Sharpe is Senior Lecturer and former head of English and Creative Writing at Lancaster University. He is the author of well-reviewed studies of Vladimir Nabokov, T.S. Eliot and Wallace Stevens, alongside various essays in books and journals reflecting his research interest in modern poetry.

Routledge Guides to Literature

Routledge Guides to Literature offer clear introductions to the most widely studied authors and texts. Each book engages with texts, contexts and criticism, highlighting the range of critical views and contextual factors that need to be taken into consideration in advanced studies of literary works. The series encourages informed but independent readings of texts by ranging as widely as possible across the contextual and critical issues relevant to the works examined, rather than presenting a single interpretation. Alongside general guides to texts and authors, the series includes 'sourcebooks', which allow access to reprinted contextual and critical materials as well as annotated extracts of primary text.

Already available*:

Geoffrey Chaucer by Gillian Rudd
Ben Jonson by James Loxley
William Shakespeare's The Merchant of Venice: A Sourcebook edited by S.P. Cerasano
William Shakespeare's King Lear: A Sourcebook edited by Grace Ioppolo
William Shakespeare's Othello: A Sourcebook edited by Andrew Hadfield
William Shakespeare's Macbeth: A Sourcebook edited by Alexander Leggatt
William Shakespeare's Hamlet: A Sourcebook edited by Sean McEvoy
John Milton by Richard Bradford
John Milton's Paradise Lost: A Sourcebook edited by Margaret Kean
Alexander Pope by Paul Baines
Jonathan Swift's Gulliver's Travels: A Sourcebook edited by Roger D. Lund
Mary Wollstonecraft's A Vindication of the Rights of Woman: A Sourcebook edited by Adriana Craciun
Jane Austen by Robert P. Irvine
Jane Austen's Emma: A Sourcebook edited by Paula Byrne
Jane Austen's Pride and Prejudice: A Sourcebook edited by Robert Morrison
Byron, by Caroline Franklin
Mary Shelley's Frankenstein: A Sourcebook edited by Timothy Morton
The Poems of John Keats: A Sourcebook edited by John Strachan
The Poems of Gerard Manley Hopkins: A Sourcebook edited by Alice Jenkins
Charles Dickens's David Copperfield: A Sourcebook edited by Richard J. Dunn
Charles Dickens's Bleak House: A Sourcebook edited by Janice M. Allan
Charles Dickens's Oliver Twist: A Sourcebook edited by Juliet John
Charles Dickens's A Tale of Two Cities: A Sourcebook edited by Ruth Glancy

* Some titles in this series were first published in the Routledge Literary Sourcebooks series, edited by Duncan Wu, or the Complete Critical Guide to Literature series, edited by Jan Jedrzejewski and Richard Bradford.

Herman Melville's Moby-Dick: A Sourcebook edited by Michael J. Davey
Harriet Beecher Stowe's Uncle Tom's Cabin: A Sourcebook edited by Debra J. Rosenthal
Walt Whitman's Song of Myself: A Sourcebook and Critical Edition edited by Ezra Greenspan
Robert Browning by Stefan Hawlin
Henrik Ibsen's Hedda Gabler: A Sourcebook edited by Christopher Innes
George Eliot by Jan Jedrzejewski
Thomas Hardy by Geoffrey Harvey
Thomas Hardy's Tess of the d'Urbervilles edited by Scott McEathron
Charlotte Perkins Gilman's The Yellow Wallpaper: A Sourcebook and Critical Edition edited by Catherine J. Golden
Kate Chopin's The Awakening: A Sourcebook edited by Janet Beer and Elizabeth Nolan
Edith Wharton's The House of Mirth by Janet Beer, Pamela Knights and Elizabeth Nolan
Joseph Conrad by Tim Middleton
The Poems of W.B. Yeats: A Sourcebook edited by Michael O'Neill
E.M. Forster's A Passage to India: A Sourcebook edited by Peter Childs
D.H. Lawrence by Fiona Becket
Samuel Beckett by David Pattie
W.H. Auden by Tony Sharpe
Richard Wright's Native Son by Andrew Warnes
J.D. Salinger's The Catcher in the Rye by Sarah Graham
Ian McEwan's Enduring Love by Peter Childs
Arundhati Roy's The God of Small Things by Alex Tickell
Angela Carter's Nights at the Circus by Helen Stoddart

For my parents

W.H. Auden

Tony Sharpe

LONDON AND NEW YORK

First published 2007
by Routledge
2 Park Square, Milton Park, Abingdon, Oxon, OX14 4RN

Simultaneously published in the USA and Canada
by Routledge
270 Madison Ave, New York, NY 10016

Routledge is an imprint of the Taylor & Francis Group, an informa business

Typeset in Sabon and Gill Sans by RefineCatch Limited, Bungay, Suffolk
Printed and bound in Great Britain by
The Cromwell Press, Trowbridge, Wiltshire

British Library Cataloguing in Publication Data
A catalogue record for this book is available from the British Library.

Library of Congress Cataloging in Publication Data
Sharpe, Tony, 1952–
W.H. Auden / Tony Sharpe.
p. cm.—(Routledge guides to literature)
Includes bibliographical references.
1. Auden, W.H. (Wystan Hugh), 1907–1973—Handbooks, manuals, etc.
I. Title
PR6001.U4Z82 2007
811′.52—dc22
2007008405

ISBN10: 0–415–32735–0 (hbk)
ISBN10: 0–415–32736–9 (pbk)
ISBN10: 0–203–35874–0 (ebk)

ISBN13: 978–0–415–32735–0 (hbk)
ISBN13: 978–0–415–32736–7 (pbk)
ISBN13: 978–0–203–35874–0 (ebk)

Contents

Acknowledgements ix
Abbreviations x

Introduction **xiii**

1: Life and contexts **1**

Life 1

English Auden 1
Post-English Auden 4

The literary context 8
The historical context 13

Signs of the times: poetry and politics 13
Auden 'in our time': the Great War, the General Strike, economic slump 16
England, their England 19
An age of anxiety – and Auden's response 22
Looking beyond this island: to Iceland, Spain, China and the USA 25

The personal context 28

Family; sexuality; education 28
Auden's fantasy world 31
Ideas, ideology and Christianity 33

2: Works **39**

Auden's books of poetry 40

Poems (1930) 40
The Orators (1932) 43

Look, Stranger! (1936) 49
Letters from Iceland (1937); *Journey to a War* (1939) 52
A note on Auden as dramatist 54
Another Time (1940) 55
The Double Man; *New Year Letter* (1941) 56
For the Time Being (1944) 58
The Age of Anxiety (1947) 59
Nones (1951) 61
The Shield of Achilles (1955) 63
Homage to Clio (1960) 63
About the House (1965) 65
City Without Walls (1969); *Epistle to a Godson* (1972); *Thank You, Fog* (1974) 65

Poems individually considered 67

'The Watershed' 67
'The Letter' 69
'The Secret Agent' 71
'1929' 72
'Consider' 76
'A Summer Night', 'On This Island' 78
'Lullaby' 82
'Spain', 'In Time of War', 'September 1, 1939' 84
'Musée des Beaux Arts', 'The Shield of Achilles' 91
'In Memory of W.B. Yeats', 'The Sea and the Mirror' 94
'In Praise of Limestone', 'Amor Loci' 98
'Horae Canonicae', 'Bucolics', 'Thanksgiving for a Habitat' 101

3: Criticism 110

Critical contours: Auden and his readers 110
Critical perspectives 117

Inventing Auden and the 1930s 117
Auden and others 124
Early Auden – later Auden 128
Auden theorised 132
Poets' Auden 136

Chronology 142
Further reading 149
Select bibliography 153
Index 158

Acknowledgements

The publisher and author would like to thank the following for permission to reprint material under copyright:

Extracts from W.H. Auden, *The English Auden: Poems, Plays and Dramatic Writings, 1927–1939; Prose, Vol II: 1939–1948; Collected Poems, Prose and Travel Books in Prose and Verse Vol I: 1925–1938*, by permission of Faber and Faber Ltd.

'Cover' from *The Age of Anxiety* by W.H. Auden. © copyright 1947 by W.H. Auden and renewed 1975 by Monroe K. Spears and William Meredith, executors of the Estate of W.H. Auden. Used by permission of Random House, Inc.

'As It Seemed to Us', © copyright 1943, 1945, 1955, 1959, 1960, 1962, 1963, 1964, 1965, 1966, 1967, 1968, 1969, 1970, 1971, 1972, 1973 by W.H. Auden. Originally appeared in *The New Yorker*, from *Forewords and Afterwords* by W.H. Ayden selected by Edward Mendelson. Used by permission of Random House.

'The Public vs The Late Mr William Butler Yeats', W.H. Auden. Copyright © 1939 by W.H. Auden. Reprinted by permission of Curtis Brown Ltd.

Every effort has been made to trace and contact copyright holders. The publishers would be pleased to hear from any copyright holders not acknowledged here, so that this acknowledgement page may be amended at the earliest opportunity.

Abbreviations

AS I, *AS* II, *AS* III:	*Auden Studies* vols I, II, III – see Bibliography, under Bucknell
AtH:	W.H. Auden, *About the House*, London: Faber, 1966
C&HK:	*Christopher and His Kind* – see Bibliography, under Isherwood
CDLCP:	C. Day-Lewis, *The Complete Poems*, introduced by Jill Balcon, London: Sinclair-Stevenson, 1992
CW:	W.H. Auden, *A Certain World: A Commonplace Book*, London: Faber, 1970
CWW:	W.H. Auden, *City without Walls*, London: Faber, 1969
DH:	W.H. Auden, *The Dyer's Hand and Other Essays*, London: Faber, 1963
EA:	*The English Auden: Poems, Essays and Dramatic Writings 1927–1939*, ed. Edward Mendelson, London: Faber, 1977
Early A:	*Early Auden* – see Bibliography, under Mendelson (1981)
EF:	W.H. Auden, *The Enchafèd Flood*, London: Faber, 1951
EG:	W.H. Auden, *Epistle to a Godson*, London: Faber, 1972
F&A:	W.H. Auden, *Forewords and Afterwords*, selected by Edward Mendelson, London: Faber, 1973
FTB:	W.H. Auden, *For the Time Being*, London: Faber, 1945
HtC:	W.H. Auden, *Homage to Clio*, London: Faber, 1960
Juv:	*W.H. Auden: Juvenilia* – see Bibliography, under Bucknell (2003)
LA:	*Later Auden* – see Bibliography, under Mendelson (1999)
N:	W.H. Auden, *Nones*, London: Faber, 1952
NYL:	W.H. Auden, *New Year Letter*, London: Faber, 1941
Plays:	W.H. Auden and Christopher Isherwood, *Plays and Other Dramatic Writings, 1928–1938*, ed. Mendelson, London: Faber, 1989
P I:	W.H. Auden, *Prose and Travel Books in Prose and Verse, Vol. I: 1926–1938*, ed. Mendelson, London: Faber 1996
P II:	W.H. Auden, *Prose, Vol. II: 1939–1948*, ed. Mendelson, London: Faber, 2002
SA:	W.H. Auden, *The Shield of Achilles*, London: Faber, 1955
SP:	*W.H. Auden: Selected Poems*, ed. Mendelson, London: Faber, 1979

Tribute: *W.H. Auden: A Tribute* – see Bibliography, under Spender (1975)
WHACP: *W.H. Auden: Collected Poems*, ed. Mendelson, New York: Vintage International, 1991
WWW: *World within World* – see Bibliography, under Spender (1951)

Cross-referencing

Cross-referencing between sections is a feature of each volume in the Routledge Guides to Literature series. Cross-references appear in brackets and include section titles as well as the relevant page numbers in bold type, e.g. (see Life and contexts, **pp. 14–15**).

Introduction

W.H. Auden is an important poet whose work has at various junctures challenged, intrigued, amazed, offended, gratified and disappointed his readership, sometimes by being cleverer than us, at others by seeming less serious than we suppose ourselves to be. His canon has been provokingly inconstant, flouting any notions of art's monumental fixity: he subjected poems to authorial revision or derision, even to complete suppression. Any critical summary of his career, therefore, risks offering a sedatively reasoned account of something which was in many aspects unshapely and unreasonable.

I may not have been able entirely to avoid writing such a book, since its elements conspire to impose narrative shape: divided into three parts, it focuses on Auden's life and times, on his successive volumes of poetry and a range of individual poems, and on the critical responses. The reader I have principally envisaged in writing it is one either coming to grips with Auden for the first time, or refreshing an acquaintance that has staled (which does not, therefore, exclude the jaded scholar); and I hope that by the end of it such a reader will have found justification for an excitement with Auden's work, a way of formulating that interest, and the means of taking it further. In the first section, I have tried to imagine what my reader needs to know, in order to establish the broad contours of the career and the debates it has engendered; the core lies in the second section, which outlines the nature and impact of Auden's individual volumes of verse, and offers what I hope will be experienced as fresh readings of poems, some of which (in certain cases to his dismay) have become trusty anthology pieces. I present a variety of critical perspectives in which his work has been considered, in hope that this will incite closer exploration of those found stimulating; I do not, of course, invariably agree with the critics I examine, and on occasions I cite a critical formula that does not obviously support my own position, in order to suggest how discussion might be extended or a particular issue differently perceived. Auden continues to be the object of sustained attention within universities and, interestingly, in the world beyond (evidenced by the frequency with which he is referred to in newspaper articles not directly concerned with poetry); his approaching centenary makes it certain that more critical studies will appear, so the final section does not aim at an exhaustiveness that could only be momentary.

The majority of the poems I discuss are to be found in the *Selected Poems* (ed. Mendelson), which is the text likeliest to be on readers' shelves; this prints the first stabilised versions of the poems included, and in that conforms to my own scholarly preference. I have also been guided by some words of William Carlos Williams at a poetry reading, when he declared 'You should never explain a poem, but it always helps, nevertheless.' Although, naturally, I hope a reader will find my discussions interesting and helpful, they are not intended to displace either close acquaintance with a poem itself or that reader's own response to it; they are certainly not intended to exhaust poetry in explanation, and if my reading provokes strong disagreement, then that, equally, can be a means of clarifying response. Constraints of space have combined with the voluminousness of Auden's output to enforce difficult but necessary omissions, some with a high element of self-denial; I have also omitted close attention to the dramas and the work in prose. I hope enough remains not to misrepresent the career, and to suggest why Auden continues to be valued; I shall certainly have failed if I do not communicate something of my own enthusiasm for his work.

This book is part of a larger project of research, during which I have studied Auden material in libraries great (the British Library, the Bodleian, the Berg Collection at New York Public Library) and smaller (Carlisle City Library); to all I am grateful, as to Lancaster University for enabling it. I should also pay tribute to my wife Jane and our children Eva and Ned, who have found themselves – sometimes unwittingly – conscripted into forays down lead-mines and up the obscure valleys of Auden country, here in his favourite North of England. The book's dedication falls short of repaying an unquantifiable debt.

Tony Sharpe
2006

1

Life and contexts

Life

The first two subsections, on 'English' and 'post-English' Auden, offer a relatively factual account intended to provide an overview of the principal events in Auden's life, which can then inform a reading of the following part, where that life is set successively in its 'literary', 'historical' and 'personal' contexts. The latter two categories are lengthier, and have also been thematically subdivided in hope that such indications of content will be found helpful; these are intended as aids rather than definitions, and I have not wanted to police the boundaries between categories with any dictatorial rigour. Although the book can be read continuously from beginning to end, so as to impart – I trust – a sense of intellectual accumulation in the process, I have also borne in mind the needs of the reader who wishes to use it for purposes of more specific or piecemeal consultation. Whichever kind of reader you are, I hope this book repays the attention you give it, and enhances your engagement with Auden's writing.

English Auden

Born on 21 February 1907, Wystan Hugh Auden was the youngest of three brothers and the last child of his parents George and Constance Auden. His father had a successful medical practice in York, which he nevertheless left the year after Wystan's birth to move to Birmingham, in which city he pursued a distinguished career as School Medical Officer and (additionally, after 1918) Professor of Public Health at Birmingham University. The family were 'High Church' Anglicans who started the day with prayers and, Auden recollected, tended to look down on less elevated forms of Protestantism – a tone which came especially from his mother, who was unusual for her time in having a degree, and who had met her future husband when nursing in a London hospital with a view to joining a Protestant medical mission to Africa. On the outbreak of the Great War in August 1914, George Auden enlisted in the Royal Army Medical Corps and was posted overseas; the family house in Solihull was relinquished, and the war years were spent staying with relatives, friends and in boarding-houses during the holiday periods. In 1915 Auden joined his brother John at preparatory school in Surrey, and although there was much he enjoyed about these nomadic years – which gave him, on holiday in Derbyshire, his first sight of lead-mining country – looking back he thought that his father's long absence, and his own consequent exposure to the influence of his mother, had been decisive factors for him.

At the school in Surrey, Auden first enountered his future friend and collaborator Christopher Isherwood; he remembered Isherwood's wearing a black armband when his father had gone 'missing in action'. George Auden, however, unlike so many fathers of that era, returned from the war, acquiring a house in Harborne, near Birmingham. From 1920 to 1925 Wystan boarded at Gresham's School, Holt, in Norfolk; during this period he became more aware of his homosexual orientation and also had revealed to him, in early spring 1922 during a Sunday afternoon walk with an older boy on whom he had a crush, that what he really wanted to be was a poet and not, as he had hitherto supposed, a mining engineer. Nevertheless, in autumn 1925 he went up to Christ Church, Oxford to read natural sciences, switching briefly to politics, philosophy and economics before settling on English – where he particularly enjoyed the Anglo-Saxon and Old English parts of the course. During this period he became acquainted with some of the aspiring Oxford poets with whom his name would later be linked – Cecil Day-Lewis, Louis MacNeice and Stephen Spender – and also with one for whom his affinity was less remarked and a little more surprising – John Betjeman (whose poetry he would recommend to T.S. Eliot and, later still, introduce to America). He re-met Christopher Isherwood in London, and through him met Edward Upward, Isherwood's friend. At Oxford, Auden further explored his homosexuality, meanwhile acquiring, not without effort, the reputation of being a brilliant eccentric, literary leader and poetic genius. Before the beginning of his final year, Auden had already written the poem subsequently called 'The Watershed', which is the earliest work to survive into his self-selected canon; shortly after his graduation, Stephen Spender privately printed a pamphlet edition of his poetry. Auden's third class honours surprised his friends: in that era there was even a fourth class to signify negligent disdain, nor had he – like Isherwood at Cambridge – deliberately thrown his degree.

This appears to have been a difficult period: not only was his result a disappointment, but Auden was also sufficiently concerned about his homosexuality to undergo in August 1928 some sort of psychoanalysis at Spa, Belgium, intended to correct what he inclined always to believe was 'wrong' with him. He became engaged to be married, like his father before him to a nurse; he had probably already lost his heterosexual virginity (on a trip to Austria in 1926), and there would be later occasions when he proposed marriage or entered into sexual relations with a woman. Despite this, however, when George Auden offered to finance a post-university year, Wystan chose to spend it in Berlin: partly in reaction against the dominant Francophilia that sent so many aspiring artists to Paris, but also because he was allured by the reputed sexual adventurousness of the Weimar Republic's capital. He left for Berlin in October and, apart from short visits back, was in Germany almost continuously until late July 1929, when he returned to England and started looking for a job. For some of this time in Berlin he was joined by Isherwood, whom he had visited during a Christmas break in England. Since meeting up again their friendship had deepened, and Auden regarded Isherwood as an important literary counsellor to whose judgement he deferred, submitting drafts of poems for his approval. As well as this, their relationship became physical: Isherwood's biographer believes Auden to have been the more in love, but they certainly reinforced each other's homosexual inclinations, which for both were confirmed in Berlin. When Auden returned in the summer, one of the first things he did was to break off his engagement.

His father's allowance came to an end, and he needed to earn his living. The new decade opened with the publication in T.S. Eliot's prestigious journal *The Criterion* (January 1930) of Auden's charade 'Paid on Both Sides', written before Berlin but there revised and enlarged. This was a startling debut, in which a saga-like story of feuding families, intermingled with elements derived from Mummers' plays and music-hall, takes place in a geography Auden based on Alston Moor in Cumberland, with whose landscape of decaying lead-mines he had become familiar since 1919 – a fascination he would never entirely outgrow. The individuality of Auden's new talent was further underscored by the publication, that autumn, of his first commercial volume, *Poems* (1930), issued – again under Eliot's *imprimatur* – by Faber & Faber, who would thereafter be his British publisher. This appearance as a poet coincided with his taking up a profession which he found, on the whole, to be unexpectedly congenial: from the summer term of 1930 to the end of the school year 1935 Auden worked as a schoolmaster, first at the Larchfield Academy at Helensburgh near Glasgow, and then, from Autumn 1932, at the Downs School at Colwall near the Malvern Hills. Larchfield, where Auden succeeded his friend Day-Lewis in the job, was then a fading establishment; during his time there he wrote his second book of poetry, *The Orators* (1932), to which the Helensburgh background contributed many details. The Downs School was a Quaker boys' school, and near enough to Cheltenham, where Day-Lewis taught, for the two poets to visit each other. At Colwall, Auden passed what were certainly his happiest years in England, and possibly of his life: the poem later called 'A Summer Night' (1933) commemorates this period.

At this time he was also writing drama, stimulated by an association with Rupert Doone's 'Group Theatre', which aimed at small-scale experimental productions: at one such evening in London, Auden's first play *The Dance of Death* (1934) was performed alongside Eliot's 'Aristophanic melodrama' *Sweeney Agonistes*. Subsequent dramas were the result, sometimes through several versions, of collaboration with Isherwood (*The Dog beneath the Skin*, *The Ascent of F6* and *On the Frontier*; published respectively in 1935, 1936 and 1938); and in the latter part of the decade, Auden was involved in further collaborative ventures. He left his job at the Downs School to work with the GPO Film Unit in London, principally as writer but also in other roles; the most memorable result of this was the short film *Night Mail*, with music by the young Benjamin Britten, at this period very much impressed by Auden. Other collaborations were with Louis MacNeice on their travel book *Letters from Iceland* (1937); and on the book *Journey to a War* (1939), where prose mainly by Isherwood and poetry and photographs by Auden recounted their 1938 travels to the Sino-Japanese conflict taking place. Before then Auden had, at the beginning of 1937, celebratedly if somewhat anticlimactically paid a shorter-than-anticipated visit to the Spanish Civil War, to show sympathy and give support to the anti-Franco forces; the chief literary consequence of this was the poem 'Spain' (May 1937), which he subsequently altered and would eventually exclude altogether from his collected poems.

The dissatisfaction implicit in Auden's retrospective acts of self-censorship is perhaps also to be seen in the restlessness, that so often took him beyond the England in which he established himself as the dominant poetic voice of his generation. During this decade he visited Austria, Yugoslavia, Switzerland, Czechoslovakia, Hungary, Denmark, Portugal, France, Egypt, China, Japan, and the USA, as well as countries already mentioned. His collection *Look, Stranger!* (1936; published as *On This Island* in the USA, 1937) had sold well and been well-received by critics; he had accepted the King's Gold Medal for Poetry from George VI. Having himself been influenced by Eliot, in an era in which a considerable number of aspiring poets were turning out unintentional imitations of the Master's style, Auden was unique in influencing Eliot's poetry in his turn. Despite all this, he was not settled, and he was not personally happy. Evidently he did not feel guilty about or encumbered by his homosexuality, and had love affairs (most notably with the sleeping youth addressed in the 1937 poem subsequently called 'Lullaby'); but the relationships had not lasted, and according to Isherwood, on the last stage of their voyage back from China, Auden had tearfully confessed his fear that he would never be truly loved. On his return Auden spent little time in England, before moving to Brussels for a month, by which stage, according to John Auden who visited him there in September 1938, he had made up his mind to emigrate to the USA: in January 1939 he and Isherwood set sail for New York. Although published after the move to America, his next collection, *Another Time* (1940), containing some of his best-known shorter poems (such as 'Lullaby', 'Musée des Beaux Arts', 'In Memory of W.B. Yeats' and 'September 1, 1939'), really represents the last poetry of his English phase: according to his editor Edward Mendelson, this is suggested by the volume's title.

Post-English Auden

Auden and Isherwood had arrived in cold, snowy New York two days before Yeats's death, which provoked the famous elegy, first published in March 1939. Auden now set to work to establish himself in the new country, earning money by commissioned reviews and articles as well as poetry and by teaching at adult education and college levels. His first volume of poetry written in America was published as *The Double Man* (1941) in New York, and as *New Year Letter* in London – the British title coming from the long poem that was its major component. This 'letter' was addressed to Elizabeth Mayer, whose psychologist husband was a Jewish refugee from Nazi Germany; Auden had met her through Benjamin Britten and Peter Pears, and in her small Long Island house he had enjoyed much-valued hospitality. He and Britten (who spent the early years of the war in the USA) were renewing the collaboration which had previously seen the composer set some Auden poems to music; this time they were attempting something larger, and the fruit was the opera *Paul Bunyan*, which was performed at Columbia University in May 1941, and thereafter sank without very much trace. Britten and Pears briefly shared the chaotic ambiance of the house on 7 Middagh Street, Brooklyn, over which Auden presided; other occupants included the writer Carson McCullers and the stripper Gypsy Rose Lee. This was not for them, however, and they decided to return to wartime England; there then commenced an evident cooling of Britten's regard for Auden, which caused the poet some distress.

In Elizabeth Mayer, Auden felt he had found a surrogate mother; and when his own mother died in 1941, he sent Mrs Mayer a photograph of himself as a baby in Constance's arms, implying the extension of Elizabeth's maternal duties. She was not, however, the most momentous of the new acquaintances he made in America: that person's identity had already been signalled by the dedication of *Another Time*, 'To Chester Kallman'. Auden had met Kallman in April 1939, when the latter attended a reading he gave in New York along with Isherwood and MacNeice, and followed up with a visit to their apartment, ostensibly to undertake an interview for his college magazine. Aged 18, Kallman was fourteen years younger than Auden; the son of a Jewish dentist, his mother had died when he was four, and subsequent stepmothers had treated him coldly. In 1939 he was a good-looking blond, well-read, quick-witted and happy to signal his sexual availability; within a little while Auden had fallen in love, buying gold rings to signify that Kallman represented the love of his life, the person whom he had tearfully told Isherwood he feared never meeting. He wrote excitedly about this new relationship to confidants in England, and his sense of attachment and responsibility, as of a husband to a wife, gave him an additional reason for not returning when war broke out in September 1939. By that stage he and Kallman had undertaken a long bus journey across America, including a stay at the D.H. Lawrence ranch in New Mexico and a visit to Isherwood, now transplanted to California. This was intended as their honeymoon but, notwithstanding, Auden still found time to work on a book of prose called *The Prolific and the Devourer*, partly aphoristic and partly autobiographical; he abandoned it on their return to New York, which they reached just before war was declared in Europe.

A poem such as 'The Prophets' (1939), which represents Kallman as the destined culmination of Auden's boyhood enrapturement with illustrated books of machinery and then landscapes of decayed lead-mining, showed something of the importance its writer attributed to this love. It suggests, also, something of the pressure such expectations would place on a contentedly promiscuous young man; for a short while Auden's happiness in their relationship was unalloyed, as Kallman introduced him to opera as well as to the particular ambiance of his New York Jewish roots, but in July 1941 came a crisis. Auden viewed their relationship as marriage, duly monogamous; but Kallman saw matters differently, and when, that month, the poet confronted him over his infidelity, the young man rebelled, making plain that he was not prepared to submit to any requirement of exclusivity and that, moreover, he would in future not consent to be Auden's sexual partner at all (their particular preferences were not especially compatible, in any case). Despite this calamity, Auden did not renounce his side of the commitment, nor abandon what he saw as the truth of their love; instead, he set himself the task – undertaken at what some observers would feel to be enormous personal cost – of being 'the more loving one', in a relationship that obliged him to tolerate Kallman's promiscuity alongside his inability ever to earn his own living.

The reputation Auden had acquired in England during the 1930s was of a poet committed to the political left; he now wished to withdraw from that arena and write a different kind of poetry, less publicly engaged. His literary reaction to his mother's death came in the form of a 'Christmas oratorio' called *For the Time*

Being, finished in July 1942 but not published until September 1944. Auden had hoped this would be set to music by Britten, but its eventual length made this impractical, and although the composer did set parts of it, his coldness towards Auden was beginning. The oratorio's theological concerns were the emphatic signal of an interior development as momentous as, externally, Auden's crossing of the Atlantic had been: for in 1940, at almost the same time that he had set in motion the process by which he would attain American citizenship six years later, he had also rejoined the 'high' Anglican communion of his childhood (or as near to it as he could come in New York). Soon after finishing this work, Auden began a long poem based on Shakespeare's *The Tempest*, which he wrote during the period when he was teaching at Swarthmore College, Pennsylvania, and spending summers in New York. 'The Sea and the Mirror' was published in *For the Time Being*, and almost simultaneously in August 1944 Auden was starting to work on his next long poem, published three years later. In April 1945 his American publishers, Random House, brought out *The Collected Poetry*, notable for its curt authorial foreword giving voice to the cold eye Auden now cast over much of his earlier work, which he had discontentedly re-read in order to compile the book, and also for his method of arranging poems in alphabetical order of their first line. This was designed to disrupt any assumptions about the nature of his development which over-familiar readers and reviewers might otherwise bring to this first collected volume.

That same month, Auden flew the Atlantic, attached to the US Strategic Bombing Survey as a uniformed civilian with rank equivalent to major; the purpose was to undertake a study of the effects on German morale of the intensive Allied bombing. He was able to spend a few days in England on the outward and inward flights, visiting his father and also Spender, but intervening weeks were spent among the ruined cities of Germany, undertaking interviews which were at times harrowing. Also on this assignment was his friend the writer James Stern, who probably took the photograph (*Tribute*: 82–3) showing Auden aboard a jeep in devastated Nuremberg; miraculously preserved in the background, a statue of Dürer perhaps suggests how Art triumphantly transcends historical disaster. Auden's view of matters, however, was different; increasingly suspicious of art's self-applaudingly magical orderliness, his scale of values is better illustrated by Stern's reminiscence of having inadvertently interrupted his early-morning prayers, and registering Auden's anguish at the intrusion. He and his wife Tania had been dedicatees of 'The Sea and the Mirror', and shortly after the return from Germany in mid-August 1945, they and Auden shared ownership of a shack on the not-yet-fashionable New York resort of Fire Island, where Auden spent the summers: visitors noted the map of Alston Moor prominently displayed on one of its walls. In adddition to what he earned from poetry, Auden made money by teaching at a variety of colleges and by undertaking reviews and editing anthologies. That autumn he rented the first of a series of apartments in New York, later shared with Kallman.

In July 1947 the publication of *The Age of Anxiety*, subtitled 'A Baroque Eclogue' and dedicated to John Betjeman, brought to a close the series of long poems which had been his chief output in these American years. In the spring of 1948 he sailed the Atlantic with Kallman, for whom it was the first visit to Europe, where Auden introduced him to English friends and to his father, now retired and living in what had formerly been their holiday cottage ('Far Wescoe') near Threlkeld in the northern Lake District. In May they were in Paris, thence travelling, via Florence, to Forio on the Isle of Ischia, which enchanted them. In August they were back in London, and spent two weeks at Wescoe before returning to America in the autumn. This extended trip to Europe inaugurated the pattern which would obtain for ten years; in 1949 Auden rented a house at Forio, where he and Kallman would go during the summer. In 1948 his rediscovery of the scenery of the North Pennines and first acquaintance with the limestone landscape of Italy had inspired his celebrated poem 'In Praise of Limestone'; Auden's European re-entry was also marked by Faber's publication of *Collected Shorter Poems 1930–1944* (1950), which for the most part resembled Random House's 1945 collection.

The relationship with Kallman had its turbulences, but was settling down to a companionability of minds, in which sharing lives did not depend on sharing a bed. Their chief area of collaboration was in writing libretti for opera, most notably that for *The Rake's Progress*, to music by Stravinsky, which was produced in Venice in 1951; Stravinsky had initially been taken aback by having Kallman foisted upon him as Auden's equal collaborator, but in the event had felt his talent merited it. Meanwhile Auden was working with characteristic steadiness: in 1949 he had been invited to deliver the prestigious Page-Barbour Lectures at the University of Virginia, published the following year as *The Enchafèd Flood*; in 1951 his collection *Nones* was issued, followed in 1955 by *The Shield of Achilles*. In 1956 he was elected, not entirely without controversy, to the Oxford Professorship of Poetry; the tenure was for five years, entailing a commitment to deliver three public lectures in each year: these were timed so as to enable Auden to continue his practice of using the New York autumn and winter to earn most of his income, and devoting the summers to Europe. This was in most ways a triumphant return to the university where his undergraduate result had been so disappointing; on his visits Auden happily reinhabited his old college, but even in the 1950s Oxford was changing from what it had been in his youth.

Also lessening was the pleasure he derived from living in Forio, and his receipt of a remunerative Italian literary prize paradoxically enabled him to sever connections with the Mediterranean south that had never entirely suited his 'nordic' temperament or skin-type. In 1958 he bought his first and only home, an old farmhouse in Kirchstetten, Austria, where a separated upstairs workroom provided Auden with a space in which to write, and a modern kitchen was installed to suit Kallman, an accomplished cook. This became their summer destination for the ensuing years. In 1960 his collection *Homage to Clio* was published, and in 1962 his second book of prose, based on his Oxford lectures, was published as *The Dyer's Hand*. Subsequent volumes of poetry were *About the House* (1965), *City Without Walls* (1969), *Epistle to a Godson* (1972), and, posthumously, *Thank You, Fog* (1974); Auden's individual volumes of poetry are all described in Section Two. In 1966 his *Collected Shorter Poems 1927–1957* was published, which abandoned the alphabetical arrangement of the earlier collection and reinstituted chronological sequence; but its foreword also made clear that Auden had grown sick of some earlier poems and had thrown them out; others had been modified.

In these latter stages Auden looked the part of Grand Old Man of Letters, his elderliness underlined by the extraordinary appearance of his face, which collapsed into its famous network of furrows and wrinkles. His premature ageing may have had a medical basis, but was likely to have been exacerbated by his heavy smoking, drinking, and indiscriminate use of stimulants to start and tranquillisers to end each day (from which chemical regime he began to wean himself in the 1960s). Given his literary stature and their personal association, Auden was the obvious choice to inaugurate the series of T.S. Eliot Memorial Lectures in 1967, published the next year as *Secondary Worlds*; but these were rather a muted performance, lacking the vigour and inventiveness of earlier essays. Despite his celebrity, Auden was not especially happy; in 1963 Kallman had decided to overwinter in Athens, rather than return to New York with him, and this meant that the winter months were spent by the poet in circumstances that became increasingly squalid, lonely and even hazardous. At length he saw the necessity of leaving America, and managed to secure a base at his old Oxford college, where a former brewhouse was converted for his use; but the university to which he returned in October 1972 was even more radically changed than he had found it in the period of his professorship: the streets were choked with traffic, and dons' lives centred less upon the senior common-room. Whilst Auden's idiosyncrasies – the extreme inflexibility of his personal routines and the monological repetitiousness of his conversation – could be tolerated by friends with fond memories of a formerly brilliant companion, they antagonised some Christ Church colleagues who merely felt themselves imposed upon by a booming old bore; in consequence, his first period of residence there was more of a tribulation than a haven. The Sterns, at whose Wiltshire home he spent the Christmas of 1972, were aware how little he desired to return to Oxford, and it was perhaps another sign of flagging powers of invention that he could ever have supposed it a good idea to do so. He was able to escape to Kirchstetten for the summer of 1973, but it was after closing the cottage in advance of an anticipated return to Christ Church for the coming winter, and having given a poetry-reading in Vienna, that on 29 September Auden suffered a fatal heart-attack in his hotel room, where Kallman discovered his body in the morning. He was buried at Kirchstetten, in the graveyard of the local Catholic church from whose gallery, as a card-carrying Anglican, he had enthusiastically joined in Sunday services.

The literary context

Every writer is to some extent indebted to the authors whose work impressed him in childhood, or whose example she seeks to emulate or challenge at a formative stage of development. Auden acknowledged these two kinds of influence: to the books which had seized his imagination as a child, and which he more than once defined as his 'nursery library'; and later, to the writers whose work offered models for his own. A chief characteristic of this 'nursery library' was its belonging to a phase of life before he had understood his desire to become a poet, and before any question of literary judgement (as opposed to more instinctive 'liking' or 'not liking') entered into its selection. In fact, some of its significant items were technical rather than imaginative writing, and his list included books about lead-mining and its machinery, as well as the more predictable children's authors and

Icelandic sagas. These books will therefore be considered under the ensuing heading of his 'personal context'. In looking here at the 'literary context', what will be considered are the conceptions of poetry by which Auden was formatively influenced once his sense of vocation had been established, on a Sunday afternoon's walk across a muddy field with his school-friend Robert Medley:

> Kicking a little stone, he turned to me
> And said, 'Tell me, do you write poetry?'
> I never had, and said so, but I knew
> That very moment what I wished to do.
> ('Letter to Lord Byron', *EA*: 194)

As Auden saw it, reviewing his own development in 1940 (in 'A Literary Transference'), from birth to early manhood he had witnessed a radical change, which he expressed in a chiasmus contrasting Victorian and Modernist poetry: 'Whatever its character, the provincial England of 1907, when I was born, was Tennysonian in outlook; whatever its outlook, the England of 1925 when I went up to Oxford was The Waste Land in character' (*P* II: 42). His own emergence as a poet in 1930, published in the *Criterion* and by Faber & Faber, naturally suggested a close affinity with T.S. Eliot, then a dominant presence in English letters, even down to the detail that each used his initials rather than first name: both seemed to exemplify the challengingly new and difficult writing required by this modern era. Although during this decade Eliot was to produce poetry and drama informed by the Christian perspectives he now embraced, his influence on contemporary poetry depended more upon earlier work such as 'The Love Song of J. Alfred Prufrock', *The Waste Land* (1922) and 'The Hollow Men' (with which poem he had closed his first collected volume, in 1925). Auden's discovery of Eliot towards the end of his first year at Oxford was decisive, and such as to make him decide to tear up all his previous efforts (so the story goes); but the poems he had been composing up to that point, and copying out to show his mother and send to certain friends, revealed the poets by whom he had hitherto been influenced, and these represent a fuller version of the tradition than that embodied in Eliot or recognised by criteria he espoused. Despite his admiration for Eliot as man and as poet, to assume that Auden continued the Modernist trajectory he exemplified is to overlook important differences between them, as well as to miss qualities Auden found to emulate in certain poets Eliot did not consider praiseworthy. His ability to learn from unusual sources, and to incorporate such lessons beyond the phase of straightforward imitation, was what enabled Auden to develop and then to preserve his 'voice' despite the influence of some quite distinctive masters – and mistresses, since at various stages Emily Dickinson, Laura Riding and Gertrude Stein were audible in his work.

In his 'Letter to Lord Byron' (Part III), Auden was to evoke the 'terror' to be anticipated by poets brought before the judgement seat in the afterworld, where they would be obliged to recite their collected works, including juvenilia. As an increasingly critical appraiser of his own poetry, he would have had his own apprentice-work in mind here; but even if the quality of much of the verse gathered in Katherine Bucknell's edition of his *Juvenilia* (2003) justifies the fears he light-heartedly confided to Lord Byron, it also offers a fascinating record of the emergence of a distinctive talent, with – as Bucknell notes – an acceleration, as he matured, of the speed with which he assimilated succcessive influences. The first poem Auden could remember having written was a sonnet inspired by Blea Tarn in the Lake District; no trace remains of this effusion, which nevertheless suggests that the earliest of his models was Wordsworth. Even in his youth he seems to have understood that it might be better not to imitate a giant, and Wordsworth and then Keats ('official poetry', as he described it in *The Dyer's Hand*) gave way to slightly more manageable figures such as Walter de la Mare and W.H. Davies. Auden himself identified Thomas Hardy as the first serious literary influence – in fact, his first literary 'love', first read in the summer of 1923. Apart from the incidental advantage of resembling Auden's father, Hardy was principally useful in being good, 'but not *too* good' (*DH*: 38), offering his disciple a ' "modern" rhetoric which was more fertile and adaptable to different themes than any of Eliot's gas-works and rats' feet which one could steal but never make one's own' (*P* II: 48).

In fact, Auden had already written a poem called 'By the Gasworks, Solihull' (June, 1924; *Juv*: 55), having become familiar with that place in boyhood when – as he would much later recall in the poem 'Prologue at Sixty' – he had been taken there in the belief that the fumes in its vicinity would alleviate bronchitis. The early poem, however, was no industrial evocation nor childhood memory, but a tribute to nature's ability to make the most of what humans have spoiled or neglected; its close observation of the vigorous weeds and the insects and birds profiting from the site is strongly reminiscent of the poet who succeeded Hardy in Auden's personal pantheon, Edward Thomas. If from Hardy Auden developed an abiding interest in experimenting with different kinds of stanza and metre, from Thomas he may have learned the value of an unassuming and unsentimental accuracy, and an ability to be satisfied with apparently modest effects: a kind of honest pastoralism. Both Hardy and Thomas exemplify a certain kind of Englishness; Thomas's American friend Robert Frost, whom Auden also read at this time, clearly does not; but from Frost's work he seems to have understood how to deploy colloquial speech within the context of regular verse; and what Hardy, Thomas, and Frost all have in common is their use of traditional verse-forms.

This traditionalist feel to their work, in form and in theme, was part of what made them uncongenial to a Modernist innovator like Eliot; and although, when Auden entered his Eliotic phase, his impulse to start afresh implied that he now found his earlier work – and by implication those writers it built upon – hopelessly old-fashioned, the lessons they had taught him remained, to survive this later period of enthralment. If for a while Eliot's imagery resonated in Auden's verse, and he espoused the ideals of a poetry that was classic and austere (as he put it in 'Letter to Lord Byron'), Eliot was supplanted or augmented in his turn by Yeats, the other major figure of English poetry. It can be argued that Yeats was more immediately important in enabling Auden to reach his own voice than Eliot; for one of the earliest poems in which we can hear something that could justly be described as 'Audenesque' is 'I Chose this Lean Country' (June/July 1927; *Juv*: 211; *EA*: 439), which was indebted to the third section of Yeats's 'The Tower', whose publication in the *The Criterion* (June 1927) Auden admiringly noted. Auden's greater enthralment by Yeats may be one of the reasons why, later, he felt it necessary to denounce Yeats's influence on his work, as he never did with Eliot's. Although he could make Eliot the butt of some of his jokes – using his name in an intricately disrespectful palindrome, or imagining him obliged to share a room with Walt Whitman as a means of achieving Purgatorial cleansing – he usually referred to him with affection and admiration, both in private and in published comments. His sense of the difference between the two poets is perhaps illustrated by his remark that whereas Yeats never had mystical experiences he spoke about them all the time, and Eliot had them all the time but did not refer to them. Yeats seems to have worried Auden more, and perhaps the most telling sign of that worry was seen in 1964, when he declined Spender's request to write something about the Irish poet, because he had come to represent for Auden 'my own devil of unauthenticity', that tempted him to fill poems with 'false emotions, inflated rhetoric, empty sonorities' (quoted Carpenter 1981: 416). This may explain why the poem of his against which he turned with the greatest ferocity was 'September 1, 1939', which in metre as well as in title was modelled on Yeats's famous 'Easter, 1916'.

It was in 1939, in his elegy for Yeats, that Auden provocatively declared that poetry made nothing happen; this seemed precisely to contradict the sense of poetry's necessary engagement with the problems of its era, which had seemed to many one of the defining characteristics of Auden's own work of the previous decade. He had praised his friend Isherwood's writing for making action urgent and its nature clear and, as Valentine Cunningham has suggested, the air of self-certainty or epistemological assurance communicated by Auden's poetry (with its frequent imperatives, or directions to focus on 'this' thing or 'that' event, see Criticism, **pp. 117–18**) gave the appearance of doing much the same. Yet the reversal was neither as absolute nor as sudden as it may have seemed, and Auden's desire in 1937 to be in communication with Lord Byron might have suggested there was a model of what a poet could be that he found more attractive than those by which he had been guided into public attention.

For it was Byron the urbanely playful satirist and not Byron the political activist by whom Auden was most animated; shortly after *Letters from Iceland*, he engaged in compiling the *Oxford Book of Light Verse* (1938), which further showed his commitment to a poetry that was neither classically austere nor strutting around on stilts. If Eliot and Yeats had been important way-markers on Auden's road to his own poetic self-conception, he had further to go: this would involve dissociating himself from notions of the importance or essential seriousness of poetry, implicit in the practice of those earlier masters. For even if Eliot, by 1928, felt able to declare in *The Sacred Wood*'s second edition that poetry was no more than 'a superior amusement', his own reliance on a process remarkably akin to that of Romantic inspiration made each poem a momentous event: of composition for the poet and of publication for the reader. Yeats, whilst more routinely workmanlike (as Auden himself), gave the appearance of producing poetry out of mystical exaltation. Auden would come to feel that neither of these models did justice to the more humdrum social realities in which both poet and reader were involved.

Although his Oxford tutor, Neville Coghill, recalled undergraduate Auden aspiring to become a 'great' poet, and whilst the discipline with which he set himself to write demonstrated throughout his career a consistently professional commitment to composition, Auden grew increasingly suspicious of anything like grandiosity in poetry's conceptions of itself, and unforgiving when he found traces of such an attitude in his own work. In his own person he seems to have combined elements suggesting the desire to lead and to dominate, with genuine co-operative instincts that made possible his various artistic collaborations. Those with whom he worked were often struck, not only by the facility with which Auden could produce high-quality verse more or less to order, but also by the modesty that enabled him to throw it away if it subsequently turned out to be surplus to requirements. His desire to divest poetry of its delusions of grandeur may have become clearest after his move to the USA, but can be seen in the 1930s as well. Although *The Orators* (1932) is in most aspects the most self-consciously avant-garde book of poetry Auden ever wrote, Stan Smith has argued that the hyper-parochialism in its references to obscure local details of the Helensburgh location parodies, and implicitly reproaches, the internationalist aspirations of *The Waste Land*. The schools poetry anthology Auden co-edited with John Garrett (*The Poet's Tongue*, 1935) arranged its contents alphabetically by first line and banished details of authorship to the index; the intention being to free readers from 'the bias of great names and literary influences' and foster the idea of poetry as 'a spontaneous living product' instead of 'a cultural tradition to be preserved and imitated' (pp. x–xi). Although a preference for spontaneity above 'tradition' might imply Wordsworthian values supplanting Eliot's, Auden implicitly rebutted other Romantic notions of the heroically isolated artist, by asserting that the best art was likely to arise within a society that offered 'a community united in sympathy, sense of worth, and aspiration' (p. viii). Three years later, in his introduction to the *Oxford Book of Light Verse*, he made clear his preference for the kind of poetry arising out of a community of interest, and for the kind of poet not exaggeratedly conscious of himself as an 'unusual person'; for Auden 'light' verse was a term of approbation rather than denigration: an attitude that underlay his admiration for a poet such as Betjeman.

For a while left-leaning politics had seemed to Auden the means by which his poetry could achieve this desirable social integration, but his decision to leave Britain signalled his loss of confidence in the project; Mendelson has argued that he emigrated in order to renounce his role as court poet of the left, and Auden himself later claimed that he did so to avoid being absorbed into 'the British establishment': either would have been a falsified social relation, and the move to America implied a corresponding decontextualisation. In the late 1930s it was perhaps easier for Auden to see what he did not want to be, than what he did; by the time he arrived in the USA he was an established reputation beyond the stage of being formatively influenced by any other poet, and perhaps the most significant author for him, in his early American years, was Henry James, the novelist indefatigably concerned with the moralities of perception. Auden was not, however, too proud to learn, and Marianne Moore's use of syllabics (rather, perhaps, than her poetry itself) was something to which he confessed a debt; as he also took an interest in the poetry of William Carlos Williams, and its experiments with the 'stepped line' as a mode of attempting a distinctively American poetic. Despite some slightly ostentatious declarations of his new nationality, however, Auden was not principally concerned to transform into an 'American' poet, and certainly did not succeed in doing so; in 'Journey to Iceland' he had written that travelling

North symbolised rejection, and it is possible that going to America principally involved an abjuration of the type of poet he might have become, had he remained in England. In 1964, in his poem dedicated to the memory of Louis MacNeice, Auden envisaged himself becoming 'a minor Atlantic Goethe'; that is, a modest version of a great writer, owing only an oceanic allegiance. He had, perhaps, expressed a similar aspiration in 1936, writing for the Workers' Educational Association (WEA) magazine, when he complained that 'Personally the kind of poetry I should like to write but can't is "the thoughts of a wise man in the speech of the common people" '(*P* I: 165): citing Aristotle to outline a Wordsworthian goal that stressed the democratic ideal, rather than any isolated sublimity such as he may have tried to voice in his lost sonnet about Blea Tarn.

The historical context

Signs of the times: poetry and politics

The fact that an Oxford-educated poet, born into the superior middle-class of Edwardian England, found himself in the mid-1930s involved with the WEA and invoking 'the common people' was a sign of the times and of an awareness shared by many intellectuals that they could not ignore the 'class struggle'. Although in a December 1935 diary entry Betjeman described Auden as 'an avowed Communist' who declared (surely with tongue in cheek), 'I feel it is my duty to make notes and report on the bourgeoisie' (Hillier 2002: 64), he had in fact moved beyond the dutiful proto-communism that was most stridently audible in his 1932 poem 'A Communist to Others'. Auden was, however, still strongly enough convinced of his duty to resist Fascism to envisage fighting in the Spanish Civil War (in the event he went intending to drive an ambulance). By the time he was writing 'The Prolific and the Devourer' in summer 1939, he explicitly rejected the notion that one could become a major writer only through participation in the class struggle, and dismissed the left-wing posturing of many 1930s writers, who had embraced politics 'as an exciting new subject to write about'. There is little doubt that he included himself as one of those whose revealed 'follies' should now lead to a self-appraisal which took due account of the negligible effect artists and intellectuals had had: 'As far as the course of political events is concerned they might just as well have done nothing' (*EA*: 403).

Auden left 'The Prolific and the Devourer' unfinished and unpublished, but these sentiments chimed with his recent declaration in the elegy for Yeats that poetry made nothing happen, and with the mood that would soon underlie his disillusioned characterisation of the low and dishonest decade, in 'September 1, 1939'. This writing came at a pivotal moment in his career, when his repudiation of the era in which he had himself achieved prominence comprised, as well, a repudiation of the kind of writer he had seemed content to be during it, alongside a renunciation of his citizenship. It also involved a redefinition of his conceptions of the artist's relation to the times he lived in and to 'history', which continues to be the focus for critical debate regarding the quality of the poetry he wrote before and after his expatriation. The poetry he wrote from 1940 onward ceased to be 'Audenesque', as that term had been used – since 1933 – to denote his characteristics of tone, setting and subject-matter; later he turned most savagely against those of his poems which had seemed to make the largest claims in their historical diagnosis or for the artist's interventionary power: in 1964, alongside 'Sir, no man's enemy . . .' and 'A Communist to Others', he dismissed 'August for the people . . .', 'Spain' and 'September 1, 1939' as 'trash' which he was ashamed of having written (see *Early A*: 306). 'August for the people . . .' (1935), composed for Isherwood's birthday and commending that writer's ability to make action 'urgent' and its nature 'clear' (echoing phraseology Auden had used earlier the same year introducing *The Poet's Tongue*), ends with a notable image that contrasts the peaceable harbour on the Isle of Man in which Auden had been observing the activity of pleasure-craft, with deeper, more destructive currents defining human lives:

> And all sway forward on the dangerous flood
> Of history, which never sleeps or dies,
> And, held one moment, burns the hand.
> (*EA*: 157)

As we have seen, Auden judged that he had been born into a world essentially Tennysonian in its attitudes and that by the time he went up to Oxford in 1925 it more closely resembled the world of *The Waste Land*; ten years later, lines such as these concluding 'August for the people . . .' suggest some of the reasons why that uneasy decade seemed to many to bear the particular stamp that Auden's writing gave to it, and why Samuel Hynes's influential study of 'Literature and Politics in England in the 1930s' would bear the title of *The Auden Generation* (1976). The dangerous flood of history has seldom, either at the time or in retrospect, been so apparent as it was in the mid-1930s, amid widespread premonitions of another major European war. Auden's birthday tribute to Isherwood, offered in part as a critique of the false values embodied in earlier phases of their friendship, is acute in observing the displacement strategies by which people tried to divert themselves from awareness of the gathering storm, and is alert to the contemporary importance of the wireless as a means both of drawing popular attention to and of distracting it from such realities. Curiously, the poem's analysis of what is wrong occurs by means of eighteenth-century personified abstractions, essentially depicting the Triumph of the False and Defeat of the True everywhere the poet looks; there is no overt linkage to what the radio may be talking about – perhaps because he assumed the contemporary reader could easily imagine this. Yet with its insistence on an atmosphere of 'crisis', 'dismay' and 'disaster', the poem communicates a sense of threat that world events would shortly validate: Mussolini would invade Ethiopia (October 1935), and Hitler would stage the Nuremberg Rally, after which anti-semitism in Nazi Germany became *de jure* as well as *de facto* (September 1935).

Auden seemed especially adept at reading the signs of the times and at expressing what was to become their meaning; the very urgency and assurance of this address to contemporary history set him apart from the previous literary generation. Joyce's Stephen Dedalus notoriously describes history as 'a nightmare from which I am trying to awake', and Eliot explicated and deepened that disdain: in '*Ulysses*, Order, and Myth' (1923) he described 'the immense panorama of futility and anarchy which is contemporary history', and saw Joyce's deployment of mythic parallels as the best means for art to restore order to experiences which, without it, could only amount to muddle. His comments, many have noticed, threw as much light on *The Waste Land* as on *Ulysses*; but in Joyce preferring his imaginatively reconstructed city to the real Dublin, as in Eliot observing social and cultural decay through the mixed registers and elegiacally ironised historical allusions of his poem, can be seen the high Modernist impulse that valued the selective discriminations of artistic process above the inclusive confusion of what Henry James dismissed as 'clumsy Life . . . at her stupid work' (preface to *Spoils of Poynton*). Neither mandarin disengagement nor dismayed withdrawal were particular features of Auden's writing for much of the 1930s, despite its occasional postures of detachment. Rather, its dominant mode might be described as the 'present imperative': for whatever the diagnosis of human energies wasted by collusion with decaying and corrupted systems, his was a rhetoric apparently insistent on the need to measure up to an actual or imminent crisis ('To-day the struggle' is the culminating formula, in 'Spain'), and on the responsibility of each implicated onlooker. Marx, in the *Theses on Feuerbach* (1845), had declared that 'the philosophers have only *interpreted* the world in various ways; the point is to *change* it', and there was much in Auden's work that appeared to enforce something similar. For this reason, his willingness to be a non-participant, when Europe was eventually convulsed by the disaster he had seemingly predicted, was a point of great difficulty for some admirers: it was as if the poet who had so memorably denoted the 'dangerous flood / Of history' now believed he need not get his feet wet.

Yet the tension, in that poem, for Isherwood, between contemporary detail and Augustan diction (anachronistic, albeit appropriate to a poem set in August) reminds us that Auden seldom presented an uncomplicated picture, either in his poetry or as a man. The holidaymakers he observes disembarking from their pleasure-craft wear contrastingly emblematic clothing: their striped blazers evoke the tiger, while their white shoes evoke the dove. The mixed messages thus sent reflected the different reactions observable in the larger world: the first six months of 1935 saw Germany repudiate the disarmament imposed on it by the Versailles treaty, and Britain announce significant expansion of its airforce, including development of a new heavy bomber; but they also saw British efforts to appease the militarism of Mussolini, and a 'peace ballot' organised by the League of Nations Union in Britain which attracted 11.6 million votes in favour. At the close of 1938, Auden was rushing about addressing public meetings on the Sino-Japanese conflict from which he had recently returned, in order to enlist support for the Chinese cause, and giving every appearance of being a committed left-wing activist; yet he had already made up his mind to leave England, had ceased to trust his political impulses and in fact had never joined the Communist Party. This is not to attribute to him any hypocrisy; rather, it is to reinforce the necessary *caveat* that no retrospect of a life or an era can do justice to the complicating and confusing realities experienced by those living through them.

Auden 'in our time': the Great War, the General Strike, economic slump

When in the mid-1970s Spender read Bernard Bergonzi's literary study of the 1930s, he noted in his journal that the book tended to treat the decade as if it had somehow been thematically self-contained, whereas for his own part, as one of the actors in its drama, he was aware of continuities with the earlier two decades. Although with great historical convenience Auden became visible as a writer in January 1930, his first mature poetry had been written in the late 1920s, and he had already been affected by significant events. The first of these was the Great War, which deprived him of his father during formative years of his boyhood, when even boarding schools constituted themselves as a kind of home front: he remembered being reproached by a master, having helped himself to a second slice of bread and margarine, with 'Auden, I see, wants the Huns to win' (Spender experienced something similar at his school; friends and family noted Auden's gluttonous tendencies, so the reproach probably struck home). While it is true, as Paul Fussell has argued in *The Great War and Modern Memory*, that the 1914–18 war retrospectively assumed iconic status in the later twentieth century as a fall from innocence, this mythic interpretation does not entirely contradict the facts. Subjectively, an ex-combatant such as J.B. Priestley, in his *Literature and Western Man*, asserted that the sense of alteration was 'something that nobody born after about 1904 can ever fully appreciate. . . . 1919 was a ragged shadow of 1913' (1960: 329). More dispassionately, the historian Eric Hobsbawm, in *Age of Extremes: the Short Twentieth Century*, notes that 'in 1914 there had been no major war for a century'; but that five years later '[n]o old government was left standing between the borders of France and the Sea of Japan' (1994: 22, 29). The Russian, Ottoman and Hapsburg empires had all been swept away; and if the British Empire appeared to have survived and even enlarged, the reality was that Britain had lost half a million men under the age of thirty (casualties among the upper classes, which furnished the junior officers who led so many doomed assaults, had been severe), and effectively 'the country had ruined its economy by fighting a war substantially beyond its means' (ibid.: 30). Events of this magnitude have complicated consequences. Artistically, the Modernist momentum that had preceded the outbreak of war was interrupted and irretrievably altered by the loss of so many individual talents (a waste bemoaned, for example, by Ezra Pound in *Hugh Selwyn Mauberley*). Politically, an enormous boost was given to the forces of Communist radicalism, conspicuously successful in Russia where the Tsarist regime had been overthrown, and looking to reproduce these effects elsewhere; this in its turn nourished counter-reaction, in the several forms of European Fascism that would emerge.

For Auden, twelve years old in 1919, the cessation of hostilities was chiefly signalled – he recalled in 'Letter to Lord Byron' – by the return of butter to the table and his father to the family: George Auden came home having suffered no worse injury than frostbite at Gallipoli (which intermittently troubled him thereafter). A sense of insularity and insulation was what Spender recalled from the circles he moved in, looking back on the ensuing period in his autobiography *World Within World*:

> It is true that the Slump had caused a certain uneasiness, and the fall of the pound still more. But with the recovery from those disasters, during the years of the Baldwin Government, not only were these forgotten, but English middle-class life was characterized by a refusal to contemplate further disasters. The middle years of the 1930's were symbolized in England not by Hitlerism or even the Spanish war, but by the Royal Jubilee.
>
> (1953: 142)

Of course, Auden knew that those living in Warrington and Wigan (that is, in areas marked by the Depression and its aftermath) would see things differently; he too had identified and responded to the class-complacency alluded to here, trying to puncture it and make it change. But just as Spender speaks of a relatively restricted social group that for him emblematised the *Zeitgeist*, so it should be remembered that Auden – who in America in 1939 defined the 'ordinary' British man as one who 'left school at 14 and [is] earning less than $20 [about £4] a week' (*P* II: 17) – reflects and effectively interacted with a comparatively small set. It is chastening to note – as Valentine Cunningham does (1988: 297) – that *Look, Stranger!* was considered a runaway success when it sold 2,350 copies within three months of publication in 1936; but that this contrasts with the sales achieved by the versifying moraliser Patience Strong, whose first book (1937) sold over 100,000 copies within a year. In 'Squares and Oblongs' (1948) Auden acknowledged as much: 'It is a sobering experience for any poet to read the last page of the Book Section of the Sunday *Times* where correspondents seek to identify poems which have meant much to them. He is forced to realize that it is not his work, nor even the work of Dante or Shakespeare, that most people treasure as magic talismans in times of trouble, but grotesquely bad verses written by maiden aunts in local newspapers' (*P* II: 348).

By 1948 Auden evidently read the papers; but looking back on his 'frivolous' Oxford years, he claimed to have existed in a state of negligent ignorance regarding the wider world and the political implications of what was happening:

> I find it incredible how secure life seemed. Too young for the war to have made any impression upon us, we imagined that the world was essentially the same as it had been in 1913, and we were far too insular and preoccupied with ourselves to know or care what was going on across the Channel. Revolution in Russia, inflation in Germany and Austria, Fascism in Italy . . . went unnoticed by us. Before 1930, I never opened a newspaper.
>
> (*F&A*: 511)

Auden may not have been disproportionately affected by the war itself, but it cast its shadow over the years in which he grew to youth and manhood, despite the fact that his family was able to resume a life of relatively comfortable normality. Although envious of the private means of friends such as Isherwood and Spender, he was also alert to the comparative advantages of his own position (a university education, for example, was a privilege fiercely rationed between the wars, decided more by money than ability).

The chief political event which occurred during his Oxford years was the General Strike of early May 1926, during which many young gentlemen from the universities volunteered to keep the country going. Auden retrospectively ascribed such strike-breaking to the perennial boy's desire to drive a train or bus, rather than to class-animosity; his own decision to side with the strikers (as a driver for the TUC) he put down to 'sheer contrariness', but it was likely also to have been provoked by some sense of social justice – even if the only sacrifice it entailed was his loss of a lunch, when a cousin's stockbroker husband ordered him out of the house on discovering his affiliation. The strike had originated in miners' resistance to the imposition of longer hours and lower wages by pit-owners, so Auden's boyhood fascination with life underground may also have influenced his choice. The General Strike only lasted nine days and ended in defeat for the miners' cause (they themselves held out longer, but to no avail). In spite of the bitterness and recriminations engendered, it seemed to many at the time a less-than-fully-serious affair: Graham Greene, who had enrolled as a special constable, recalled in his biography that 'the great depression was still some years away; the middle classes had not yet been educated by the hunger-marchers' (Sherry 1989: 302). This corroborates Auden's own somewhat flippant retrospect; but the strike itself, and what it revealed about the middle and upper classes' ignorance of working-class realities, serves to remind us that the majority was excluded from the excitations of a decade otherwise denoted by tags such as 'the roaring Twenties' or 'the Jazz Age'.

The Wall Street Crash of late October 1929 inaugurated a global recession generally called the 'Great Depression' or 'The Slump' that intensified the suffering of those already economically disadvantaged and extended it to many who had once been comfortably off. Industries ground to a halt and mass unemployment became a fact of life, particularly visible in industrial communities and insufficiently alleviated by the rudimentary, insensitive schemes set up to address it. Hobsbawm has argued that the bursting of this bubble, rather than the Great War itself, marked the irreversible severance between modern Britain and an obliterated era of stability: 'It was a catastrophe which destroyed all hope of restoring the economy, and the society, of the long nineteenth century. The period 1929–33 was a canyon which henceforth made a return to 1913 not merely impossible, but unthinkable' (1994: 107). This evident collapse of the capitalist system gave greater credibility to the alternative proposed by Communism; a credibility augmented by the fact that it was difficult to ascertain exactly what was going on inside the Soviet Union (effectively under Stalin's control since 1926), and abetted by the gullibility of some high-profile foreign visitors there, such as Bernard Shaw. Furthermore, Socialism seemed to many preferable to the extreme right-wing authoritarianism manifesting itself in Italy, and becoming audible elsewhere.

During his post-Oxford months in Germany, Auden's interests had been principally amorous and intellectual rather than political; but the 1930 in which he achieved his first serious publication, started looking for a job and – by his own account – opened his first newspaper was also the year in which he wrote two notable poems of bossy denunciation and energetic declamation: 'Consider This and in Our Time' (March 1930) and 'Get There If You Can and See the Land You Once Were Proud To Own' (April 1930). The second of these Auden wrote during a walking tour of Hadrian's Wall and Alston Moor undertaken in the company of his Oxford friend Gabriel Carritt, who had already joined the Communist Party in America and would become an activist within the British Communist Party. Both poems contain obscurely personal references, as well as gleefully identifying antagonistic authority figures such as financiers, dons and clergymen – all of whom are menaced by an impending social apocalypse prefigured in the imagery of silted harbours, derelict works, rotting wharves and choked canals. These landscapes of simultaneous industrial and agricultural decay implied the question that, a year later, would be posed with parodical directness by the Old Boy giving the 'Address for a Prize-Day' in *The Orators*: 'What do you think of England, this country of ours where nobody is well?' (*EA*: 62).

England, their England

'England' was being looked at, and for, in various ways; as Cunningham (1988) has remarked, in the interwar period there was a rash of attempted definitions, ranging from the nostalgic pastoral reflectiveness of H.V. Morton's much-reprinted peregrinations *In Search of England* (1927), to the post-Slump stock-taking pragmatism of J.B. Priestley's *English Journey* (1934), among many others. Auden's England is closer to Priestley's (indeed, the detail in the fourth of Auden's '1929' poems, of children at play on a fuming alkali tip, strikingly prefigures Priestley's observation (p. 336) of industrial spoilheaps at Shotton, which smoke sulphurously and on one of which 'a very dirty little boy was tobogganing'); but perhaps it is significant that the book which he would mine for images at different stages of his career was Anthony Collett's *The Changing Face of England* (1926, reissued 1932). This was much more concerned with English landscape and its evolution than with people or institutions, and with geological rather than political events – although as the title suggests, it does not view 'England' with quiescent nostalgia, but as the site where contending forces produce change: the caption to its first photograph reads, 'This hill-stream is attacking the scrub and pasture which cover its ancient bed'. Such a perspective, continuously dynamic as well as implying the impersonal antagonisms involved in processes of modification, offered a particular stimulus to Auden's imagination.

To observe that there might be something wrong with England was not a novel perception; Eliot's *Waste Land* had seemed to suggest as much, and Pound had railed against 'an old bitch gone in the teeth, . . . a botched civilisation' ('E.P. Ode . . .', V): what discriminated the younger poets from that previous generation was not their diagnosis, so much as that they admitted the possibility of cure. It is fair to say that some relish was detectible in their anticipating how any necessary remedy might afflict the comfortable, as in these lines which close 'Part Three' of Day-Lewis's 1933 book of poems *The Magnetic Mountain*:

> Drug nor isolation will cure this cancer:
> It is now or never, the hour of the knife,
> The break with the past, the major operation.
> (*CDLCP*: 162)

Auden's early poetry – by which Day-Lewis had been strongly influenced – resounded with declarations that it was time for the destruction of error, that the game was up, that it was later than people thought. His message seemed to amount to 'You'll be for it!'; whereas by 1938, in one of the sonnets provoked by witnessing a Japanese air-raid in China, he implicated himself in the imminent threat: no longer the 'lone flyer' and 'bully boy' envisioned by Day-Lewis in *The Magnetic Mountain* (*CDLCP*: 151), he looked up at threatening aircraft and acknowledged that it is 'we' who are about to suffer 'now' (see *EA*: 256).

Again unlike Eliot's or Pound's, this vision of England did not involve any simple distaste for the present, nor the implicit judgement that it was inferior to some ideal version of the past. The Oxford poets with whom Auden was grouped, the slightly older Day-Lewis and the slightly younger Spender, as well as MacNeice who was the same age (but with whom Auden did not become friendly until after Oxford, although they met as undergraduates), were collectively identified as the 'Pylon' school, a nickname which referred specifically to Spender's 1933 poem 'The Pylons', and generally to their habit of including in their work images of industrial modernity such as factories, arterial roads and power-stations. It also encoded their left-leaning politics, since celebrations of technological progress in industry and agriculture were characteristic of Soviet artistic output at this period (leading in 1935 to the institutionalisation of 'Socialist Realism' as the official Party aesthetic). Their grouping was not simply an anthologist's construction, even if the claims made for them by editors such as Michael Roberts reinforced its visibility; a sense of common purpose was amplified by their various public tokens of mutual esteem. Auden dedicated 'Paid on Both Sides' to Day-Lewis, *Poems* (1930) to Isherwood, and *The Orators* (1932) to Spender; Spender dedicated his *Poems* (Second Edition, 1934) to Isherwood; Day-Lewis dedicated *Transitional Poem* (1929) to Rex Warner (another leftward-leaning Oxford poet) and *The Magnetic Mountain* to Auden, who dedicated one of the six Odes in *The Orators* to Warner's infant son, John, and another to Edward Upward, whom Isherwood deferred to as a literary authority in much the same way that Auden had deferred to Isherwood, whose *Mr Norris Changes Trains* (1935) was dedicated to Auden.

They also received walk-on parts in each other's poems. A certain circularity was noticed and waspishly commented on by some, as was the poets' tendency to draw on the boys' school for their analogies, in ways that suggested a limited experience and reluctance to grow up: 'The Prep School atmosphere: that is what I want', Auden declared to his 1929 Berlin journal, indicating the kind of drama at which he aimed (*EA*: 301). Of those listed above, Day-Lewis, Auden, Warner and Upward all worked as schoolmasters during the 1930s. Yet what could be dismissed as immature cliquishness was not without its point or its object, as Richard Davenport-Hines has pungently observed:

> It may seem that Auden and his friends were juvenile in their railing against authority and the dull malevolence of officials. It is too easy to forget the noxious, pompous stupidity that leaked over their epoch like gas-fumes from a defective stove.
>
> (1995: 143)

An example of what Davenport-Hines means is shown in an episode from mid-decade, when Day-Lewis found himself reprimanded by the chairman of governors of the Cheltenham school where he was teaching, for having given a sympathetic talk about collective farms (Stalin's programme of agricultural reform): 'D'you realise what would have happened to you if you'd done this sort of thing in the Regiment? The Colonel would have handed you over to the subalterns' mess and when they'd finished with you you'd have been asked to join some other regiment' (Sean Day-Lewis 1980: 90). This rebuke, administered by one who was a peer of the realm and privy councillor, illustrates that analogies based upon regimental life could be every bit as limitingly puerile as those deriving from school. Later on, Day-Lewis would become the object of clandestine surveillance by British 'intelligence', as a probable Communist sympathiser – when his tendency to go hatless was noted as an apparently sinister inclination.

As it happens, he was wrong about the Soviet collectivisation of agriculture (whose imposition we now know to have inflicted brutal suffering on peasant smallholders, as well as causing disastrous food shortages); Day-Lewis ended his life as Poet Laureate and pillar of the literary establishment, sending his son to the same public school he had himself attended. Auden, too, changed, albeit in different ways; and so did most of their group of literary associates (Upward held the longest to a doctrinaire Communist line); but this does not prove – despite what Auden himself implied in 'The Prolific and the Devourer' – that they were insincere or mistaken in all their beliefs: to have been wrong about 1930s Russia does not mean they were also wholly wrong about England. Auden's poetry tended to combine what resembled political comment with a melodramatic tone that seemed idiosyncratically personal in its choice of objects of attention. He was never as overtly committed to a left-wing agenda as Day-Lewis or Spender were, but the early 1930s were years in which he evinced a greater awareness of the condition of England and the need to change it.

The Weimar Republic, in which he had spent his postgraduation 'year' and – as he later acknowledged – his father's money, was the product of a vindictive post-war settlement which had imposed on Germany a heavy burden of reparations for the war that compromised the economic reconstruction on which such payments would depend. The resulting instabilities produced an environment that was not only hospitable to certain forms of artistic and sexual self-expression, but also to the reaction against these embodied in the person of Hitler and his growing number of supporters. In July 1929 Auden returned to an England which had since June been governed by a non-majority Labour administration under Ramsay MacDonald: a change of government he might have viewed auspiciously. MacDonald had presided for a few months in 1924 over the first-ever Labour administration, but from November that year the country had been governed by the Conservatives under Stanley Baldwin: a period that had seen acute industrial and social unrest occasioned by the economic legacy of the war, itself exacerbated by Britain's ill-advised return to the gold standard at pre-war exchange levels. But MacDonald's new government was itself shortly to be blown off course by the stockmarket crash and ensuing slump; and when the punitive cuts proposed in order to balance the budget met with demurral from Labour colleagues, in August 1931 he resigned, to emerge the next day as titular head of a national government, which faced the electorate that October seeking approval for its 'Doctor's

Mandate' (showing, as Stan Smith has pointed out, how metaphors of disease and healing were politically as well as poetically current). Expelled from the Labour Party, which like the Liberal Party split into two camps and seemed headed for extinction, MacDonald presided over a 'national' government overwhelmingly stocked with Conservatives, operating measures such as the infamous 'Means Test' for state relief that were offensive and injurious to mainstream Labour voters, until he was put out of his misery by Baldwin's succeeding him as prime minister in June 1935 and out of parliament by losing his seat in the general election that November.

An age of anxiety – and Auden's response

This prime minister, perplexed about his own loyalties, might stand as symbol for the ambivalence of the entire decade, which simultaneously embraced the future (as in its architecture) and feared what it might bring (as in its preoccupation with war from the air). 'Man is changed by his living; but not fast enough,' Auden asserted with characteristic impatience in the first chorus of *The Dog Beneath the Skin* (1935), 'In the hour of the Blue Bird and the Bristol Bomber, his thoughts are / Appropriate to the years of the Penny Farthing' (*EA*: 282–3). The references here were highly topical: in 1935 Sir Malcolm Campbell broke his own land speed world-record in his car 'Bluebird', but that year also saw the more ominous acceleration indicated by the second item, alluding to *Daily Mail* proprietor Lord Rothermere's gift to the nation of a new Bristol 142 twin-engined passenger aircraft for development into a prototype bomber; airforce chiefs to whom it was demonstrated had been impressed by its ability to fly faster than their latest fighter plane. Television sets first went on sale in Britain in 1930, when one was also installed in the prime minister's residence, although radio ownership remained far more widespread; but the decade's numerous technological advances were malignantly accompanied by advances of a military nature.

In 1931 Japanese forces moved into Manchuria; in Germany in January 1933 the Nazis came to power and straight away took firm measures to secure it; in 1935 Italy invaded Ethiopia, dropping mustard gas on civilians from aircraft; in 1936 Britain established its first civil defence anti-gas school, Germany violated the Treaty of Versailles – with impunity – by moving troops into the demilitarised Rhineland, and civil war broke out in Spain, where in 1937 the Basque city of Guernica was bombed by German aircraft acting on behalf of General Franco; that same year Japanese troops moved beyond Manchuria into China. In 1938 German troops crossed into Austria and the two countries were (consensually) united, Britain acquiesced to the Italian occupation of Ethiopia, and Prime Minister Neville Chamberlain flew to Munich, in order to meet with Hitler and agree to the latter's demands that the Sudetenland in Czechoslovakia be ceded to German control; his return to Heston aerodrome, emerging from his aircraft with a sheet of paper which he proclaimed to represent 'peace for our time' and 'peace with honour', was broadcast on television. The British and French had obliged the Czech government to comply with Hitler's requirements, but by March 1939 he discovered that more *Lebensraum* was needed, so Germany and Hungary between them took the rest, and even Poland got in on the act; only Slovakia remained semi-independent. Later the same month Hitler made new territorial demands, this time of Poland, provoking Britain and France to agree a pact of mutual assistance with that country, and Italy invaded Albania. Also in April the Soviet Union proposed that Britain and France enter into a triple alliance, and when that failed of the desired response, Stalin concluded a non-aggression pact with Hitler in August (which secretly ceded parts of Poland to Soviet control). On 1 September 1939 German forces rolled into Poland, where newsreel captured their tanks being charged by a magnificently futile Polish cavalry. Having received no reply to its consequent ultimatum, Britain, with France, declared war on Germany on 3 September: their pact with Poland was, thus, one of the very few treaties or agreements numerously made between European states in the 1930s to be honoured, rather than reneged on.

'From 1931 onwards,' Spender recalled in his autobiography, 'I felt hounded by external events' (*WWW*: 137), and the foregoing sequence suggests why that might have been; by the time it reached its dire conclusion Auden was in America, writing a poem of disillusioned retrospect on what the decade had amounted to. Earlier in his career he had been fascinated by notions of the 'Truly Strong Man', and had at times adopted an interventionist or apocalyptic rhetoric in his writing; now events had unfolded, indicating the kind of apocalypse to which strong-arm interventionism might lead. At this juncture he told more than one correspondent that listening to radio news, as events led towards war, had reduced him to tears. 'September 1, 1939' bade a sour farewell not only to the exploded hopes of a self-deluding era, but also to his own complicity in its delusions: the fourth stanza finds a guilty face staring back in the mirror. Yet Auden would later turn against this poem, regarding it as insufficiently cleansed of the kind of poet he had previously tried to be: he had, if you like, not been 'changed fast enough' to avoid some of the old pitfalls. And indeed, despite its initial protestation of fear at what events portend, the poem quite quickly modulates into a didactic historical analysis of what has happened, that seems in its assertiveness to be at odds with the uncertainty laid claim to at its outset: the poet is still functioning as an immodest diagnostician, in possession of the answers.

After Auden's death, Rex Warner summed up the distinctive energies that had made him such a commanding figure at the outset of his career:

> Faced with the apparent absoluteness of crisis of the thirties, Wystan always had, or thought he had, some curative or specific, often based on some medical or psycho-analytic theory, things which at that time were somewhat strange and consequently exciting. He used to snatch up ideas, information, scraps of conversation with the assiduity of a jackdaw and would neatly label and catalogue his findings with enormous rapidity.
> (*Tribute*: 46)

Auden's intellectual omnivorousness, which found him intrigued by the developing social sciences of psychology and anthropology as well as by literature, saw him move beyond thinking of neurosis in a personal context, to apply theories of pathology to political analysis: it was not just the individual psyche, but the body politic itself that was sick and needed to be cured ('Freud's error,' he wrote in his 1929 Berlin journal, 'is the limitation of neurosis to the individual. The neurosis involves all society'; *Early A*: 52). Warner also highlights Auden's zest for aligning apparently disparate phenomena under some often idiosyncratic system of classification: what might otherwise be dismissed as merely incidental was found to be symptomatically significant, in ways that could be made to yield meaning, but could also (as in some of the lists in *The Orators*) suggest a richly comic paranoia. The method in part depended on a technique of dispassionate observation, such as might be exercised by hawk or helmeted airman – the figure whose appearance in his work derived from Auden's admiration for Hardy's 'hawk's vision, his way of looking at life from a very great height'. This detached onlooker with an apparently objective aerial view, who might be a fledgling social scientist, also had links with the techniques later put into practice by such enterprises as the 'Mass Observation' programme (set up with Tom Harrison in 1937 by Charles Madge, an enthusiast for Auden's poetry), where the wide-ranging collection and collation of data about everyday life offered the potential for decoding collective patterns, undiscernible on an individual basis.

Associates such as Spender commented that an air of dispassionate objectivity also tended to characterise Auden's attitude towards his friends, as if they, too, were so many case studies. This may in part have been a line of defence on the part of one who felt himself an outsider, memorably inciting those in the know to tell him the truth about love; on the one hand, Auden the onlooker with his lists and tabulations affected the pose of the scientist, on the other, he was the author of some of the century's most enduring poems about love. In fact, for most of the decade he was preoccupied by the need for change in two areas: in his emotional life, where he desired stability and reciprocation of affection; and in the state of the nation, where he desired greater honesty and a more equitable distribution of benefits. The cure he prescribed for both conditions, following the example of those he most admired as 'healers in this English land', could be summed up in the word 'love'; that is, a state in which knowledge would combine with passion to issue in right action, as he advised the homosexually hesitant Benjamin Britten: 'Act from thought should quickly follow: / What is thinking for?' (*EA*: 160). The role that poetry might play was outlined by Auden in his preface to *The Poet's Tongue*:

> Poetry is not concerned with telling people what to do, but with extending our knowledge of good and evil, perhaps making the necessity for action more urgent and its nature more clear, but only leading us to the point where it is possible for us to make a rational and moral choice.
> (p. ix)

This moderate definition (surprising, perhaps, from the author of so many imperative poems) occurred in an anthology for use in schools; and for a while schoolmaster Auden had wished to persuade himself that being a teacher might be the means to effect the social change he desired: in 1934, in a review of books on education for the magazine *Scrutiny*, he had declared that educationalists 'must always be revolutionaries' (*P* I: 66). But he also became aware that the kinds of independent boys' boarding-school in which he himself taught were not the vehicles of social change, but helped perpetuate the wrong kind of love: this is suggested by the earliest version of the poem he later called 'A Summer Night'

(1933), where the pleasures of his outdoor sleeping in the grounds of the Downs School, in a moonlit atmosphere of love, were contrasted with the plight of those hungry masses excluded from this *locus amoenus*. The previous autumn had seen a hunger march, in which poverty-stricken unemployed had converged on London from as far away as Glasgow for a mass gathering in Hyde Park, where protestors were baton-charged by mounted police; 1936 would see a similar event, when men marched from Jarrow in north-east England. Auden's involvement in documentary film-making, after leaving the profession of schoolteacher, may be read as an attempt to engage in a contemporary art-form that might make a difference; the documentary movement was itself affected by doctrines of social realism, and prefigured the generalised interest in the lives of ordinary citizens implied by Mass Observation later on. He quickly became disenchanted with the potential of that medium for discovering or presenting the truth, arguing that middle-class film-makers were unlikely to understand working-class realities. His forays into drama with the Group Theatre, undertaken mostly in collaboration with Isherwood, were also attempts to reach a wider audience in a more immediate setting than was possible by his issuing books of poetry; but it cannot be said that their experiments were successful, and Auden presents the unusual spectacle of a dramatist whose work, from *Paid on Both Sides* to *On the Frontier*, becomes less interesting as it progresses.

Looking beyond this island: to Iceland, Spain, China and the USA

The effect Auden had on his friends and many readers, of a young man with an important message to deliver, was one part of a whole that also included a defiantly unexalted view of what poetry should be for. When Geoffrey Grigson solicited opinions on the desirability of setting up his magazine *New Verse* in 1932, unlike some other respondents Auden affected bemusement: 'Is it as important as all that? I'm glad you like poetry but can't we take it a little more lightly. . . . I hope you'll keep it gay' (quoted in Davenport-Hines 1995: 127). It was in a spirit of gaiety, in all senses, that after leaving the GPO film unit Auden undertook his next project, which was to travel to Iceland and, with Louis MacNeice whom he also enrolled in the project, to produce a travel book of sorts. This idea of visiting Iceland had germinated when he learnt that Michael Yates was to go there with a party from Bryanston School, where Yates was a pupil; Auden had fallen in love with him during Yates's last year at the Downs School (in his company Auden had also undertaken a journey across Europe memorialised in the prose piece 'In Search of Dracula' (1934) and, more obliquely, the 1965 poem 'Since'). Iceland was a northern island, so – as Auden wrote – the journey there implied both rejection and escape; but the self-indulgences of the project were intruded on in more ways than one: Auden was shocked by the bloody shambles he encountered on a visit to a whaling-station; he bumped into Herman Goering's brother's entourage of Nazis visiting Iceland; and while he was there the news about the outbreak of the Spanish Civil War came through.

Auden's reaction, along with that of many others, was that this was a cause requiring him to make a real commitment. The major element in the book *Letters from Iceland* was his tonally casual but metrically intricate long poem of autobiography, addressed to Lord Byron; but if there was something 'Byronic' in the standard sense about his decision to go to Spain, the upshot resembled Byron in a less exalted light. One of the last people Auden met before his departure from London was Britten, who gushed into his diary about Auden's phenomenal bravery in going; but just as Byron travelled to enlist in the Greek fight for freedom carrying a helmet modelled on that of Achilles, but died of sickness before seeing any military action, so Auden was not used even in his proposed capacity as ambulance driver. He came back to write the poem 'Spain' which he later disowned, but was reticent about the overall experience, beyond recording he had been shocked to have been shocked by the compulsory closure of the churches in Barcelona. It was possibly a sign of his need to regain his bearings as much as his need to earn a living that he then went back to teach for the summer term of 1937 at the Downs School.

The prevalent contemporary view of the Spanish conflict was that it represented a crucial historical moment, on whose outcome the shape of Europe's future would depend. As much was expressed in the exhortative tone of Auden's poem, and implied in the willingness of so many foreign left-wing sympathisers to enlist in the International Brigade, in order to turn back the tide of Fascism in Europe. Hobsbawm has more recently asserted that 'contrary to the beliefs of this author's generation, the Spanish Civil War was not the first phase of the Second World War' (1994: 156); it was, however, an arena in which the views of many foreigners who engaged in it were unexpectedly modified (George Orwell and Arthur Koestler are examples of this). After his return from Spain, Auden was involved with Isherwood in planning what was to be their final play, and intended to go back to Spain with him for a conference designed to demonstrate the international left-wing intelligentsia's sympathies for the Republican side; but there were difficulties with visas and the trip did not occur. Instead, armed with a publisher's commission to write about the East, the two of them set off in mid-January 1938 for their six-month trip to China; outward via Egypt and Hong Kong, and inward via Japan and the USA. According to Isherwood, they had chosen that destination because, unlike the Spanish conflict, it had not been over-populated with writers looking for good copy; he reports Auden predicting they would 'have a war all of our very own' (*C&HK*: 217).

The apparent flippancy of that remark reflects something of the spirit in which they undertook the trip, which was motivated more by the itch to get away from England than to find a cause to espouse. The title of the book they produced gave a slightly misleading impression of its writers' purposive involvement in conflict: *Journey to a War* was not published until March 1939, after they had left for the USA in what would strike some to have been a decisive journey *away* from a war. Their departure for the East had been duly photographed and reported in the press: two young literary celebrities going off to take a closer look at history's dangerous flood. They came back convinced that the Japanese were the aggressors, and sympathetic to the Chinese, in whose cause Auden gave some speeches. Yet despite the fact that they witnessed little fighting, the trip was a jaunt that became serious, as Auden understood more of the atrociousness as well as the haphazardly unjust outcomes of war; also, similar to what happened in Iceland, while abroad news came of Germany's annexation of Austria. The sonnets that he wrote reflecting on these matters achieved a gravity that did not depend on overestimation of what the role of a poet could be in such matters. Ironically, the kind of poet he was interested in becoming was not the kind of poet he had been widely perceived to have been, nor yet the kind of literary figure England would value during the years of conflict to follow. Indeed, some thought Auden still wanted the Huns to win (and it would turn out that after returning to Europe he lived principally in countries formerly allied with Hitler). He had legitimate reasons for the move to America, consistent with positions developed over the preceding years and unrelated to any personal cowardice (as if it did not require some courage to uproot and start afresh); yet he never candidly acknowledged the reality of a sense of desertion engendered in fellow-countrymen by his departure – presumably because that was a function of the celebrity he wished to cast off.

Cometh the hour, goeth the poet: at a stroke he placed himself outside the frame of historical immediacy in which he had been perceived, and ceased to be able to offer the kind of reassuring presence and consistency that – for example – Eliot could, producing his last three quartets in wartime England. Nor could he measure up to a situation of crisis, as he had envisaged Isherwood doing in 'August for the People . . .', or accomplish what, in December 1940, Graham Greene asserted J.B. Priestley had done for the nation by means of his series of Sunday evening radio broadcasts, which began in the summer of 1940 after Hitler's onslaught had resulted in the catastrophically rapid fall of France and the scrambled evacuation of the British army from Dunkirk:

> We shall never know how much this country owed to Mr Priestley last summer, but at a time when many writers showed unmistakable signs of panic, Mr Priestley took the lead. When the war is over we may argue again over his merits as a novelist: for those dangerous months, when the Gestapo arrived in Paris, he was unmistakably a great man.
>
> (quoted in Sherry 1989: 441)

As Mendelson has pointed out, in the months leading to his expatriation Auden wrote many poems set outside England, as if prefiguring the event; and after his move to America, the titles of his poems signified an interest in time, rather than place. Yet that time was not indicated by the hour of the Bristol Bomber, nor the contemporary struggle; Auden foresaw a different role: he had, as asserted in 'September 1, 1939', only a 'voice' with which to combat the spread of untruth. But even this 'voice' was, in the historical moment which it addressed, less immediately effective than some others – as Greene also said of Priestley's broadcasts:

> [A]fter the disaster of Dunkirk, he became a voice: a slow, roughened voice without the French polish of the usual B.B.C. speaker; we had been driven off the Continent of Europe with a shattering loss of men and material . . . and the voice on Wednesday, June 5th, began to lead the way out of despair.
>
> (1989: 440)

In other words, Priestley here achieved Auden's earlier aim of uttering 'the thoughts of a wise man in the speech of the common people'; yet for all that, the voice in the poem Auden disowned for its glib historical relevance and falsifying sonorities about love, has outlasted that of the wartime radio programmes limited by topicality. The history with which he increasingly engaged, after his move to America, was not that being constituted by world events, momentous as these were, but that registered in patterns of cyclical recurrence or relating to the religious calendar.

For this reason, and because Auden actively sought to disinvolve himself from public life, the 'historical context' becomes of much lesser moment after 1940. He contacted the British embassy soon after war broke out, but was told that only citizens with essential skills were required; when, after American entry into the war at the end of 1941, he became liable for the military draft, he was rejected because of his homosexuality. He chafed a little, and considered trying to join the merchant marine in order to make a tangible contribution; but largely he spent the war years teaching and writing, and did not – as in Spain and China – observe the conflict itself, only its aftermath when he was part of the bombing survey in Germany. At the beginning of the 1950s, the spy scandal involving the defection to the USSR of double-agent Guy Burgess involved Auden, for Burgess (whom he knew slightly) had tried to contact him, hoping to stay at Auden's house in Forio: for a while, Auden found himself under watch. Later that decade, his candidacy for the Oxford Professorship of Poetry revived some discontents concerning his wartime absence. But for the most part he contentedly slipped out of the kind of limelight that had once shone on him, and disburdened himself of the expectations it entailed.

The personal context

Family; sexuality; education

Auden was opposed to biographical approaches to an author's work. Nevertheless, he tended in his own consideration of other writers to adopt such an approach, and biographical scholarship has made clear how much events from his own life informed the poetry he wrote. He described his own childhood position in his family as that of the naturally lucky and indulged third son, who in the fairy-tale sequence will succeed where the elder two must fail. Externally, the Audens enjoyed a middle-class prosperity that enabled the education at public schools of their three sons, the employment of domestic servants and the possession of a holiday cottage in the Lake District. Internally, the dynamic was more complicated, even though Auden seems never to have doubted that he was loved.

His father was an affectionate man, in a rather remote way, as Auden recalled:

> [T]o some degree I lost him psychologically. I was seven . . . when he enlisted . . . and I didn't see him again until I was twelve and a half. I think this is probably the reason that, although we got on amicably enough (all my rows were with my mother), we never really came to know each other. He was the gentlest and most unselfish man I have ever met – too gentle, I used sometimes to think, for as a husband he was often henpecked.
>
> (*F&A*: 501)

His father's absence led to the loss of a fixed abode for the family, which Auden claimed to have enjoyed, and coincided with his surprisingly late circumcision, which he did not: in America he would recall this last to have been 'quite something' (Carpenter 1981: 21). Davenport-Hines (1995) has speculated on possible reasons, and on the consequences for one who throughout his life manifested both negative and positive fixations regarding penises (the smallness of his own; the oral pleasurableness derivable from others'). It is generally agreed that Auden started at his Surrey prep school in September 1915, when he was eight, but he tended to claim that this had occurred a year earlier: in 1939 he wrote that his political education began 'at the age of seven when I was sent to a boarding school' (*EA*: 398; *P* II: 415), and he repeated the error in 1965, asserting that the Great War started a month before he left for school (see *F&A*: 503). In memory, private and public upheavals overlapped, reconfiguring the outbreak of war, his father's five-year absence, the disestablishment of home, his circumcision and his going away to school, as seismically simultaneous.

From his father's side, Auden judged himself to have inherited his robust health, and from his mother's a tendency to hysteria and neuroticism; George Auden represented common sense and reality, Constance, eccentricity and fantasy – which clearly made it appropriate that he should gather his earliest poetic effusions into notebooks which he presented to her. She stipulated that these should *not* be returned to him, as she was fearful he would destroy this earliest work; this underlines the dissonances referred to in Auden's parenthetical aside, above, that were part of their uncomfortable closeness: 'My mother, whom I understood very well, could be very odd indeed. When I was eight years old, she taught me the words and music of the love-potion scene in *Tristan*, and we used to sing it together' (*F&A*: 501). When he was an undergraduate, a visiting college friend witnessed Auden being reduced to tears by an argument with his mother – who struck some as a rigid and censorious presence, little enough exemplifying the eccentricity and fantasy she would symbolise in her son's retrospect. Tears, at other times, would constitute her response to evidence of his sexual preferences; and there may have been other tensions in the family, contributing to a desire to suppress unwelcome kinds of knowledge: during the war, George Auden seems to have had a love-affair with a nurse in Egypt, which cannot have made easy the resumption of his marriage to a woman whose son John declared of her, 'Mummy doesn't play; she punishes', and whose youngest recalled that 'Mother was often ill' (1929 Berlin journal; *EA*: 397).

All three sons took up pipe-smoking as their mark of manhood; Auden later became a notoriously immoderate cigarette-smoker. All three seem to have felt the need to move far away from home: Bernard to Canada and John to India, while Auden kept himself as unrooted as possible. Apart from his schoolmastering, which provided accommodation, he tended to use his parents' houses at Harborne and Wescoe as bases from which to operate; the tensions this created were partly ameliorated, in Birmingham, by his friendship with E.R. Dodds and his wife, at whose house he could take refuge: Dodds was then a colleague of George Auden's, as Professor of Classics at Birmingham University, and had appointed MacNeice to his staff. Auden did not find either parent wholly congenial company: he had hated a holiday to Yugoslavia taken with his father, and he would do his best to secure invitations to friends' houses or, failing that, to entice them to stay with him, in order to mitigate his parental exposure. The need was acutely felt during long stays at Wescoe with his mother.

Adopting a basically Freudian model, Auden inclined to connect both his creativity and his sexuality to the nature of his relationship with his mother, whose death – unlike that of his father, later – he commemorated with a long dramatic poem. Early rummagings in his father's library had meant he was precociously aware of the 'facts of life', before Constance Auden took it upon herself to try to explain them to him during her husband's absence; but perhaps for that very reason there tended to be a certain objectivity in his grasp and – some would aver – his practical applications of this knowledge. Educated entirely in single-sex establishments from prep school to Christ Church (women were a rarity at Oxford, and were themselves carefully segregated in separate colleges), there was scant opportunity for Auden to extend his heterosexual knowledge beyond the theoretical, for which he probably had little personal inclination in any case. Although he seems to have lost his virginity while an undergraduate, to an older woman in whose house he was staying on a trip abroad, this led to no Pauline conversion – except insofar as he found himself predominantly falling in love with unattainably heterosexual men at Oxford. His father came to tolerate his orientation, although there is no sign that his mother did; it is not obvious, however, that Auden became engaged in response to overt parental pressure, so much as because he believed he could change himself by an act of will. In 1935 he actually married Erika Mann, Thomas Mann's (lesbian) daughter, but this was entirely to furnish her with a means of leaving Nazi Germany, where she was about to be deprived of her citizenship. In 1946 Auden commenced a sexual relationship with Rhoda Jaffe, a young woman who had done some secretarial work for him; this was conducted over an extended period with the knowledge of Chester Kallman, and came to a close without any obvious bitterness on either side; later still, he twice proposed marriage to women, apparently more as a means to palliate potential loneliness than for any other reasons. But notwithstanding his sustained heterosexual involvement with Jaffe (which he later felt to have been wrong), Auden seems to have found penetrative sex with either gender objectionable – describing it in his 1964 Berlin journal as 'an act of sadistic aggression' or, passively, of masochistic submission (although he often defined himself as a 'bugger', he used the term generically, to denote 'homosexual' rather than 'participant in anal intercourse').

Despite the fact that homosexual acts between men were illegal in Britain and would remain so into the 1960s, the 1920s and 1930s were more tolerant – or simply less knowing – than the post-war period would prove to be. Two men could share the same room at an inn, for example, without arousing excessive suspicion; and in the circles in which Auden moved it was necessary only to be moderately discreet in one's behaviour. Some degree of subterfuge was required, and the threat of blackmail hung over anyone vulnerable to scandal; but the worst Auden had to endure in this line seems to have been the five pounds with which he bought his college bedmaker's silence, after being found in bed with Betjeman. It was perhaps ungallant of Auden to comment later that it had not been worth it, but at that time five pounds was more than a week's wage for many; the size of the bribe also indicated that the stakes were high: he would have been sent down from Oxford, and the offence was one for which imprisonment was possible. Certain kinds of self-censorship were required, therefore, and a homosexual poet – defiantly if covertly encoded in such a line as 'Different or with a different love' (*EA*: 25) – needed to leave ambiguously gendered the subject of any amorous verses; but these impositions were not necessarily perceived by Auden as damaging either to art or erotics. In his 1929 Berlin journal he confided that 'the attraction of buggery is its difficulties and torments. Heterosexual love seems so tame and easy after it'; the decadent secret guarded in the enemy's territory, the glamour of espionage, the dangerous crossing of frontiers, all featured in the atmosphere of the 'Audenesque', and constituted more of a resource than a repression – as, later, Caliban would declare: 'without these prohibitive frontiers we should never know who we were or what we wanted. It is they who donate to neighbourhood all its accuracy and vehemence' (*SP*: 154; *FTB*: 37).

Much the same could be said of the boarding-schools Auden attended, which he was to perceive as social structures metonymically corresponding to rudimentary (prep school) and evolved (public school) stages of collective organisation. 'Every English boy of the middle class,' he wrote in 'The Prolific and the Devourer', 'spends five years as a member of a primitive tribe ruled by benevolent or malignant demons, and then another five years as a citizen of a totalitarian state' (*P* II: 415). His prep school gave him a thorough grounding in Greek and Latin, and also provided his first homosexual experience, as he seems at the age of thirteen to have become involved with the recently arrived school chaplain: an episode in which the religious and erotic concerns of his life first coincided (*LA*: 266n). This kind of teacher–pupil relationship may then not have been as altogether uncommon as, now, we might wish; doubtless it grew out of the feverish atmosphere in which adolescent Auden prepared for confirmation, itself the culmination of a period of religious intensity. The following year he moved to Gresham's, where he drifted into agnosticism – although it is likely he was not as disencumbered of old beliefs as he supposed, since Robert Medley remembered that his asking Auden whether he wrote poetry was to cover the awkwardness of having angered this new friend by attacking the Church.

The regular religious routine of Auden's childhood, augmented by the frequent compulsory chapel-going that boarding-school involved, gave him a thorough exposure to the rituals and liturgy of the Church of England, as well as familiarising him with a good deal of the Bible, and embedding in his choirboy's memory the hymn-tunes he would delight to thunder out on pianos in adulthood. It also provided him with raw material for the satirical mock-sermons he was wont to perform for friends, and which would feature in his writing as well. Finally, it offered him a public and social world-view, to a version of which, after some years of errancy, he would return in adulthood; but he was in these formative years more preoccupied with private and asocial concerns, driven by his particular desire to situate himself in his own mythic landscape.

Auden's fantasy world

This derived from a 'North' which was initially imaginary, mediated by books, but was subsequently based upon locations in the North Pennines visited during the period of his enthusiasm for lead-mining. His initial imaginative compass-bearing came from the sagas his father read to him, believing that the family name had an Icelandic derivation: Auden would record this book among the contents of his 'nursery library'; which contained some surprising other items, alongside more conventional ones such as tales by Hans Christian Andersen and Hoffmann's *Struwwelpeter* poems. The unusual books bore titles such as *An Account of the Mining District of Alston Moor, Weardale and Teesdale* (1833), *Mines and Miners; or Underground Life* (1869), *Machinery for Metalliferous Mines* (1894) and *Lead and Zinc Ores of Northumberland and Alston Moor* (1923). The last, published when he was sixteen, could hardly properly qualify as a 'nursery' item, although Auden listed it as such; the first three all helped him in the childhood creation of a 'secondary world' which, although preceding his sense of poetic vocation, he regarded as directly linked to it. 'Most of what I know about the writing of poetry, or, at least, the kind I am interested in writing, I discovered long before I took an interest in poetry itself', he recalled in *A Certain World* (1970):

> Between the ages of six and twelve I spent a great many of my waking hours in the fabrication of a private secondary sacred world, the basic elements of which were (a) a limestone landscape mainly derived from the Pennine Moors in the North of England, and (b) an industry – lead mining.
>
> (*CW*: 423)

The characteristics of this world which linked it to poetry-writing were that, although intensely based in his imagination, it drew its materials from the primary 'given' world; and that in his disposition of those elements, the child Auden came to understand the nature of creative responsibility:

> As I was planning my Platonic Idea of a concentrating mill, I ran into difficulties. I had to choose between two types of a certain machine for separating the slimes, called a buddle. One type I found more sacred or 'beautiful', but the other type was, as I knew from my reading, the more efficient. At this point I realised that it was my moral duty to sacrifice my aesthetic preference to reality or truth.
>
> (*CW*: 425)

This imaginary phase, also consisting of 'a series of passionate affairs with pictures of, to me, particularly attractive water-turbines, winding-engines, roller-crushers, etc.', was superseded by his becoming familiar with the actual places in which lead-mining occurred. Auden seems to have paid his first visit to Alston Moor in 1919 when, at Rookhope in Weardale, he had the formative experience he most fully described in 'New Year Letter' (1940); 'I was never so emotionally happy as when I was underground' he recalled, a few months before writing that poem (*EA*: 398). The austere, depleted landscapes he saw then and revisited later, littered with abandoned workings but amid which, here and there, a few mines were still operational, became of immense symbolic significance to him: he continued to visit such places long after he had abandoned his pretensions to a career in mining, and evoked them throughout his writing career. Part of their appeal for him lay, he came to see, in the stoic endurance implicit in their states of unreproachful desertion; he greatly preferred the mute pathos of abandoned machinery to the clatter of an operational mine, and valued nature only as the poignant setting for such evidence of obsolete industrial endeavours: the remote moorland settings of many lead-mines heightened this effect (which is Auden's equivalent to the uncompleted sheepfold of Wordsworth's Michael).

He candidly described his fantasy world as 'autistic': self-sufficient and unshareable, it significantly lacked any human presence. People did not begin to interest him until adolescence, and for the most part theories preceded and modelled his responses to them. He once announced to the matron of his prep school that he liked to see the various types of boys, and perceiving people typologically remained a habit: in adulthood, he analogised a public schoolboy's progress from new entrant to sixth-former as a rise through the social classes, commenting that school offered an 'admirable laboratory for the study of class-feeling and political ambition' (*P* II: 416). Public schools then constituted a rigidly hierarchical system of possibilities, into which it was fairly easy to slot: the role Auden filled, of the short-sighted non-sporty intellectual eccentric, was no less a recognisable type than that of the hearty athlete on whom he tended to fixate. His undergraduate years which followed he described to a Yale audience in 1941 as having been the most unhappy of his life; one reason for which may have been that Oxford presented social and emotional challenges that could not be aloofly contemplated nor satisfactorily categorised like a laboratory experiment. In this speech, he looked back on his undergraduate self as having for the first time become conscious of the importance of personal relationships, and recalled the humiliations he suffered before learning that 'unlike his relation to his parents, love and friendship have to be worked for, carefully nourished, and above all, deserved' (*P* II: 119).

These were the self-perceptions of one then in the act of reviewing and reconstructing his life in the light of emigration and his not-yet-disappointed love for Kallman, which seemed to show he was at last able to confront the complications of reciprocity inherent in fully human relationships. Such difficulties were evaded by the scientist's objective stance he at times affected; all the same, the laboratory and its attitudes were important to Auden, who had gone to Gresham's School because it was strong in the sciences, at a time when they were sometimes marginalised by a curriculum still dominated by notions that a gentleman's education should be classical. His father's example had taught him that there need be no division between these areas, and Auden's interest in scientific method was a distinctive feature, leading him to look for causes underlying observed phenomena, in much the same way that a geological knowledge derived from his interest in mining made him alert to the rock strata beneath a landscape's surface. His switch from natural sciences to English at Oxford did not mean that he renounced his former training, so much as that he brought that to bear on his new interests; for this reason, the criticism of I.A. Richards, with its mimicry of scientific method in the business of literary evaluation, was more congenial to him than Eliot's.

Ideas, ideology and Christianity

The most influential discourses affecting the era in which Auden grew to maturity were those generated by Marx and by Freud, of whom he observed, in 'Psychology and Art To-day' (1935):

> Both Marx and Freud start from the failures of civilisation, one from the poor, one from the ill. Both see human behaviour determined, not consciously, but by instinctive needs, hunger and love. . . . The difference between them is the inevitable difference between the man who studies crowds in the street, and the man who sees the patient, or at most the family, in the consulting-room. Marx sees the direction of the relations between outer and inner world from without inwards, Freud vice-versa.
> (*EA*: 341)

George Auden wrote articles on psychology, so his omnivorous son might naturally take an interest in Freud, whose ideas in England were mediated by men like W.H.R. Rivers (who during the Great War played a decisive role in the lives of Wilfred Owen and Siegfried Sassoon, and whose work George Auden admired), and also by D.H. Lawrence in disputatious books such as his *Fantasia of the Unconscious* (1923), which for a while captivated Auden. Freud appealed to Auden as a healer and explicator, but he was more attracted by flashier or more dogmatic approaches such as Lawrence's, or those embodied in the writings of Georg Groddeck, and in the person and conversation of John Layard, a former associate of Rivers whom he met in Berlin. His relations with Layard were lurid, complicated, but finally stimulating (see accounts in Carpenter 1981; Davenport-Hines 1995; Page 1998); Layard's mentor had been Homer Lane, whose doctrine of 'original virtue' argued that disobedience to the inner law of our own nature was the only sin; in 'Get There If You Can . . .' Auden grouped Lane with Blake and Lawrence, as 'healers' whose remedies the English had ignored. What these had in common was a belief in the importance of unconscious or instinctual drives which, when thwarted, break out distortedly in neurosis or physical ailments; and alongside the ideas of Groddeck with their uncompromisingly psychosomatic analysis of illness (whereby a sore throat could be the consequence of lying), notions such as these pervaded the early writing. In his 1929 Berlin journal, Auden declared that 'Be happy and you will be good' was a truer maxim than 'Be good and you will be happy'; and since he was in Germany to cast off the shackles of his conventionalism, his application of this creed was practical.

In 'The Prolific and the Devourer' he asserted that the value for the artist of frameworks of general ideas or any explanatory theories – whether political, psychological, or religious – lay more in their 'immediate convenience' as ordering devices than in their 'scientific truth' as verifiable hypotheses (*EA*: 403–4). Younger Auden was an intellectual opportunist who tended to inhabit and exhaust ideas: thus, in 1934 he praised Lenin and T.E. Lawrence as figures whose lives exemplified 'what is best and significant in our time, our nearest approach to a synthesis of feeling and reason, act and thought' (p. 321), but he would outgrow those admirations. In 'The Good Life', written in 1935 shortly after 'Psychology and Art To-day', he suggested that psychology and communism were 'both concerned with unmasking hidden conflicts' (p. 351); and despite the contrasts that essay goes on to draw between them, looking back in 1955 Auden described his interest in Marx as having been more psychological than political: 'we were interested in Marx in the same way that we were interested in Freud, as a technique of unmasking middle-class ideologies' (*Early A*: 307). Yet this does not mean that the impetus they gave Auden's thought was superficial, because 'unmasking' was supremely important: in his 1934 essay, 'The Group Movement and the Middle Classes', he declared that 'to-day the light which has been shed by Freud and Marx on the motivation of thought makes it criminal to be uncritical' (*P* I: 48); and this necessary critical stance included the recognition that self-interest invariably played its part in the formulation of any intellectual position.

In his influential critical study *The Destructive Element*, Spender was concerned to suggest that for the 'highbrow' contemporary writer 'Communist' politics need not imply a proletarianism inevitably conducing to aesthetically regressive socialist realism; thinking about Upward and Auden, he described their work as 'advance-guard experimental writing imbued with Communist ideology' (1935: 236). In fact, for Auden, private highbrow experimentalism as well as public discourses such as psychology or communism could enact a similar subversion, so that the 'Mortmere' stories created by Isherwood and Upward at school, elaborated thereafter and circulated amongst a coterie of their friends, also influenced him: telling of grotesque goings-on in a parodically 'English' village whose inhabitants are barking mad but do not know it, 'Mortmere' too offered a 'technique of unmasking', albeit a superficial and unsystematic one. When Auden sent Upward a copy of his *Poems* (1930), he told him 'I shall never know how much in these poems is filched from you via Christopher' (letter dated 6 October 1930, British Library).

By the time of writing 'The Prolific and the Devourer' he was no longer interested in exposing middle-class ideologies, and was undertaking a personal redefinition that almost immediately made that piece of prose itself obsolete. During his first years in America his interest in Jung supplanted his interest in Freud, and was reflected in aspects of 'For the Time Being' and *The Age of Anxiety*; part of the attraction of Jung lay in the move beyond an individual to a collective psychological theory. But the more important intellectual adherence that became visible at this period was Auden's readoption of Christianity; 'Religion' had been the third element considered alongside 'Psychology' and 'Communism' in 'The Good Life', and it outlasted the two others in its importance for the rest of his life and writing. As will already be clear, Auden's reflections on his earlier life have about them a degree of myth-making; thus, one account he gave for his return to Christianity attributed it to the shock he had received in November 1939 when, in a Manhattan cinema, he watched a Nazi film about the invasion of Poland and heard German-Americans in the audience shouting 'Kill them!' whenever Poles appeared on the screen. This required him, he said, to consider what moral basis he had for the repugnance he felt; and this in turn led him to see that no doctrine deriving from politics or psychology could be sufficient: these were inevitably relativist, when what was needed was an absolute definition of 'good' and 'evil' that only religion could provide.

Important as that cinema in Yorkville was for him, it is clear that Auden had been aware, at least since his reactions to the locked churches of Barcelona, that Christianity still had claims upon him. The virtual simultaneity of his re-embracing Anglicanism and initiating the process of applying for US citizenship might suggest a desire to retain some aspects of the England he was disengaging from; but although his preferred form of worship resembled that of his childhood, the theology in which he immersed himself at this period was the radical Protestantism being expounded by theologians such as Paul Tillich and Reinhold

Niebuhr, philosophically related to the thought of Søren Kierkegaard, which Auden first encountered on reading Charles Williams's history of the Church *The Descent of the Dove*, early in 1940. Williams's excerpts from Kierkegaard provoked him to a more sustained engagement with the work which, he later told a friend, 'knocked the conceit out of me'; as Mendelson puts it: 'Kierkegaard's existential Christianity offered two strengths that psychoanalysis and politics could not: it perceived its relation to an absolute value; and it understood that it could never claim to know or embody that value' (*LA*: 130). Two aspects seem particularly significant: Kierkegaard's insistence on the importance of individuals' self-definition through the moral choices they make (rather than finding themselves lived by forces greater than themselves, 'behaving' rather than 'acting', as the theories of Marx and Freud tended to suggest); and the impossibility of attaining to the highest 'religious' stage of experience other than by a chosen leap of faith. Again unlike Marx or Freud, Kierkegaard did not desire to lead a movement.

Auden was appalled by the kind of unindividuated collectivism he observed manifesting itself in Nazism under the charismatic leadership of Hitler; but equally he distrusted what he had once termed the isolated personal life: Christianity offered a collectivism that absolved its believer from none of the responsibilities of individuality. One of the consequences of Auden's Christianity was to re-emphasise the limited importance of poetry compared to other things; and even if the long poems he composed during and after the war were serious in their intentions as they were ambitious in their scope, they did not commit the error of Matthew Arnold or the contemporary Wallace Stevens, of supposing that poetry should be a substitute for religion. Although, as Carpenter has suggested, Auden's return to Christianity implied, in its acceptance of the doctrine of original sin, a break from earlier beliefs approximating to Lane's doctrine of original virtue, this did not also imply that the poet had retreated to a safely transcendent theology which licensed detachment from the fallen world. Friends such as Isherwood could be enraged by what he called 'the smugness of Wystan's Christian dogmatism' (*C&HK*: 228), and in the 1950s Spender confided to his Journal the thought that 'the effect of [Auden's] cultivating a bad Christian conscience has been to free him of interest in social problems' (1985: 127); but Mendelson asserts the opposite, arguing that 'through all his later religious changes Auden retained this sense of Christianity's integration with social justice' (*LA*: 151), and Stan Smith argues for a fundamental continuity, finding that Auden's Christianity is 'neither a quietist cult of waiting for the millennium, nor a recantation of his radical past. It is, rather, the translation into a new discourse of those impulses which lay behind his thirties writing, a resistance to temporal power in all its forms' (1985: 176).

As Smith has also suggested, the Auden about whom we write and speculate is always a construct, partly dependent on our own ideological position – so that, for example, the issues around his expatriation will look different, seen from British or American perspectives; just as they looked different to him, at different times. In November 1939, he wrote to Margaret Gardiner that he never wished to see England again and that he was 'happier than I ever believed it possible to be' (Berg Collection); yet the following month, I.A. Richards wrote to T.S. Eliot of having attended a crowded lecture Auden gave at Harvard: 'He is an utterly changed man . . . thin, white, shrunk and tortured by something' (quoted in

Davenport-Hines 1995: 201); and in 1951 Auden would be writing to the Sterns, envying them their imminent return to the English countryside and climate(!). Perhaps the more balanced assessment is one he gave Mrs Dodds, in an early letter from America: 'About becoming American. I know that this is a very difficult thing to decide. What England can give me, I feel it already has, and that I can never lose it' (11 July 1939, Bodleian).

In his essay 'Morality in an Age of Change' commissioned by *Nation*, a liberal American magazine, and probably written in November 1938, Auden declared:

> But we do have to choose, every one of us. . . . No policy of isolation is possible. Democracy, liberty, justice and reason are being seriously threatened and, in many parts of the world, destroyed. It is the duty of every one of us, not only to ourselves but to future generations of men, to have a clear understanding of what we mean when we use these words, to remember that while an idea can be absolutely bad, a person can never be, and to defend what we believe to be right, perhaps even at the cost of our lives and those of others.
>
> (*P* I: 486)

Particularly in its close, this seems to show the kind of specious rhetoric that Orwell had objected to in the phrase 'necessary murder' in the poem 'Spain': there is little enough indication that this rallying cry was being uttered by one about to leave Europe behind, pursuing what more resembled a policy of isolation than active defence of what he believed to be right. But this tub-thumping tone would be repeated in an address Auden gave six months later in New York, in aid of Spanish refugees (*P* II: 15–18); and it was after this effective rabble-rousing, he told Mrs Dodds in his July letter, that he felt himself 'just covered with dirt', and determined not to repeat such a performance.

At about the same time he was telling her this, in 'The Prolific and the Devourer' Auden was criticising those 'who today seek in politics an escape from the unhappiness of their private lives' (*EA*: 405); he noted that artists were not immune to this temptation. Naturally he had himself in mind, and Mendelson has suggested that Auden's political withdrawal was a consequence of his resolving his own personal unhappiness through the relationship with Kallman. Of course, it is equally true that people can seek in their personal lives escape from the unhappiness of a political situation they wish not to confront; Auden's earlier poetry had offered its critique of such complacently sequestered selves, and John Milton, that intemperate radical, in the seventeenth century uttered the most ringing denunciation: 'I cannot praise a fugitive and cloistered virtue, unexercised and unbreathed, that never sallies out and sees her adversary, but slinks out of the race, where that immortal garland is to be run for, not without dust and heat' (*Areopagitica*). Yet there is a falsity of tone in the heat and dust of Auden the propagandist, audible at the end of his *Nation* essay and throughout his New York speech: the first summons its audience as much to the dictionary as to the barricades, and the second calls its hearers to action with an insistence that seems more indicative of Auden's own unease (putting me in mind of Emerson's observation that 'the more he talked of his honor, the faster we counted our spoons'). What was falsifying about the tone of voice he adopted was that it violated one of the fundamental principles which, he argued, psychology, Christianity and art had in common: the non-coercive mode. In 'Psychology and Art To-day' he wrote that 'the task of psychology, or art for that matter, is not to tell people how to behave, but by drawing their attention to what the impersonal unconscious is telling them, and by increasing their knowledge of good and evil, to render them better able to choose' (*EA*: 340–1); and in 'The Good Life', shortly afterwards, pursuing an analogy between psychology and Christianity he asserted that 'the only method of teaching [psychology] recognises is parabolic. . . . You must never tell people what to do – only tell them particular stories of particular people with whom they may identify' (*EA*: 347).

It would be a mistake to suppose that Auden's life and work formed a simply explicable linear progression, in which adherence to one set of doctrines or allegiances was sequentially supplanted by another; similarly, the career will not add up to a conveniently interpretable whole. Auden himself accepted the principle that the meaning of a poem could alter, depending on its reader's context, and his revisions and excisions of earlier work implicitly denied that art attains to any state of transcendent unalterability, but is continually involved in time. Yet from the early 1930s onward, he was fairly consistent in his view that poetry should persuade rather than constrain (to adopt key terms from his elegy for Yeats): the similarity between his definitions in the previous paragraph and that offered in *The Poet's Tongue* at roughly the same period is noteworthy. In 'The Prolific and the Devourer' he observed that 'If the criterion of art were its power to incite to action, Goebbels would be one of the greatest artists of all time' (*EA*: 406); later, in 'Squares and Oblongs' (1948), he scorned Shelley's view that poets were the 'unacknowledged legislators of the world' as a description more appropriate to the secret police, and went on to enforce the difference between literary and social order:

> A society which really was like a poem and embodied all the esthetic values of beauty, order, economy, subordination of detail to the whole effect, would be a nightmare of horror, based on selective breeding, extermination of the physically or mentally unfit, absolute obedience to its Director, and a large slave class kept out of sight in cellars.
>
> (*P* II: 348)

In the same piece, he offered a definition of the true attitude of a poet which was in many ways consistent with the throwaway response he had earlier given to Grigson's enquiry about seting up *New Verse*: ' "Why do you write poetry?" If the young man [*sic*] answers: "I have important things to say," then he is not a poet. If he answers: "I like hanging around words listening to what they say," then maybe he is going to be a poet' (pp. 343–4). Subordination to the power of language was for Auden as much of a prerequisite for poetry as insubordination to temporal power; but it was equally necessary to know the differences between the two.

2

Works

The first of Auden's poems published in a book was 'Woods in Rain', included in a 1924 anthology of public school verse where his name was Shakespeareanised to 'W.H. Arden'. At Oxford he was evidently well-enough known for a pastiche to appear in a university magazine, under the Joycean name of Mystan Baudom (sounding like 'Mist and Boredom'; Bucknell speculates that the author might have been Isherwood. In China the two of them would sinofy into 'Y Hsiao Wu' and 'Au Dung'). Despite these denominative variations, however, there was soon little doubt about the kind of poet Auden was: his name was used to define a brand, the 'Audenesque', which eclipsed the minor ones of 'public school' or 'Oxford' poetry in influence and importance. In an era in which schoolboys' poems and undergraduate verse were anthologised and sometimes even reviewed, it was not difficult to get into print; still less if one had a friend such as Spender, who in 1928 privately printed a pamphlet containing twenty of Auden's poems. The eventual acceptance by Eliot of a first collection of thirty poems – having in 1927 turned down an earlier proposal – was a surer sign; nine poems from Spender's pamphlet survived into this Faber volume (a further six were incorporated into 'Paid on Both Sides').

Auden's revisions and excisions of his work became more noticeable later in his career, but were apparent from the beginning; it was his habit to enter poems into notebooks, where even what seem to be fair copies were subject to modification. This process can be tracked through Bucknell's edition of his *Juvenilia*, from which it can also be seen that from early on Auden acquired the habit of salvaging felicitous bits of rejected poems for incorporation into later work (a notable example occurs in 'Who Stands, the Crux Left of the Watershed', whose line 23 and most of lines 25–8 derived from an earlier poem). This raises issues about the nature of the relationship between the poet and his work, and the work and its readers, to be touched on in due course; the next part offers a survey of the successive collections of poetry he published (including the prose and poetry collaborations with MacNeice and Isherwood; it also includes a note on his dramas). There are several reasons for doing this. To examine the particular characteristics of books marking the principal stages of his career is to observe the changing face of Auden – to 'consider [him] and in [his] time', in his own phrase. We can gauge contemporary responses to his work, and recover some sense of the original poet whom his later self revised and even censored. It also enables attention to be paid to poems, beyond those singled out for detailed discussion in the later part of the section, and to see how these suggest the broader concerns of his writing.

Auden's books of poetry

Poems (1930)

This was part of Fabers' strategy to market work by new poets. Its contents consisted of 'Paid on Both Sides', which Eliot at the last minute agreed to include, followed by thirty poems, untitled and identified solely by roman numerals. This absence of titles marked a distinctive difference from Eliot's own practice, and Yeats's: providing the reader no preliminary clue to content or meaning, it added to a sense of suddenness with which poems were encountered, forcing an unmediated engagement with unfamiliar – and, as some found, intransigent – material. It took two years for the initial print-run of 1,000 copies to be exhausted, so the book was not a meteoric success, even by the modest sales figures anticipated for serious poetry; nevertheless, it established Auden as a talent worth watching, and was more important for its impact upon a particularly influential readership: the dustjacket for *Look, Stranger!* would later claim that this first volume had 'immediately marked the author as a leader of a new school of poetry that has since established itself'. Reviewers responded both with perplexity and with excitement, and in his 1931 review of the *Criterion* printing of 'Paid on Both Sides', William Empson praised the charade because 'psycho-analysis and surrealism and all that, all the irrationalist tendencies which are so essential a part of the machinery of present-day thought' were 'made part of the normal and rational tragic form'; it had 'the sort of completeness that makes a work seem to define the attitude of a generation' (Haffenden 1983: 80). Auden's ability to effect a conciliation between tendencies in 'present-day thought' and literary tradition (rather than seeking refuge from the first in the second) was what made him seem contemporary and important: Empson's closing comment recalls that Edmund Wilson had suggested that in 1922 *The Waste Land* reflected the attitude of its generation.

Auden originally wrote 'Paid on Both Sides' for performance at the Somerset home of his Oxford friend Bill McElwee, as part of the latter's twenty-first birthday celebrations (it was vetoed, for fear of offending neighbours also invited). McElwee and his younger brother Patrick, with whom Auden fell successively and unrequitedly in love, had boarded at Sedbergh School; fascinated by their tales of its spartan northern hardiness, he duly incorporated Sedbergh into his private mythology: the first version of his charade – in which the chorus was to be dressed as rugby-players – reflected its sporting ethos, as well as evoking some local geographical features. The version printed in the *Criterion* and in *Poems* had been revised in Berlin, and in addition to introducing the surrealist elements referred to by Empson above, aligned its action more clearly across locations to the west and east of Alston Moor. In the 1940s Auden emphasised its autobiographical angle by describing it as 'A parable of English middle-class (professional) family life 1907–1929' (*Early A*: 47): the dates were his own life-span at the time of composition. The reader encountering it for the first time was challenged by the generic oddity of something called a 'charade', which contained fanciful elements within an apparently seriously intended drama of vengeful hatred triumphing over love: the hatred was principally embodied in a mother whose implacability is common to both versions, although her leg-iron had been lost in revision. A provocative disorientation, together with a theme of the interlinkage of love with conflict, featured in many of the poems which followed in the book.

When compiling his first *Collected Poems* in America, Auden created titles for those poems from this era he decided to preserve; here I treat the first line (or phrase) as the title. When choosing work for the Faber volume, Auden had not known that his charade would precede them (see *Early A*: 87n); therefore he compiled his thirty poems in the belief that they would constitute the whole book, and since they were not arranged in order of composition some other organising principle is inferrable (chronological order is followed in *EA*, which lists individual volume contents in an appendix). The first two, 'Will You Turn a Deaf Ear' and 'Which of You Waking Early', start with questions, and the first three address a 'you' which seems to implicate the reader; this markedly vocative mode continues through the invitational imperatives of the fourth ('Watch Any Day His Nonchalant Pauses') into an earlier poem written at the end of 1927, 'From the Very First Coming Down', which springs the surprise of its vocative in the emphatic 'you' with which its fourth line begins. This poem is the first in which we also encounter an 'I' whom it seems safe to identify as the author and is, Fuller asserts, one of only three in the volume to contain 'a reliably personal "I" ' (1998: 59). These first five poems offered variations of form and metre, including restrained tetrameter rhyming couplets as well as more discursive alliterative strong-stress verse.

It was difficult poetry, and early readers found it so; but it offered a different kind of problem from Eliot – who had in his essay on 'The Metaphysical Poets' (1921) influentially propounded his doctrine of the necessary difficulty of modern poetry. The first line of Auden's opening poem is a more confrontational formulation than the 'Let us go then, you and I' with which Eliot preferred to start his various collections of verse; the gnomic sparseness of 'Will You Turn a Deaf Ear' gives much less circumstantial detail, both psychological and social, than is provided in Prufrock's musings. The language of Auden's poem appears to reflect an interior logic, yet that logic is not easily discoverable, nor straightforwardly grammatical. Information available to us now makes it a little more accessible, but the contemporary reader could not have known that when he wrote it in September 1929, Auden was in London tutoring the son of an officer paralysed in the war and confined to a wheelchair; nor that his adherence to the doctrines of Homer Lane as mediated by Layard had led him to claim that Spender was so tall because he was unconsciously trying to reach heaven: both facts throw light on the poem's images. Hardly anybody knew that it also served as the prologue to a play called 'The Enemies of a Bishop', Auden's first collaboration with Isherwood, in which the bishop who uttered it was loosely modelled on Homer Lane, for that play was never performed. Yet the reader who felt obscurely upbraided by 'Will You Turn a Deaf Ear' could have noticed that the last poem in the book, 'Sir, No Man's Enemy', was probably not addressing him (and certainly not her), and that this sonnet ended with the invocation of a brighter future, involving modern architecture and changes of heart.

Having opened with numbed language and imagery of death, the collection, thus, finished on a note of rhetorical bravura, in which the intercession of a higher power may yet enable life-affirming change. Mendelson notes that Auden wrote 'Sir, No Man's Enemy' immediately after 'Will You Turn a Deaf Ear' (where he believes Auden principally addressed himself): the later poem repudiates the moral inertia dwelt on by its forerunner, anticipating possible rectification of the cowardice and automatism with which that seems preoccupied. 'Will You Turn a Deaf Ear' also introduces the imagery of plotting and espionage that forms a running strand in the rest of the volume, along with ideas concerning the risks involved – or declined – in the search for love, and a concern with heroism not easily locatable in lives sometimes deceptive in their posed assurance ('Watch Any Day . . .'). Also manifest in various poems is a slightly complacent anger directed mainly against the privileged classes (though not excluding Auden himself), whose future is seen to consist in the essentially Lawrentian choice proposed at the end of 'Get There If You Can . . .', of learning to live or deciding to die. This poem written in Tennyson's 'Locksley Hall' metre, which Auden excluded from his collected editions, may seem to indicate the truth of Yeats's dictum that rhetoric results from the quarrel with others and poetry from the quarrel with oneself; but its excesses and those of other poems in the book can be justified as a declamatoriness protesting against a climate of pervasive and unhealthy reticence: for the suppression of important truths, sometimes by a falsifying loquacity, is also a concern of several poems.

The presiding powers of *Poems* (1930) are Eros and Thanatos, exerting urges which are not invariably contrary, since in different ways each can lead to entropy and despair, and each to rebirth. In his Berlin journal, Auden had written that 'the real "life wish" is the desire for separation, from family, from one's literary predecessors' and, separately, noted 'the Tyranny of the Dead' (*EA*: 299). These preoccupations surface in several poems, including one composed in Berlin in April 1929, 'The Strings' Excitement, the Applauding Drum', to which far-from-lucid poem Auden later gave the title 'Family Ghosts'. Written in a *terza rima* that breaks its own pattern to produce an internal division resembling that between a sonnet's octave and sestet, it analogises the emotional and sexual quandary of its speaker to a city under siege: knowing that ancestral ghosts will approve a certain – possibly heterosexual – choice of partner, the effects of that choice appear to lead to the 'despair' of glaciated incommunicative indifference in the final image. It is one of several poems written in sequence that deal with the 'tyranny of the dead' and express the challenges of love in military or conspiratorial metaphors (see *EA*: 29–36); this one, emerging at a time when Auden was becoming more convinced that his homosexuality was the unalterable truth of himself, but was still engaged to be married, appears to present the emotional predicament of its speaker as one of dark extremity.

Auden's personal situation would, of course, have been known only to a handful of readers; but the rest could nevertheless have been alert to his book's depiction of a society half in love with easeful death. They could, whilst being impressed by its not sounding like Eliot, pick up occasional echoes of him, and of a variety of other voices – Shakespeare, Hopkins, Emily Dickinson, Gertrude Stein, Laura Riding and Yeats – without ever feeling that the work was merely derivative; they could also have noticed the specialised terminology appearing in more than one poem, where Auden lifted phrases from books on psychology or anthropology he had read. As Spender was to observe, Auden had 'plagiarized on an heroic scale' (1935: 259); but his borrowings were made part of a larger and different whole. Readers would also have been struck by imagery of industrial decline and high fells beleaguered by weather, that seemed to suggest a northern geography: the two aspects came together memorably in 'Who Stands, the Crux Left of the Watershed', but were present in several other poems as well as 'Paid on Both Sides'. They might have been startled that the word 'buggers' slipped past the censor (in one of the poems excluded from the second edition, 'Which of You Waking Early').

The book, finally, was not a neatly thematised totality; the principal obstacle lay in the impenetrability of many of its pieces, and even if MacNeice put the best gloss possible on this by noting in his review that the poems were not tyrannised by the necessity of meaning, Auden conceded to another basically appreciative reviewer, Naomi Mitchison, that the obscurity she had noted was a bad fault. Part of the problem is foregrounded in the very label 'charade' to describe 'Paid on Both Sides'; the dictionary defines this as an acted riddle, and although – as MacNeice suggested – vivid acting might compensate for a finally impenetrable puzzle, the notion of *private* performance also implicit in the notion of a charade suggests the tiresome exclusiveness of an extended in-joke ('That is what friendship is. Fellow-conspiracy', the Berlin journal noted). Most of the poems had been written during or after Auden's spell in Berlin, and some of the names and episodes they referred to derive from that period; but only one, 'This Lunar Beauty', was written after he took up his job at Larchfield. Consequently, whatever personal advances Auden had made in Germany, until he secured the steady if unremunerative employment as schoolmaster he was, during the composition of most of these poems, at least semi-dependent on his father; this in turn may have contributed something to the themes of inauthenticity connected to ancestral domination that are apparent in several poems. The conspiratorialism was doubtless also connected to his homosexuality, which of itself enforced secretive behaviour; and however matter-of-fact Auden may have been about this, he was living in a society which condemned him as illegal in expressing his true nature. It is as if life only could amount to a charade, lived in the shadow of elders who could always pull rank by having fought a war you were born too late to be involved in, and who disapproved of the way you were; but by his next volume, Auden offered a different and more boisterous governing metaphor for inauthenticity: oratory.

The Orators (1932)

The book's subtitle was 'An English Study', but he wrote most of it in Scotland, using details of Helensburgh and its surroundings; this is noteworthy, because the experience of being beyond the border was important to him, not least because it seems to have helped him see England more clearly and crystallised his responses. Earlier examples of this process were the poems 'Who Stands, . . .', written shortly after returning from a holiday with his father in Yugoslavia, and 'From Scars where Kestrels Hover', which was written in Berlin, yet obviously evoked a northern British landscape. Fuller comments, of a later uncollected poem set above Helensburgh ('A Happy New Year', *EA*: 444), 'it is as though from such a height, even though in Scotland, he can see the whole of England' (1998: 180). In the case of *The Orators*, mostly written between spring and autumn 1931, the self-assurance of Auden's 'take' on the England he studied resulted in a self-consciously complicated picture, rather than any clairvoyant panorama. His initially mixed feelings about this book later hardened into a sense of its having failed, which led him to exclude the greater part of it from his *oeuvre*: by 1944 he would dismiss it as a 'fair notion fatally injured' in the foreword to his first *Collected Poems*; and twenty years later, his introductory remarks to a new edition confessed bemused estrangement from a work which seemed to have been written by a talented fellow on the brink of insanity and Nazism. Unlike his other 1930s volumes, the contents do not easily lend themselves to extraction, which reflects the fact that its parts do not satisfactorily function in isolation from each other: when first published, the blurb – probably written by Eliot – described it as 'not a collection, but a single work with one theme and purpose'. Because this volume was a significant step in Auden's career, and because overall it does not contain the sorts of anthology pieces amenable to close reading out of this context, I shall pay it extended attention here.

Although its difficulty and unconventionality were noted by reviewers on first publication, they also found much to praise; and whatever the shortcomings its author diagnosed, this was the book by which he drew ahead of the field. Haffenden (1983) includes fourteen reviews of *The Orators*: more than for any other of book of poetry or drama Auden published. This is a significant quantity of attention, indicative of the status the poet was accruing: 'Those who like to keep up with the newest developments of English literature have known his name for some time', noted one (Haffenden 1983: 94); and considering that its almost aggressive experimentalism makes it the most consciously avant-garde of his books, there were some suprisingly affirmative responses, even from those who made no secret of their bafflement. Its aggression was, in fact, one of the features found appealing by some: Geoffrey Grigson (an Auden enthusiast) thought it justifiably 'savage' and 'violent' (1983: 106), and the *TLS* reviewer judged it 'insolently but exhilaratingly new' (1983: 98). Although F.R. Leavis sounded the note of concern about Auden's schoolboyish propensities that would in time become his *leitmotiv* in increasingly dismissive evaluations, here he conceded this book's 'remarkable' qualities, which caused him to entertain high hopes of the contribution Auden could make to modern English poetry. Leavis, along with others, noted that Auden belonged to the generation whose boyhood had coincided with the Great War; but more significantly three of its reviewers (Grigson, Parkes and John Hayward in his *Criterion* review) drew explicit connections between *The Orators* and *The Waste Land*, first published ten years previously: Hayward claimed it as 'the most valuable contribution to English poetry' since Eliot's poem (1983: 15). There is no doubt that the example of Eliot had created a climate in which a work such as *The Orators* could be projected; but that climate itself was, in part, a source of objection: the link with *The Waste Land* has been more recently – and differently – elaborated by Smith, who argues that Auden's book stands in an adversarial relation to Eliot's poem (in 'Remembering Bryden's bill . . .').

The Orators went into a second edition in 1934, when Auden omitted two poems and a paragraph of prose; it is this version which Mendelson prints in *The English Auden* (giving the excised material in appendices), and to which I refer here. Auden made further alterations in his 1960s reprinting, rendering that less reliable as a means of recapturing the book's first impact three decades earlier. What confronted readers was a book that mixed poetry with a considerable quantity of prose; it included lists and diagrams, along with names of places and people they had little chance of decoding, since many referred to the people figuring in Auden's life as friends and colleagues, and to the places familiar to him from his Helensburgh surroundings. Some commentators therefore assumed that this was an in-joke which would be transparent to the poet's intimates; but they, despite being included by direct reference and as dedicatees, were no better equipped to make sense of it than most others. It is an obscure book, but its references to the Helensburgh locale, Smith has argued, function as a democratic rebuke – by means of a deliberately minimising inversion – of the metropolitan swagger of *The Waste Land*: if people were supposed to know about the Strand or King William Street in London, why should they not also and equally know about Helensburgh's Craigendoran Pier or Sinclair Street? The obscurities were deepened by unreferenced borrowings from a variety of sources (for examples, Wolfgang Köhler's *Gestalt Psychology* (1930), and John Layard's papers on ritual practices in the Malekulan Islands, published in the *Journal of the Royal Anthropological Institute* in 1928 and 1930). The book was spreading its net far beyond conventional literary sources, and in fact shortly before publication its author became alarmed that he might have gone too far, and proposed to Eliot, at Faber's, the inclusion of an apologetic foreword: 'I feel this book is more obscure than it ought to be. I'm sorry, for obscurity, as a friend once said to me, is mostly swank' (quoted in *Early A*: 96). Eliot, however, advised against any such concession to readerly perplexity.

The Orators consisted of a Prologue (the poem 'By Landscape Reminded Once of His Mother's Figure') followed by three 'Books'. The first was titled 'The Initiates' and comprised four sections: 'Address for a Prize-Day' (first published in the *Criterion*); 'Argument' (itself sub-divided into three numbered subsections); 'Statement' (also in three parts); 'Letter to a Wound'. All of Book I was prose. The second, 'Journal of an Airman', consisted of groupings of prose paragraphs, diagrams and lists, interspersed by six (originally eight) poems. Book III contained 'Six Odes' of varying lengths and metres, the earliest from October 1930 and the latest from November 1931. Finally, an Epilogue balanced the Prologue: ' "Oh Where Are You Going?" Said Reader to Rider' (echoing the traditional ballad, 'The Cutty Wren'). These first and final items, two poems from Book II and two of the Odes were all that Auden wished to preserve when, late in life, he finalised his *oeuvre*. Whether this indicated a loss of interest in any notion of an 'English Study', or whether it was principally because he distrusted the nature of his analysis (so far as he could later understand it), are matters for speculation; but what seems less speculative is that later Auden was much less attuned to the kinds of intellectual and stylistic extravagance that *The Orators* displays, and had developed an impatience with such bravura performances.

Ideas of 'performance' are particularly relevant to *The Orators*, since oratory, as public speaking, implies an immediacy of relation between linguistic performer and audience: such performance is a 'live' rather than a deferred one (as when reading a printed essay or a poem). The book offers various types of public speaker, from the Old Boy giving his prize-day speech to the soapbox 'windbags' noted in Ode IV; whether as official invitee or self-appointed street preacher, they share the conviction of a particular responsibility to set the world to rights. In this Ode, Auden both discriminates himself from such presumptuousness and gives the grounds for his own right to address us, in the jubilantly bathetic declaration, 'It is John, son of Warner, has pulled my chain' (*EA*: 101: the low-cistern w.c. condemns this image to a lingering death). At work on 'The Journal of an Airman' in August 1931, he told Mitchison that formally he was attempting to write 'abstract drama – all the action implied' (*Early A*: 97), which again underlines a concept of performance; but the journal as a form, along with the claustrophobic intimacy of 'Letter to a Wound' preceding it, are paradoxically secretive types of utterance, intended for their recipient's eyes only. They are not, strictly speaking, acts of oratory; and in fact, a journal or diary implies the most self-reflexive and internalised kind of communication. *The Orators*, then, offers extremes of discursive behaviour, from the complacent egotism of the public speaker sounding off, to the introverted narcissism of the writer focused on the insides of his body ('Letter to a Wound' – suggested by Auden's 1930 operation for an anal fissure) or his head ('Journal of an Airman').

This is a simplifying schema, but one which corresponds to a distinction instigated by the volume's epigraph, which prefers private faces in public places to public faces in private places: persons who remain true to themselves in public are 'wiser and nicer' than persons who obtrude a public self-importance into the private sphere; or, it is better to see those you love inhabiting the public world than to have as a lover someone more committed to that world than to you (a public face in a private place might also summon up for certain readers the outrageously subversive vision of receiving oral sex from, say, a prominent politician). Yet in what does truth to self consist, and how does it transfer into the public realm? These were questions of particular importance to a practising homosexual like Auden, whose private self was legally excluded from public recognition – except punitively. The private–public dichotomy was relevant to 'Paid on Both Sides', a performance or drama implicitly public, yet intended – as 'charade' – for private consumption. Indeed, the public school atmosphere of *The Orators* draws attention to the paradox that such establishments are private and hierarchically exclusive, characteristically defined by limited accessibility (Smith notes the further paradox that Larchfield was 'an *English* public school in Scotland' (1985: 95)). The book is a public statement with an intensely and covertly allusive private agenda, most radically signalled in that passage of the 'Journal' where apparently nonsensical personal reminiscences (of Auden's) which dissolve into impenetrably infantile private nicknames are synchronised with the collapse – and some would say, subsequent class-treachery – of MacDonald's Labour government in August 1931 (see *EA*: 87–8). This, too, can be seen to point up the ways in which Auden's attitudes differ from Eliot's in *The Waste Land*: for whereas Eliot's poem evoked the past and its great episodes and personages, undertaking a transcontinental sweep that included the Ganges and north Africa, Auden remains defiantly localised, refers to his own circle of friends, and relates his writing to contemporary events unfolding during its composition.

The political contexts of *The Orators* have been incisively set forth by Smith, and its structure and sources investigated by Mendelson in *Early Auden* and Fuller in his *Commentary*, with a thoroughness making replication here unnecessary. Fuller, enlarging on the work's function as an 'English Study', suggests that 'it is a portrait of a culture sketched both by social and political allusion, . . . a self-referential display of literary and verbal forms, and . . . a quasi-anthropological analysis of a variety of socially embedded rites of initiation, conflict and sympathetic magic' (1998: 86). The novelty of subjecting English society to an anthropological scrutiny customarily reserved for the tribal practices of peoples at more 'primitive' stages of development was itself subversive; although it is perhaps unclear whether the enforcement of parallels between 'savage' and 'civilised' behaviour need be exclusively critical, bearing in mind D.H. Lawrence's diagnosis that an abiding enfeeblement of modern Western societies lay in their estrangement from older forms of 'blood-consciousness' (ancestor-worship is proposed by the airman as one means to counteract the 'enemy'). Indeed, in his letter to Mitchison cited earlier, Auden went on to explain that Book I, 'The Initiates', was in some ways his memorial to Lawrence, and its theme 'the failure of the romantic conception of personality'; the four parts, he suggested, corresponded to the four ages of man, from boyhood to old age, and 'are stages in the development of the influence of the Hero (who never appears at all)' (quoted in *Early A*: 97). This was one version of the book, and he gave others: as Mendelson points out, in his correspondence Auden made more efforts to explain *The Orators* than any of his other works, which almost certainly indicated his growing dissatisfaction with what he felt had been achieved in it.

Some of the confusion generated by the book was partly because, as with Lawrence, the attitudes it expressed alternate between the authoritarian and the libertarian; although the Old Boy's address apparently incites an insurrection in which the school's authorities are made away with (compare the apocalyptic ending of Lindsay Anderson's 1960s British film *If*, where a public school also symbolises a repressively hierarchical *ancien régime*, finally put to the machine-gun by young rebels), he is hardly unambiguously admirable as he scuttles off to catch his train, having sown the seeds of mutiny. Yet his address has been more stimulatingly odd than any ordinary prize-day speech; Auden had endowed him with some of his own brilliant quirkiness (diagrammatic definitions of 'excessive', 'defective' and 'perverted' love are found in Auden's notebook of this period, for example), and the question he poses, 'What do you think about England, this country of ours where nobody is well?' (*EA*: 62), reverberates throughout the book, and through much of Auden's work of the period. But if the question was clear, its answer was not: when in the 1940s Auden reprinted the fifth Ode ('Though Aware of Our Rank and Alert to Obey Orders', dedicated to his pupils at Helensburgh), he called it 'Which Side Am I Supposed to Be On?' – a title catching some of the central uncertainty of *The Orators*, that had led Grahame Greene in his review to observe that it was hard to tell whether the author's sympathies were Communist or Fascist. The book's several evocations of the Great War, into which so many idealistic young men had been destructively sucked, commemorate an era of possible heroism at the same time that they suggest those heroics to have been delusionary, leading as they have to the failure of contemporary politics and economics manifested in the deepening slump.

Just as the 'hero' never appears, in Auden's account above, so the secret into which we are to be initiated is never revealed, while the air remains thick with secrecy. Thus we move from the furtive conspiratorialism of 'Letter to a Wound' to Book II and the airman's 'Journal', composed by one afflicted in the public sphere by the sense of an 'enemy' who has infiltrated the Helensburghers and is about to seize the initiative, and privately by self-reproach concerning bouts of a kleptomania that seems connectable with masturbation guilt and his growing identification with the secret society of homosexuals. When at the end the airman apparently meets his death above the clouds, it is not evidently the result of any 'lonely impulse of delight' such as prompted Yeats's 'Irish Airman' to his existential choice, but is a more ambiguous self-sacrifice. He is another hero who never appears, and the Odes which follow add to the sense of lives helplessly circumscribed (III: 'What Siren Zooming Is Sounding Our Coming'), schoolmasters locked into their roles or their perplexed pupils into theirs (V); the only heroes envisaged are extravagantly written-up schoolboy or pre-school types: the captain of the first XV or the infant Warner upon whom England's future is, hyperbolically, to depend (Odes II and IV). The Epilogue anticipates one who breaks free from the litany of fears and doubtings – its last line repeating the refrain, 'As he left them there, as he left them there' (*EA*: 110): but it cannot be clear what world awaits him.

Yet this dour commentary misses the extravagance that is the keynote of Auden's performance in *The Orators*, as well as the humour that crackles through its farcically prejudicial categorisations ('Three signs of an enemy house – old furniture – a room called the Den – photographs of friends', *EA*: 82). Part of its aggressive energy – and in particular the insistent allusions to an 'enemy' – harks back to the overstated boisterousness of Wyndham Lewis in his most incendiary phase of *Blast*; but it draws as well on the 'Mortmere' stories of Isherwood and Upward, and Old English writings which it parodies (perhaps in riposte to the mournfully respectful evocations of the past encountered in *The Waste Land*). It throws off highly assured poems in difficult forms like rhyme royal ('Beethameer, Beethameer, bully of Britain') and sestina ('We Have Brought You, They Said, a Map of the Country'), and in Ode II, as Fuller points out, creatively varies a Pindaric model. Mendelson has observed that *The Orators* 'reads like an expressionist autobiography' (*Early A*: 95); it is replete with personal circumstance of minor and of major importance to its author, but always heeds its own suggestion that 'practical jokes' are an effective way to unsettle the enemy. For its very tonal elusiveness was of strategic origin, being mercurially different from typical 'enemy' discourse ('His collar was spotless; he talked very well,/He spoke of our homes and duty and we fell', *EA*: 81); *The Orators* is a kind of surrealist handbook intended to prevent its readers falling for the enemy's pitch by perversely disrupting his lines of communication with extravagant diversionary tactics. Against his certain certainties it opposes its clownishly affirmative dissociation of sensibility, to counteract a relentless consistency threatening to bore you to death:

> The enemy's sense of humour – verbal symbolism. Private associations (rhyming slang), but note that he is serious, the associations are constant. He means what *he* says.

> Practical jokes consist in upsetting these associations. They are in every sense contradictory and public, e.g. my bogus lecture to the London Truss Club.
>
> (*EA*: 78)

From one perspective which Auden himself came in time to inhabit, *The Orators* fails because its construction prevents any successful recovery of meaning or authorial intention: that single theme promised by the blurb. But from another, it is wholly and successfully true to itself in ceding to the reader so much responsibility for creating what it amounts to: it means what *we* read.

Look, Stranger! (1936)

The 'abstract drama' of *The Orators* had something in common with the unperformed plays Auden had been writing (1929's *The Enemies of a Bishop*, and *The Fronny*, composed in his first summer at Larchfield); these too were trying to combine a critique of England with cartoonish exaggerations not always distinguishable from schoolboyish cock-snooking. In a 1934 review of a book on poetic drama, Auden observed that drama was 'essentially a social art' (*P* I: 70), and one of the problems he was trying to solve at this period was how poetry, as well, could fulfil this function. His visible new publications between *The Orators* and *Look, Stranger!* (appearing almost simultaneously with the first English version of *The Ascent of F6*) were his plays *The Dance of Death* (1933) and, with Isherwood, *The Dog Beneath the Skin* (1935) – which he abbreviated to 'Dogskin'. But as well as the poems which went into this next collection, after writing *The Orators* and 'A Happy New Year' he had set to work on a long poem that he called his 'epic', 'In the Year of My Youth . . .', a commentary on England modelled on Langland and Dante, which he abandoned after writing 1,300 lines of alliterative verse (some of which was recycled in his plays; the surviving text has been published with an introductory essay by Lucy McDiarmid in *Review of English Studies* (1978)). The abandonment of that project signalled a loss of confidence in the poet's role as any kind of prophetic denouncer, and along with it went a move further away from Modernist assumptions concerning the necessary difficulty of poetry and the need for challenging innovatoriness of style. He would never again write a book so radically disruptive as *The Orators*; henceforth his playfulness would take different forms, some of them more overtly traditional; it is perhaps not surprising, then, that *Look, Stranger!* was the collection for which he received the King's Gold Medal for Poetry.

Auden was furious about the title of this third volume of verse, imposed by Fabers; when an American edition was published the next year, he insisted on its being called *On This Island*. It may be that his irritation was provoked by the continuity implied with the disinvolved or anthropological perspectives more characteristic of its predecessors: the American title stresses locatedness rather than estrangement. Although being 'on this island' suggested an extension of that study of England announced in *The Orators* and carried forward in plays and his abandoned epic, what becomes apparent in *Look, Stranger!* is an identification with, rather than a repudiation of, the island looked at; even if, as Mendelson suggests, the identification was willed rather than felt, and somewhat derivative in its nature (he cites Auden's reliance on *The Changing Face of England* for some memorable topographical images). *The Orators* had been dedicated to Spender, who at that period was unambiguously a member of what Auden in his 1929 journal called the 'great secret society' of 'Buggers'; *Look, Stranger!* was dedicated to Erika Mann, who although not identified as such was legally Auden's wife: while this attachment did not signify any abatement of the homosexual inclinations of either party, it did denote a public and social commitment Auden had undertaken. The dedicatory lines to her, again unlike the private/public formulae prefacing *The Orators*, use the adjectives 'extravagant', 'baroque' and 'surrealist' – all of which might have beeen applied to that earlier book – to indicate rejected styles, installing in their place a more truthful 'narrow strictness'.

The new volume received mixed reviews: those who liked their Auden energetic and anarchic missed him here, and those who disliked his marks of immaturity continued to find them. The most perceptive response came from Dilys Powell, who correctly noted that a different mode predominated, which defined the volume as 'a collection of non-dramatic verse' (Haffenden 1983: 217). This drew forth from the poet a grateful letter confirming her perception: '[t]he non-dramatic quality of the poems is of course intentional. I want lyric verse to be really lyrical, because at least in my own work when I get into the dramatic lyric I hear far too often the shrill tones of the hockey-mistress' (quoted in Haffenden 1983: 214). There was, then, a deliberate muting of the hectoring address of some earlier work, and the lyrical qualities of this collection were perhaps best signalled by the fact that three of its poems were identified as 'songs', and several would be set to music: principally by Britten, to whom two items were dedicated, but also by Lennox Berkeley. Necessarily much less visible was the identity of the person who had stimulated several of the poems: the teenager Michael Yates, now at Bryanston School, with whom Auden had fallen in love during Yates's final year at the Downs School, where Auden moved in autumn 1932. There had been, according to Carpenter, a moderately happy relationship at Helensburgh with a young man called Derek, who was mentioned in *The Orators* and provoked two poems in this next collection ('That Night When Joy Began' and 'The Chimneys Are Smoking . . .', in order of composition though not of their placing in the volume); but the three years Auden spent at Colwall were amongst his happiest, and the greatest proportion of the poems in *Look, Stranger!* derived from this period.

The volume contained thirty-one poems, including a 'Prologue' ('O Love, the Interest Itself in Thoughtless Heaven') and 'Epilogue' ('Certainly Our City . . .'): effectively implying that the contents proper consisted of the material they framed, so endowing the second and penultimate poems with additional significance as the beginning and ending of this inner book. These were, respectively, 'Out on the Lawn I Lie in Bed' (later titled 'A Summer Night') and 'August for the People . . .', Auden's birthday poem for Isherwood (see Life and contexts, **pp. 14, 15**); thus the 'inner book' begins and ends with two summer poems, from 1933 and 1935, as co-ordinating points in time, and the co-ordinating point in space throughout is 'this island', metonymically representing England (even though the phrase actually denoted the Isle of Wight). 'Look, Stranger, at This Island Now' furnished titles for both English and American volumes; Auden's alteration of his original 'at' to 'on' changed a democratic immediacy of observation to a more distanced supervision, implying the act of looking *down* on; this may reflect a disillusionment that was itself suggested by the move between the first poem, evoking heaven, to the last, quite sourly surveying the all-too-fallen city we inhabit; as from the second poem's serene garden sleeping, to the penultimate's nervous undulation on the dangerous flood of history.

If *The Orators* had at its centre an isolated and ultimately thwarted individual, perplexed by the impossibility of love or true community, in Auden's next collection the 'Stranger' enjoined to look is perhaps also encouraged to join in; the collection opposes various images of insularity to notions of communal obligation: 'islands' and 'cities' are two of the prescribed line-endings of the sestina 'Hearing of Harvests Rotting in the Valleys', whose final line prefers civic reconconstruction to dreams of isolation. If complete mastery of the air was proposed by the Airman as an effective counter to the enemy's power, then *Look, Stranger!* is by contrast 'to gravity attentive' (the phrase occurs in 'Out on the Lawn . . .'), and the 'Prologue' underlines this with its prayer that Love should

> . . . make us as Newton was, who in his garden watching
> The apple falling towards England, became aware
> Between himself and her of an eternal tie.
>
> (*EA*: 119)

This poem's linkage of England with 'love' indicates a strongly thematic structuring of the book, which constantly enquires what love can be and where it can take place, which impulses nurture and which defeat it. This is visible, for example, in the longer poem 'Here on the Cropped Grass of the Narrow Ridge I Stand', specifically set upon the Malvern Hills behind Colwall, from which elevation the poet can survey England, and whose last line is 'Love one another' (*EA*: 141–4). The Downs School, lying below that ridge, was the setting for 'Out on the Lawn . . .'; it, too, addresses themes of love, community and place within a traditionalist metric that leads Mendelson to argue that Auden's writing 'a poem like "A Summer Night" at the crest of the Modernist wave was a manifest gesture of independence' as well as a prefiguration of his 'allegiance to the augustan literary tradition' (*Early A*: 176).

Auden's contentment within the 'narrow strictness' of metrical and stanzaic regularity discontented some (including to a certain degree Eliot), but it was of a piece with poems that were trying to seek reconciliation with the possible life rather than the fantasised escape (for example, in a poem such as 'Now from My Window-sill I Watch the Night'). This is not to say that for Auden the strident hockey-mistress offering social or political comment was entirely absent: the poem 'Brothers Who When the Sirens Roar' shows this (when first published in 1932 it was called 'A Communist to Others'; see the detailed discussion in *AS* I: 174–95), and so perhaps does the later Yeats-influenced 'O For Doors to be Open . . .'. But the dominant endeavour of *Look, Stranger!* is suggested by 'To Settle in this Village of the Heart', which tries to believe that neighbourhood, whatever its vulgarities, can be more fulfilling than the erotic kindnesses of strangers. Yet it is not clear, finally, that this conviction carries, and the unease explored in 'Out on the Lawn . . .', about how to justify individual emotional gratifications in a context of deprivation or disaster in the wider world, becomes more insistently present. 'Easily, My Dear, You Move, Easily Your Head' (*EA*: 152), about Michael Yates, was written in 1934 following the trip they had taken through Hitler's Germany and beyond, intending to reach Dracula's castle (the journey was written up by Auden for the Downs School magazine; during it – if not before – the 1965 poem 'Since' suggests, their relationship was sexual). Yet however alluring the presence of the beloved, the poem is full of doubts about what his future may contain, and invaded by the big figures of contemporary history who were soon to bring about the worst of all possible worlds: the Hitler and the Mussolini who were laughed at in *The Orators* assert themselves more seriously here. *Look, Stranger!* opens with evocations of love, but the uncertainties audible in 'August for the People . . .' have resolved into dismayed despair by the time the 'Epilogue' answers its own question: 'Can/Hate so securely bind? Are They dead here? Yes' (*EA*: 166). The poem – and the book – ends with a dispirited ad-man's jingle, which at one stage Auden considered as a potential title.

Letters from Iceland (1937); *Journey to a War* (1939)

The idea of visiting Iceland, whence his father believed – probably wrongly – the family name derived, came to Auden when he learned that Yates was to visit that northern island with a small party from Bryanston School in the summer of 1936. He made a proposal to Fabers that he might write a book about Iceland, which was accepted, and he enlisted the collaboration of Louis MacNeice in the project. This involved the sort of extended trip that Auden enjoyed; he left for Iceland in early June, and spent several weeks there alone, doing some sight-seeing but principally learning to ride a horse and hitting on the idea of writing a long verse-letter to Lord Byron as a structuring feature of the book. MacNeice joined him in August, a week or so before the small party from Bryanston arrived, which the two poets joined on a pony-trek round the Langjökull icefield. Auden was annoyed that MacNeice hadn't bothered to equip himself properly for the expedition and ended up sharing his tent, but beyond those minor irritations they greatly enjoyed each other's company. Yates stayed on after the others left, returning to England with Auden and MacNeice in September.

The volume was published a year later and agreeably reviewed, although its unusual nature – neither a travel book nor a collection of poetry, but sharing some features of each – made it difficult to classify, as well as posing the problem of dual authorship (Auden judged he was responsible for two-thirds). It had, however, secured impressive advance sales, and was remuneratively adopted by the Book Club for offer to its members. The five parts of 'Letter to Lord Byron', inspired by Auden's reading *Don Juan* on the voyage out, are distributed throughout the text, interspersed with other poems by him and MacNeice, prose letters including some from Auden to his wife Erika – to whom in effect he pretended to be married – and a long piece, 'Hetty to Nancy', in which MacNeice pretended to be a jolly young woman writing to her sophisticated metropolitan chum; Auden appears in this as 'Maisie'. Its recipient was intended as Anthony Blunt, MacNeice's friend from schooldays at Marlborough, and it has been noted that the names encoded their respective sexual preferences: 'Hetty' is the heterosexual MacNeice, 'Nancy' the homosexual Blunt. (This latter would pursue a notably bifurcated career as respected art historian and keeper of the Queen's pictures, and Soviet double agent – the disgrace of exposure as which, late in his life, consumed the honours of his other role, although the immunity from prosecution he secured showed how the class-system continued to look after its own, even in treachery.) The book ended with a jointly written 'Last Will and Testament', full of private allusions and potential libels that had to be toned down for fear of prosecution, followed by MacNeice's verse 'Epilogue', whose last line ominously conjured up the image of a gun-butt rapping against the poet's door. Scattered throughout were a series of Auden's photographs, showing him to be an unconventional but not unskilful composer of scene (all reproduced in *P* I).

If the aspects of private associations and subterfuge continued themes observable in earlier Auden, *Letters from Iceland* marked a difference, principally seen in the relaxed autobiographical tone of 'Letter to Lord Byron'; here Auden gave his own version of the growth of a poet's mind, in ways that underlined his move away from Modernist notions of impersonality towards a conception of poetry as conversation or light verse, using the convention of the 'private' letter intended for publication that further enfolded the paradox of its being addressed to a dead recipient. He eschewed the *ottava rima* of *Don Juan* as too difficult, but returned to rhyme royal, in which his versification seemed as effortless as it was accomplished – even drawing attention to its own shortcomings, when he broke off to denounce the flatness of one of his lines. Readers learned about Auden's preference for industrial scenery to pastoral landscape, his views on education, his aversion to Wordsworth; they might also have been struck by how different the relationship envisaged with Lord Byron was from that of Eliot with his master Dante. In being a collaboration, the book also underlined a characteristic of Auden's work throughout the second half of the decade: since leaving teaching he had worked collaboratively with Britten and others in documentary film-making, as well as on his dramas with Isherwood in association with the Group Theatre; his next book would also be joint authored.

Although Auden had initiated the trip to Iceland in a holiday spirit, his encountering Nazis there and hearing of the outbreak of war in Spain had intruded the note of ill-omen more characteristic of contemporary events. Even before the manuscript of *Letters from Iceland* had been finalised, he had left for Spain, and the resulting poem was published as a pamphlet in May 1937. Within two months his next venture, with Isherwood, was taking shape: initially commissioned by Random House to produce a book about the far East, the Japanese aggression decided them to go to China. If at the outset there had been an element of escapism fuelling this project – a 'designer war' for them to sample – during their long trip news came of Hitler's move into Austria, and of the reverses suffered by Republican forces in Spain which signalled Franco's impending victory, while Britain and France looked on in hand-wringing inactivity. The world was becoming a darker place, and the book the two produced reflects – particularly in Auden's poetry – a deepening response, in which the strangers who went to look found themselves involved in what they saw. By the time of its publication (March 1939, London; August, New York) they had already left for the USA, but the volume was not unappreciatively reviewed in England: it was as predictable that Evelyn Waugh should sneer at most of it, and especially at Auden, as that Grigson should salute him as 'something good and creative in European life in a time of the very greatest evil' (Haffenden 1983: 297). The book resembled *Letters from Iceland* in being a literary collaboration, in containing poetry and a prose travelogue, and also in Auden's photographs, but despite the occasionally airy tone of the 'Travel-Diary', its note was more serious, as the scenes witnessed were more challenging. The book started with a dedicatory sonnet to E.M. Forster, followed by six poems by Auden (predominantly sonnets); then the long prose Travel-Diary, which was principally by Isherwood, although he incorporated material from Auden's journal as well as his own. The photographs were, at Auden's request, grouped in a section together, and contained many more pictures of individual people than of places; these were followed by 'In Time of War', described as a 'Sonnet Sequence with a verse commentary'. Although the sonnet sequence has proved to be the most durably admired component (*pace* Waugh), Fuller comments that the book functions as a whole in which relations between its parts should be remembered, and Smith (1985: 109) argues that the 'tension between the relaxed informality of the picaresque prose, and the formal, structured narrative episodes of the poetry' produces the particular self-consciousness of this text's engagement with historical event.

The poems which Auden wrote on the outward voyage, in the section titled 'London to Hongkong' (the point from which the Travel-Diary starts), are sceptical meditations on the personal predicament of the traveller, and concern themselves with the motives for travel and the kinds of person encountered on board ship. The section was completed by two sonnets, 'Macao' and 'Hongkong', written in Brussels after his return: both places are seen as curious intrusions of European sensibility and values translocated into Asia, and to that extent continue themes of personal displacement and the contrast between Occident and Orient. Of 'In Time of War' Fuller asserts that it 'represents a new scope of historical understanding and new powers of generalisation and condensation in Auden's work' (1998: 234); Mendelson, whilst disliking the orotund tercets of the 'Commentary' – he thinks Auden was tempted to pomposity by unrhymed triplets – wonders whether the sonnet sequence does not constitute 'perhaps the greatest English poem of the decade' (1981: 356). Smith sees the book as one in which the 'history of class struggle . . ., diachronic, mythic, impersonal, complements the personal, synchronic, autobiographical prose account of two young men's journey towards realizing and accepting that history' (1985: 109). Certainly, the sense of China being quaintly different drops away, and perhaps the movement of the book is best expressed in the contrast between a line from the first section's 'The Traveller' – 'It is the strangeness that he tries to see' (*EA*: 234) – and the perception in Sonnet XIV, 'Yes, we are going to suffer, now' (*EA*: 256), where privileged insulation falls away in a revelation that is simultaneously of personal vulnerability and personal responsibility. Auden and Isherwood may have gone only to disconnect from England, but ended appreciating their connection to something larger.

A note on Auden as dramatist

Auden himself wrote 'Paid on Both Sides' (1928/9), 'The Fronny'* (1930) and *The Dance of Death* (1933); 'The Enemies of a Bishop'* (1929), 'The Chase'*

(1934), *The Dog Beneath the Skin* (1935), *The Ascent of F6* (1936) and *On the Frontier* (1938) were collaborations with Isherwood (asterisks denote abandoned work). Despite the commitment to theatre implied by this continuity of production, these offer no good reason to doubt that Auden's true strengths lay in his poetry, as Isherwood's lay in prose fiction; it could indeed be argued that Auden's appetite for parabolic exposition and Isherwood's for naturalistic presentation did not combine successfully in this medium. An ambitious experimentalism (or impatience with form) is signalled by the variety of modes: only 'The Chase' and its successor *Dogskin* were described as 'plays'; 'Paid on Both Sides' was a 'charade', 'Bishop' a 'morality', others offered 'dance', 'tragedy' (*F6*) and 'melodrama' (*Frontier*). 'Paid on Both Sides' and *F6* each use a landscape to evoke psychological conflict which, in both, importantly relates to the coercing Mother, and in the latter there is a particular concern with the uses of heroism; several of the plays reflect the 1930s 'condition-of-England' debate but, beyond that, the contribution Auden made to the revivification of verse drama at this period was real enough. The chief influences on his dramatic technique were German Expressionism combining with Brecht's political assertiveness, and also the Ibsen of *Peer Gynt* and *Brand*; both were distorted by tonal uncertainties, deriving as much from unfocused 'Mortmere'-ish elements as from any theatre of confrontation – despite the pose of offering social or political comment observable in *Dogskin*, for example. The aborted first performance of Auden's 'charade' seems predictive of future problems in the medium, and his and Isherwood's difficulties in finding right endings were perhaps symptomatic of the compromised quality of nearly all these dramas, as dramas; nevertheless, Smith offers an account of how time might transfigure them into a kind of truth:

> *The Ascent of F6* was for years a nearly unreadable text, stodgy, old-fashioned, dealing with dead issues. A performance at the Edinburgh Festival in 1983, in the wake of the Falklands War, electrified it as a critique of jingoistic platitudes stirred up by the gutter press to con a gullible public into support for an unpopular government and to send people euphorically to their deaths.
>
> (1985: 11–12)

Another Time (1940)

It was perhaps inevitable that a collection published after the outbreak of the war which emphasised Auden's absence from England, and which contained many poems already separately published, should provoke some impatience amongst those British reviewers who did bother to attend to it. Only Empson was robust in rebuttal of the charge that Auden's talent had declined – although he was also one of the first of many who would note and deplore the alterations made to admired poems (he thought 'Spain 1937' a less interesting poem than the original 'Spain'). The book was divided into three parts, titled 'People and Places', 'Lighter Poems' and 'Occasional Poems': the first was the longest, with thirty-one poems including Auden's considerations of other poets, writers and thinkers; the second included the Cabaret Songs and sharp-toned ballads about Miss Gee, Victor and James

Honeyman, with other items; the third contained every poem with a date in its title, the memorial verses for Yeats, Freud and Ernst Toller and, finally, the 'Epithalamion' written for the marriage of his 'sister-in-law' Elizabeth Mann in America – although Fuller considers it to be concerned, as well, with Auden's new relationship with Kallman. Therefore the last word of the volume was 'joy', but while this might indicate what Auden hoped would follow from what he looked on as his true 'marriage' (as opposed to the arrangement with Erika Mann), the poem had opened with an awareness of the context of war, and the volume as a whole is no simple celebration.

Kallmann takes the place of Yates (the unconscious beloved of 'Lay Your Sleeping Head . . .') as the amorous focus here, but since many of the poems were written before Auden had met him, the dominant characteristic of the collection does not derive from this new love, albeit acknowledged in the volume's dedication. There are several poems expressing discontent with European places such as Brussels (where Auden had enjoyed a productive period at the close of 1938), Dover and Oxford. None of the American poems is particularly evocative of place, and even the setting of 'September 1, 1939' is inexact about precisely *which* of the dives on Fifty-second Street he occupies; those European places, however, seem associated with repeated and important failure. For the first time the majority of poems carried titles (some of them subsequently altered); just as the poems about Brussels evoked a sense of Europe as a broader focus than 'this island', so, although there were poems about English writers such as Housman, Lear and Arnold, there were others about Rimbaud, Pascal, Voltaire, Melville, Yeats and Freud, enlarging the scope of attention. Along with poems carrying titles such as 'The Novelist', 'The Composer' and pre-eminently 'Musée des Beaux Arts', these showed Auden's preoccupation with the role and responsibility of the artist, which he had been investigating in prose in 'The Prolific and the Devourer' (abandoned after the outbreak of war); the elegy for Yeats, and in particular its assertion that poetry made nothing happen, showed how he had changed. Although the book's tripartite division suggests its function as a receptacle rather than a unified book, the fact that it contains several of Auden's best-known and most frequently anthologised lyrics establishes its valid claim, Fuller suggests, as the best of his 1930s collections.

The Double Man (USA, 1941); *New Year Letter* (England, 1941)

After Auden's arrival in the USA, his books of poetry were usually published there before they were in England. This was his first wholly American collection; the different titles for the Random House and Faber editions repeated the pattern of *Look, Stranger!*, but were principally because of legal complications (see *AS* I: 73 n.6). At this stage, however, the USA was neutral, and intimations of double-agency latent in that title might have touched raw nerves in a besieged Britain hypersensitised to hidden enemies; moreover, any potential association of Auden's name with duplicity could well have seemed a poor market strategy. The title in fact derived from Montaigne, quoted (in translation) as the volume's epigraph: 'We are, I know not how, double in ourselves, so that what we believe we disbelieve, and cannot rid ourselves of what we condemn'. Auden came across this in Charles Williams's *The Descent of the Dove* (1939), which had a significant influence: early in 1940, as he was writing 'New Year Letter', he wrote to Williams to express his appreciation of it, and it was here that he was introduced to the thought of Kierkegaard. *The Double Man* was dedicated to Elizabeth Mayer, notional recipient of its principal item, the long poem 'New Year Letter', consisting of over 1,700 lines of tetrameter couplets (with occasional triplets), attended by almost ninety pages of 'Notes' which themselves sometimes consisted of poems. These were followed by a sonnet sequence called 'The Quest', and having started with a poem as 'Prologue', the volume ended with an 'Epilogue', notable for the specifically Christian vocabulary employed in its final stanza (reprinted as 'The Dark Years' in *WHACP*): thus the volume closed on a religious note. About this aspect Auden wrote to an enquiring graduate student in 1947: 'As to my return to the church, it was a gradual business without any abrupt leaps. *The Double Man*, written Jan.–Oct. 1940 covers a period when I was beginning to think seriously about such things without committing myself. I started going to church again just about October. It is therefore full of heretical remarks' (quoted in Bloomfield and Mendelson 1972: 48). Reviewers were struck by the religious element; Malcolm Cowley called him a 'profoundly Christian poet' (Haffenden 1983: 311) and also noted the preponderant references to German writers and thinkers, displacing the French who had been so important to the Modernist generation; Randall Jarrell enlarged on that theme, seeing that the title poem's eighteenth-century mode presaged 'the decline and fall of modernist poetry' (ibid.: 312).

The cumbersome and complained-about notes contained a good deal of material from Auden's abandoned prose work 'The Prolific and the Devourer', and would in their own turn be abandoned. But it was striking that the former *enfant terrible* of contemporary poetry was so publicly aligning himself with an Augustan mode; as that the letter he was writing now was not to any historical personage similar to Byron, but to a relatively unknown immigrant to America, celebrated as a living woman rather than as literary luminary (although as the end of its first part made clear, the poem operated the same convention of being a letter intended for the wider world as well). As the first long poem produced in what Auden by now saw would be his American life, 'New Year Letter' made unmistakably manifest his trajectory away from the Modernistic literary disruptions of *The Orators*; yet part of the 'doubleness' implicit in his decisive break from his former self is seen in the fact that his turn to the new life surprisingly entailed embracing a poetic past, and his eighteenth-century lookalike becomes the vehicle to address the future: itself a disruptive strategy. Significantly, however, Auden eschewed the heroic couplets of Pope's poetic 'Essays', which might have seemed complacently ratiocinative; he opted instead for the shorter line, which Smith relates to seventeenth-century poets such as Marvell and Butler. Its brevity forces thoughts of any developed complexity to overflow its bounds, and Mendelson argues that the tension between the limiting form and the 'anarchic whirlwind' of Auden's ideas is a defining feature (*LA*: 100).

The poem is divided into three successively longer parts, but maintains the temporal fiction that it occurs within a 'present' constituted by its subtitling date of 'January 1st, 1940': each section starts by alluding to the festivities audible from the street below. Its 'doubleness', then, is also constituted by its inhabiting the point of transition between one era and another, the change of year that traditionally provokes stocktaking. In some ways it can be read as a riposte to 'September 1, 1939', that view of the preceding decade Auden later disowned: 'New Year Letter' looks forward to the decade that will ensue. The anticipation is, of course, qualified by his awareness of the world at war, and in other ways the poem could be seen to start from the perception contained in the final sonnet of the earlier sequence 'In Time of War', that humanity is articled to error. For 'New Year Letter' resembles 'Letter to Lord Byron' in offering an account of the poet's life, but in a darker, self-accusatory tone that, for example, in the first part envisages his arraignment before a judicial panel consisting of Dante, Blake and Rimbaud, and throughout hints at awareness of an impending judgement that is of even greater consequence: if the poem assesses his responsibilities to art, to his self, and to the wider community, behind all these is a growing sense of a responsibility before God.

This is connected to, but is much larger than, a justification of his having left England; in a notable passage in Part III (sixty-six lines beginning 'No matter where, or whom I meet' and ending 'And I was conscious of my guilt'), Auden clarifies the nature of his Englishness in terms of an actually specifiable landscape that doubles as a moral geography by which all his life becomes interpretable. This is the lead-mining locality of his beloved North Pennines, expounded here more fully than ever before or after, in ways that make clear its furnishing a set of symbols which are his permanent possession: this England he can never desert, yet its revealable meanings do not limit themselves to any particular nation, but are experienced by him as universals; and in the final disclosure that leads up to this conscious acceptance of guilt, he has understood that the loving, frightening and abandoning mother-presence, sensed in the echoing darkness of the old mine-shaft, is one whom he must in his turn abandon, if he is to accept true responsibility for himself. This revelation both justifies his subsequent change of place, and makes his location in America, or anywhere, a comparative irrelevance: Mendelson notes that Auden's poetry from this period bore titles emphasising a concern with time rather than place (*LA*: 82). The twenty sonnets making up 'The Quest' continued a sense of moving through a Bunyanesque *paysage moralisé*, with the attendant perception of the choices a life is presented with and the different consequences to which these lead. What does not emerge is any secure or complacent feeling that the quest has been satisfactorily concluded; life, like poetry, is always a work in progress, and nothing could make clearer Auden's own commitment to that view than the apparent restlessness with which he reviewed and revised his earlier work.

For the Time Being (1944, USA; 1945, England)

When this volume appeared, Auden had rejoined the church and would shortly become an American citizen; the crisis in his relationship with Kallman had occurred; America had entered the war (as he was writing 'For the Time Being') and he had been rejected for military service – although by the time Spender reviewed the British edition Auden was undertaking the bombing survey in Germany. It contained two long elements: 'The Sea and the Mirror', written between 1942 and 1944, and his 'Christmas Oratorio' dedicated to the memory of his mother – from which the volume derives its title; this had been written across 1941 and 1942, and in his dedication Auden misdated the year of her birth. American reviews of the volume were markedly more appreciative than the British.

'The Sea and the Mirror' is probably Auden's best-known long poem, perhaps because its reassuringly literary reference to *The Tempest* requires a less specialised kind of knowledge than the overtly psychoanalytical or theological underpinnings of some others; he was teaching at Swarthmore during its composition, and produced for his class a carefully intricate chart of the axes along which it was plotted (reproduced in *LA* p. 240). This poem will be considered in the next section (see Works, **pp. 95–8**); 'For the Time Being' denotes a Christian festival where 'New Year Letter' alluded to a secular one, and arose out of two unexpected crises in Auden's life: Kallman's infidelity and his mother's death, the profundity of whose effect on him had caught him unawares. It does not succeed as an 'oratorio', for Spender could not envisage its being set to music and – more to the point – neither could Britten; nor does it wholly succeed as a long dramatic poem. Auden put a great deal of himself into the understanding of Joseph's predicament, which he felt resembled his own, and Mendelson has adduced a formal incantatory letter Auden wrote to Kallman on Christmas Day 1941, whilst at work on the poem, in which he analogised their relationship to the significant aspects of the nativity story (see *LA*: 182–3); it was here that he told Kallman that he believed that 'mothers have much to do with your queerness and mine'. Smith interestingly notes the similarity of title that the 'Oratorio' bears to *The Orators*, and the ways in which Herod's prose section resembles the Old Boy's speech as an unintended exposure of what Auden defined as liberal Fascism; he argues for a continuity of concern with Auden's earlier work, that corrupt structures of power should be replaced by the just city (Smith 1985: 161–5). Although in *The Orators* the hero does not appear at all, and in 'For the Time Being' the central character does not speak (as indeed the infant Jesus could not), the decisive difference is that, despite the conflicting voices in each work, there is a resolving truth available in the Oratorio.

The Age of Anxiety (1947, USA; 1948, England)

This was Auden's longest poem, at over 130 pages, and is probably the one that readers have found hardest to love. Although some reviewers were enthusiastic and the poem won a Pulitzer prize, Delmore Schwartz found it 'self-indulgent' and one British reviewer, 'persistently boring'. Despite its date of publication, Auden had started writing in July 1944, and had finished by November 1946; it was very much a wartime poem, and in places evokes fallen soldiers' bodies in the sea off landing-beaches, and emaciated corpses discovered in the Nazi concentration camps, but for all that it is not in any sense a poem of historical immediacy: whilst conceived dramatically and containing four separately identified characters, it is more similar to the 'abstract drama' he had projected for *The Orators*, with 'all the action implied'. Mendelson notes that it is 'theatrical in tone but almost entirely without drama in its action' (*LA*: 244); and a problem it presents, which *The Orators* did not, is that its tonal uniformity and more obvious schematism suppresses tension and surprise; indeed, Auden made clear that he was deliberately eschewing bravura effects or the shock-tactics of reportage; instead, he was attempting a rhetoric that advertised its own self-consciousness – 'We've had enough of Hemingway', as he said to Alan Ansen (Ansen 1991: 2). This was signalled by the subtitle's definition of the work as a 'baroque eclogue', whose uningratiating intentions were outlined by the dust-jacket blurb:

> *The Age of Anxiety* is an eclogue; that is to say, it adopts the pastoral convention in which a natural setting is contrasted with an artificial style of diction. The setting, in this case, is a bar on Third Avenue, New York City, later an apartment on the West Side, the time an All-Souls' Night during the late war. The characters, a woman and three men, two in uniform, speak in alliterative verse.

Since All Souls' Day is celebrated on 2 November (following All Saints'), it would be logically possible to deduce that the 'night' in question must have fallen in 1944 (by November 1945 both Germany and Japan had surrendered), but the poem is not really concerned with that kind of time-keeping. All Souls' is a Roman Catholic rather than an Anglican observance, when prayers are offered for the dead in purgatory; Fuller suggests that the institution of this custom by the tenth-century Church was seen by Auden as a significant event, incorporating the community of the dead into the experience of the living. The poem therefore contrasts two kinds of time, as measured by clocks and calendars and as measured *sub specie aeternitatis*, and two kinds of community, of the earthly city and of the transfigurable dead (to which the soldiers and camp victims noted above belong). The Latin epigraph invoking the Day of Judgement perhaps requires us less to be frightened than to think of acts of discrimination that potentially occur throughout our lives; it does not offer, in other words, an eschatological perspective overriding the existential choices which define ordinary lives, beset by the permanence of their anxieties. Indeed, the ordinary lives are those with which it principally deals, and despite the Christian emphasis of the foregoing account, this is no calmly salvationist view of the world; rather, as Mendelson points out, it is notable for withholding any 'consoling image of enduring love' (*LA*: 244).

In fact, the intellectual structure overtly governing the piece derives not from theology but from Jungian psychology; Auden expanded the 'Annunciation' section of 'For the Time Being', in which the 'Four Faculties' had spoken, and now associated these with the governing attributes of his four characters. In that New York bar are gathered Quant, a widower of Irish extraction in a dead-end job as a shipping clerk, yet whose enthusiasm for mythology (presumably expressing his Celtic roots) identifies him with 'Intuition'; Malin, a medical intelligence officer in the Canadian airforce, representing 'Thought'; Rosetta, representing 'Feeling', a lonely youngish woman with a successful job as buyer for a city department store, somewhat notionally Jewish, who daydreams of 'lovely innocent countrysides' in the England of her childhood (whose suburban ordinariness her fantasy suppresses); and finally Emble, a young American in naval uniform which he knows allures both sexes, who stands for 'Sensation'. Since in the ideal state all these attributes would balance harmoniously in one individual, their separation here, and their ultimate failure to create a community that lasts longer than one night, suggests disunity rather than the reverse: a state of imbalance that persists.

The poem has six parts, in the first of which their introspective reveries are intruded on by the radio with its war news, galvanising them into a shared conversation which moves them from the bar (where they sit facing a mirror) to the rudimentary social definition of a booth (where they sit facing each other). The next two parts, 'The Seven Ages' and 'The Seven Stages' consist of their illustrations of the phases of life and, more extraordinarily in the latter, their imagined journeys through a shared dreamscape which has many English attributes, in which apparently they undertake the kind of overview envisaged by the prize-day speaker in *The Orators* for his Commission of Angels on their tour of inspection of England. The short fourth part consists of a 'Dirge' occurring as they take a taxi back to Rosetta's flat, where the fifth part, 'Masque' takes place, in which they eat, drink and the two older men bow to the inevitability of Emble's success in competing for her sexual favours, and so leave in celebratory anticipation of that union: Rosetta, however, finds Emble unconscious on her bed, and Venus is thwarted (her character owes something to Rhoda Jaffe, who was Jewish and with whom Auden was having his affair at the time of writing). Finally, Part Six finds Quant and Malin walking home through New York; the four finish as atomistically separated as they had begun; the poem's end is one of deferral, or continued waiting: the truly purgatorial condition.

In the elegy for Yeats, Auden had written how each in the cell of himself was almost convinced of his freedom; but the freedom asserted here seems a renewal of bondage, a voluntary returning to the cell of self. *The Age of Anxiety* differs from 'The Sea and the Mirror' in that neither its characters nor its verse are as dramatically differentiated; yet perhaps a greater similarity can be found in the biographical subtext of each. For if Auden the poetic maker investigated the limits of (his) art in his meditation on Shakespeare, Auden as man, the being in time, may be the true subject of the later poem, compelled to the conclusion that, whatever its attractive compulsions, erotic human love does not satisfactorily answer all the evil that the world contains: neither art nor love are adequate refuges; to be anxious is to be in time. Considering Kierkegaard shortly before starting, Auden had suggested that from an existential viewpoint 'the basic human problem is man's anxiety in time' (*P* II: 214; for further discussion of Kierkegaard, see Life and contexts, **pp. 35–6**, Criticism, **pp. 129–30**); *The Age of Anxiety* has recently received extended consideration in Gottlieb (2003).

***Nones* (1951, USA; 1952, England)**

Auden's first *Collected Poems* had been published in America in 1945, and included the contents of the previous year's *For the Time Being*; 1950 saw Faber's publication of *Collected Shorter Poems*, which omitted the long poems but substituted others with British settings not included in the American edition and also, interestingly, gave several poems different titles (these are itemised in *WHACP* and Bloomfield and Mendelson (1972)), suggesting that Auden saw himself addressing a different audience on each side of the Atlantic. After his sequence of long

American poems ended with *Age of Anxiety*, *Nones* was the first collection of short poems Auden had assembled since *Another Time*, eleven years previously. All bore titles; thc first ('Prime', about waking up) and the one giving the collection its name were subsequently incorporated to the sequence 'Horae Canonicae', as published in *The Shield of Achilles*. These canonical hours are the church Offices to be observed at three-hourly intervals throughout the entire day, in commemoration of the Crucifixion which occurred at midday; 'Nones' takes place at 3.00 pm: in the eerily becalmed aftermath, therefore, of an unspeakable act of murder. The volume's dedication to the theologian Reinhold Niebuhr and his English-born wife Ursula, to whom Auden had applied for information concerning the canonical hours, underlined the religious orientation of the collection (his following three collections of new verse would also be dedicated to married couples). Having begun at daybreak with 'Prime', it closed with 'A Walk After Dark', whose deceptively jaunty demeanour dissimulates an acute sense of how the world's flagrant injustices give the lie to our complacently imposed orders (whereby the very stars in the sky are conscripted to his adopted nation's spangled banner); and he heads back to bed,

> Asking what judgment waits
> My person, all my friends,
> And these United States.
> (*N*: 72)

The Christian resonances of *Nones*, which were noted by some reviewers, concealed persisting anxieties, which were missed because of the muted rhetoric in which they were couched. G.S. Fraser correctly observed that there was 'nothing here in the old, urgent, hortatory vein' (Haffenden 1983: 381), which the *Scrutiny* reviewer was wrong to diagnose as showing a lack of 'any urgency, any real pressure or personal engagement' (1983: 387). Smith argues that '[i]t is the quietness of Auden's dissenting style, in the fifties, which misleads the critic into believing he has denounced politics' (1985: 169); Auden's disquiet seems to me to extend the question implied by *The Age of Anxiety*, of whether any 'states', political, psychological, or social, can properly be seen as 'united' or unitary, rather than (at least) 'double'. The dedicatory poem to the Niebuhrs (reprinted *WHACP*: 621–2) highlighted the difficulty of tone confronting the poet in an age when words such as 'peace' and 'love' have become debased by their stridently meaningless reiteration in the verbal marketplace (whose rhetoric of over-excitement uncomfortably reminds Auden of his old, urgent hortatory self); leaving open only the option of wry understatement in 'the suburb of dissent'. *Nones* was written at a time of happy change for Auden, when his first decade in the USA came to a close with the acquisition of a summer base on the Italian island of Ischia: an event which stimulated composition of 'In Praise of Limestone' (see Works, **pp. 98–100**), to be considered later. Yet islands (both Ischia and Fire Island off New York) are still subjected to sceptical scrutiny, despite their simulation of earthly paradises; and although 'In Praise of Limestone' and 'Not in Baedeker' contentedly amalgamate this newly discovered Italy with his sacred landscape of the North Pennines, the volume also contained 'Memorial For the City', in which he confronted his memories of bomb-damaged Germany; and several poems concerning the destruction of the Roman empire acknowledged the vulnerability of our orderly structure of circumstances. The poem 'A Household', where the public persona of an urbane capitalist overachiever contrasts with the disorderly hell of his home-life – from which business and golf-club colleagues are excluded – was acknowledged by Auden as a species of self-portrait, in this continuing themes of doubleness and fracture observable in 'New Year Letter' and *The Age of Anxiety*. Spender, in his review, hailing 'In Praise of Limestone' as 'one of the great poems of this century', also noted the doubleness it negotiated in being 'serious within the convention of an idiom which is thought of as being essentially unserious'; for Spender, this offered a link between Auden and the 'later Latin poets' in the declining empire, and highlighted the nature of his continuing struggle: 'that Auden who is often regarded on the Left as a Lost Leader, is in our time very much the leader who is fighting for the position of poetry still to say something' (Carter 1984: 44, 45).

The Shield of Achilles (1955)

Auden's next collection, which broke the pattern of titles referring to time, continued to provoke admiring perplexity amongst reviewers, some of whom, such as Donald Davie and Jarrell, worried about symptoms of decline even as they noted the unobtrusive virtuosity of the verse – 'Auden has become the most professional poet in the world' was Jarrell's double-edged appraisal (Haffenden 1983: 400). The book consisted of three sections: the first, 'Bucolics', contained seven poems, each separately dedicated and concerned with a different aspect of natural landscape; the second, 'In Sunshine and In Shade', contained fifteen poems, including the title poem in an opening group of four dealing with weapons of war; the final section was 'Horae Canonicae', in which the two poems transposed from *Nones* were accompanied by five others: the structure of the book was therefore symmetrical. Other poems in the second section considered the role of the artist ('The Truest Poetry Is the Most Feigning'), or the ways in which our experience of the world is mediated by the technologies through which we impose ourselves upon it ('A Permanent Way'; 'Ode to Gaea'): our destructive powers seem greatly in excess of any intelligence likely to govern their exertion ('Hunting Season'; 'Fleet Visit'), although humanity's ruthlessness would be acknowledged by a poem in his next collection ('The Sabbath').

Homage to Clio (1960)

This volume, offered to the Muse of History, was not especially well-received by its reviewers, several of whom were poets in their own right. Of these, Donald Hall was appreciative, but Thom Gunn thought it Auden's worst book since *The Dance of Death*, and Philip Larkin made his review the occasion for an influential summary of the career, which concluded that it had not advanced significantly beyond the work of the 1930s. *Homage to Clio* was divided into two parts, separated by an 'Interlude' consisting of the 'unwritten poem' 'Dichtung und Wahrheit', which Graham Hough, who also felt inclined to wonder what had gone wrong, was inadvertently right to see as the key to the volume. In terms of

Auden's life, this volume marked the end of his Italian period, with 'Good-bye to the Mezzogiorno' making his farewell to Ischia in the year that he and Kallman translated their summertime abode to Austria – as reflected in the poem about the installation of a modern kitchen at Kirchstetten, which was later absorbed into the sequence 'Thanksgiving for a Habitat' in his next collection. There was a set of clerihews under the collective title 'Academic Graffiti', cleverly disrespectful squibs calculated to provoke both academics and graffitists (later augmented and published as a small volume). The dedicatory verse for Professor and Mrs Dodds seemed candidly to admit to a period of dryness (see 'Bull-roarers cannot keep up . . .', *WHACP*: 572; immediately following is the dedicatory verse from *The Shield of Achilles*, which seems similarly to acknowledge dwindling creativity).

Two major elements recur in this collection, alongside its concern with history: silence and water. The title poem contrasts the animal kingdom whose cognition terminates in mere observation and exists amid incessant noise, with human consciousness, which is a formative 'beholding' and is aware of alternations of silence with 'decisive sound'; this is paralleled in the contrast between Clio, 'Muse of the unique/Historical fact' (*HtC*: 17), and the goddesses Aphrodite and Artemis whose noisy procreative and predatory compulsions govern animal and some human behaviour. It is the importance of individuality, even evidenced in unhappiness, and imaged in the self-reflective silence of the book he reads, that Auden associates with Clio, whose responsively silent beholding registers the world of human feeling – to which, he humbly implies, poetry adds very little (Smith suggests a comparison between this poem and 'Spain 1937'). In his later memorial poem for MacNeice, 'The Cave of Making', while alluding to Goethe, Auden asserted that 'Speech can at best . . . bear witness/to the Truth it is not' (*AtH*: 20–1); it is this unutterability that recurs at the symbolic centre of the book in its 'unwritten poem' (whose German title, borrowed from Goethe, means 'Poetry and Truth'), consisting of fifty short prose meditations on the impossibility of writing a true love poem; for, as he observed elsewhere, 'The girl whose boy-friend starts writing her love poems should be on her guard. Perhaps he does really love her, but one thing is certain: while he was writing about her he was thinking not of her but of his own feelings about her, and that is suspicious' (*P* II: 346). In other words, the love-poem risks becoming a grandiose form of self-regard that will not sustain the simplest test of veracity: 'Dichtung und Wahrheit' notes that poetry finds it easier to declare undying love than to assure the beloved that s/he will be loved at a specified day and time in the near future. A modest pragmatism is the informing note of 'First Things First', where Auden recalled his love for Yates (with whom and his wife he remained friends), whose name he fancies hearing enunciated by the commotion of a night-storm over Ischia which, paradoxically, summons a memory of preternatural stillness and silence from Iceland twenty years earlier. Like 'Dichtung und Wahrheit', which was not written about Kallman but anticipated the visit of a different potential lover, this poem implied the dwindling satisfactions of Auden's 'marriage'; but it avoided any invitation to self-pity, by focusing on something very practical the storm has accomplished, in replenishing his water-cistern. Water is more indispensable than love, and the ability to recall the past truthfully (which may mean wordlessly) is more valuably human than the simple preservation of happiness; as 'Good-bye to the Mezzogiorno' suggests, we can forget precisely *why* we have been happy, but 'There is no forgetting that one was' (*HtC*: 82): Clio becomes the muse of appropriate remembering.

About the House (1965, USA; 1966, England)

Fuller quotes from a letter where Auden asserts that this collection marked the first time he had felt old enough to speak in the first person; an intimacy of address that is implied by its opening sequence, 'Thanksgiving for a Habitat', in which he celebrated life in his Austrian house whose various aspects were evoked by different poems – a selective sociability emphasised by the personal dedication each bears. This evidently explains the book's title, but the sequence's use of the word 'habitat', as if a behavioural description of a species, also suggests the wider resonances of the word 'house', to denote in the largest sense the world we live in, and in the smallest our own bodies, which continually decay (Fenton (2001) also hears in 'habitat' a deliberate abstention from 'home'). The dedicatory verse ('A Moon Profaned. .', *WHACP*: 719) opposed the contemporary lunar space-race between Soviet Russia and America, together with their more deadly nuclear arms-race, to the living word and world that is poetry's domain, but for all that, the volume keeps focus on the devastations mankind has wrought: even the northernmost settlement has not escaped the vandalism of history ('Hammerfest'). Having started in his own house and grounds and domestic routines, the final two poems, 'Ascension Day, 1964' and 'Whitsunday in Kirchstetten' concerned a religious ordering of time, but although finishing at worship in the house of God, the poem is aware of Auden's partial outsidership (as non-Catholic Anglo-American singing a German hymn), and whilst finally evoking the dance of the spirit before its Creator, it acknowledges a world in which the things which are Caesar's, the East/West political divisions alluded to from the book's beginning, may forcibly require attention. Reviewers were, nonetheless, rather more struck by the tone of relaxation than of threat.

City Without Walls (England, 1969; USA, 1970); *Epistle to a Godson* (1972); *Thank You, Fog* (1974)

City Without Walls opened with a poem of dialogue, in which a long denunciation of the fallen ways and standards of 'Megalopolis' is set in quotation marks, whose function becomes clear when answered by a curt rejoinder that he seems to be enjoying his discontent, only to be told by a third voice to shut up because they'll both feel better by morning. All three voices are Auden's, thus repeating the idea of the self as a household or small congress he had used elsewhere. The main problem posed by these late volumes was whether the quarrels with himself Auden reported were really threatening, or whether this was just a grumpy old man who could not stop writing highly crafted poems, even though he no longer had much to say. Reviewers paid their usual respects to his extraordinary metrical skill, but were made uneasy by the ease with which the poet subjugated his material; it was left to Clive James, in his *TLS* review of *Epistle to a Godson*, to make an impassioned case for what Auden had achieved by thus disciplining the extravagant talent of the early writing. The poet who emerges in this late work is one who manages to sound wise rather than inflammatory, but who simultaneously evinces scepticism about the nature of his wisdom, and whose reaching for inkhorn usages only locatable in the fattest dictionary may be less ostentatious learning ('don-speak' as Seamus Heaney has called it) than a levity instinct with awareness that language, the great human invention, is threatened by neglectful obsolescence, just like the rusting machinery of his favourite landscapes.

The point of view is frequently that of an elderly person, a self-confessed 'senior citizen' doggereledly attached to the way things used to be, and losing patience with the present's laziness that masquerades as affirmation of freedom. Who could have foretold that the innovative firebrand of the early 1930s would in 1969 condemn the 'Anti-Novel' and 'Free Verse'? The sense of the ineffectiveness of poetry persists (the poem 'Rois Fainéants' may partly be about poets), and could perhaps be gauged in 'August, 1968', his response to the Russian invasion of Dubcek's Czechoslovakia, which contrasted with previous interventionist verse, such as 'Spain'. The previously noted theme of the preciousness of well-maintained language is at the centre of this short piece, which describes an ogre who is very powerful yet can only talk drivel; but it is unlikely that the Soviet leaders Brezhnev and Kosygin were deflected by such satire. It is equally unlikely that Auden supposed they would be; yet the fact remains that his poem has survived into the twenty-first century, which is more than can be said for their invasion or the Soviet Union itself ('The Garrison' partly concerns art's survivalism; Boly (1991: 128) notes that 'Like Shelley's Ozymandias, Auden's Ogre is undone by time, but through the medium of language rather than force'). The final poem in the book, 'Prologue at Sixty', whilst it looks back on his life, is not only attentive to his present Austrian surroundings, but also, as a prologue, looks forward to a 're-beginning', and finds connection with the lives of the young in the mutual possibilities of 'translation'. There is a grateful rootedness and a willingness to take sense from his life, evident also in poems such as 'Since' and 'Amor Loci', that give the collection its tone; and Mendelson has argued that 'River Profile' is 'the greatest poem of his last years, and one of the greatest and strangest poems of its century' (*LA*: 482).

The very late poetry engages with the contemporary world of scientific discoveries, or the self-indulgent blandness of 'Flower Power' philosophy (in the poem 'Circe'), but there is a deliberate diminutiveness, as the Audenesque landscape turns into that of his own body with its microscopic surface parasites or its unexplored interior ('A New Year Greeting', 'Talking to Myself'); when a genuinely epochal event occurred in the external world, it was subjected to deflatingly subversive treatment ('Moon Landing'). The world of animals and insects is inspected for its significant difference from our own (in a manner wholly dissimilar to his younger contemporary Ted Hughes); the keynote poems of his last, posthumous collection concerned themselves with the drowsy rememberings of 'A Lullaby' or the cocooning indistinctness welcomed in 'Thank You, Fog' (a poem which also obscures the thwarted festiveness of the Christmas it commemorates, felt by those who shared it with him). The dedication of this final volume to Michael and Marny Yates marked one of the most enduring relationships of Auden's life.

Alongside the individual volumes itemised here, there were the libretti (with Kallman), as well as collections of his prose. More significantly, there were the successive *Collected Poems* by means of which Auden engaged antagonistically with the image of himself cherished by many readers; 'Spain', thought by many the best poem to arise out of that conflict, and 'September 1, 1939', later extravagantly praised by Joseph Brodsky and containing the line that made Forster swoon in admiration, were eventually both jettisoned – as 'Lay Your Sleeping Head . . .' would have been, but for Kallman's intervention. As already suggested, Auden's practice implied a refusal to believe that poems stood above or outside time; but quite apart from the emotional wrench implied for readers deprived of their personal favourites, some were inclined to see it in the light of a potentially more sinister air-brushing of the historical record (Auden ruefully reflected that 'In relation to a writer, most readers believe in the Double Standard: they may be unfaithful to him as often as they like, but he must never, never be unfaithful to them', *DH*: 3). Although it would be wrong to impose a neat thematic unitariness on Auden's career, I close this part by suggesting that in much of his poetry, both at the level of form and at the level of meaning, he concerned himself with the implications contained in his advice to his godson, and in the question he posed when talking to himself: 'Be glad your being is unnecessary' (*EG*: 12); 'for who is not certain that he was meant to be?' (*EG*: 70).

Poems individually considered

Note: This section is best read with a copy of the poems to hand; most can be found in *SP*. I refer where possible to the earliest stabilised publication; with the exception of 'Spain', for poems preceding *NYL* this means the *EA* text. Later poems are referenced by the volume in which each first appeared.

'Who Stands, the Crux Left of the Watershed' (August 1927); 'The Watershed'

The earliest written of Auden's poems to survive the various culls by which he refined his canon, this shows extraordinary force and confidence. Written at his parents' home in Harborne, it dramatically evokes the lead-mining landscape of the North Pennines; in a letter to Isherwood he even called it 'Rookhope' (*Juv*: 219): thereby placing it in a chain of poems alluding to the area, which began with 'The Old Lead-Mine' (February 1924), included 'Paid on Both Sides' and concluded with 'Amor Loci' (July 1965). 'Cashwell' (l. 7), whose relocated pumping-engine Auden first described in a 1924 poem, was a small remote lead-mine on Cross Fell, near the south-western edge of Alston Moor; Rookhope, in Weardale, lies to its north-east. The manor of Alston Moor was formerly one of the country's most important lead-mining areas; causing the ingenious paraphernalia of Victorian industrial processes to be situated in some forbiddingly remote locations, above ground and below. Auden's boyhood fascination with metal-mines, which for a while seemed to indicate his likely profession, saw the family visit Rookhope as early as 1919 by his own account; he continued to visit derelict mining-sites into the early 1930s, drawn by the symbolic suggestiveness of their abandoned buildings and rusting machinery, once the locus of strenuous activity, now lying deserted amidst desolate moorland.

The poem is written in blank verse whose dramatic qualities owe something to Shakespeare, but which is masterly in its avoidance of predictable stress in the pentameter line; the short 'a' of 'stands' is repeatedly echoed throughout the first eighteen lines ('ramshackle'; 'Cashwell'), along with alliterative effects and teasing irregular half-rhymes at line-ends. We seem to be listening to a story of endurance, part-compressed by its own urgency and spoken in a kind of sonorous telegraphese; but which, having secured our attention, in the final twelve lines switches from third-person report to second-person address and dismissively rebukes us as complacent tourists. The abrupt beginning may recall the opening of *Hamlet* – 'Who's there?' (which in a 1948 lecture Auden suggested was the question implicitly answered by every work of art) – but it is part of the poem's deceptiveness that the apparently challenging interrogative 'Who stands(?)' turns out to be an abridgement of '(He) who stands' or 'Who(ever) stands': a tactic of disorientation compounded by our immediate uncertainty over what 'the crux' might be or how to situate it 'left of the watershed' (these definite articles seem especially coercive). The 'watershed' in turn we are tempted to visualise as some kind of building rather than a geographical feature (linked perhaps with the 'washing-floors', where ore was cleaned and sorted). Somewhat paradoxically, the urgent energetic voice goes on to present scenes of visible decline and diminution; next to bear witness to a valiant act of mine-repair; then to recount what seems a curiously feral reversion to death (probably prompted by local lore of an event in the Nenthead complex of mines in 1916, when a mortally injured miner had to be carried between valleys through interconnecting underground levels). Then in the second part the focus of observation shifts from that place and its people onto the reader–writer, confronted as a smug ignoramus who drives around understanding little of what he sees or hears: the lead-mining vocabulary of 'levels' and 'washing-floors', along with the obscurity of 'Cashwell' as a place, enforce this exclusion. The final brilliance of the poem is its return to the point of entry on that wet road amid the windblown grass, to revive the potential question of its opening by explicitly answering it: who stands, the crux left of the watershed? A stranger.

The country spread beneath him is an enigma ('This land, cut off, will not communicate'); neither it nor its denizens will collaborate with a sightseer's desire to commodify sights seen in picturesque retrospect – the 'inward eye / Which is the bliss of solitude', in Wordsworth's terms, recalling his Lake District daffodils (Boly reads 'The Watershed' as a *genius loci* poem, comparing it to Wordsworth's 'The Solitary Reaper'). 'Who Stands . . .' was written a week or so after Auden's return from holiday in Yugoslavia with his father, whose touristical behaviour had made his son wish he (Wystan) were dead (see the third day of his 1934 travelogue 'In Search of Dracula'). Its 'aimless' motorist is chastened by this landscape's sense of buried purpose – where even a coffined corpse apparently is able to seek out its appropriate place (ll. 14–18) – and his tourist's impulse to go away and wait for the holiday snaps to be developed is thwarted by an inability to leave ('Stranger, turn back again, frustrate and vexed'): this present refuses to be conscripted for his past. The superiority implied by his elevated perspective is a delusion, and the dictionary definition of 'crux' as 'something that occasions difficulty or perplexity' is embodied in the contradictory imperatives dismissing and then retaining him at that watershed (a high ridge from which water-systems drain to one side or the other: possible geographical locations are discussed in Fuller (1998), and by Myers and Forsythe in their 1999 pamphlet). To drive a car in these unprosperous valleys, the year after the General Strike had resulted in a worsening of coal-miners' pay, was indeed to be a privileged creature; but despite Auden's sympathies with the workers' cause, his plummy Oxford accent perpetually defined him as outsider, in regions where modernity had as yet made little impact on distinctive local dialects: when late in life he met the novelist and ex-miner Sid Chaplin in Newcastle, the latter noted that 'I doubt if he'd ever made friends with a Weardale or Alston lead-miner' (Myers and Forsythe 1999: 23). Equally, the surveillant stranger is ignorant of the nearer world of a wild creature – probably a rabbit – furtively surveying *him*: this points up the metamorphic agencies at work in the poem, whereby a machine begrudges its labour and the wind hurts itself, while a dead man behaves quite like a mole. Grass chafes, sap rises, the unnoticed creature assesses him: in this poem *he* is, in Coleridge's phrase, 'the sole unbusy thing', which heightens a sense of his exclusion from the world he looks at, 'unbaffled' in its being as he, 'frustrate and vexed', is not. Too centred in his externalised onlooking, he lacks the instinctual poise of the rabbit synaesthetically reliant on ears and nose, to which he signifies 'danger' (in 'Homage to Clio' Auden would imagine himself being appraised by the wildlife in his garden); this of course provides a closing rhyme with 'stranger', but may also evoke the possibility of 'changer': if he could change, might he go one way or another from the watershed, this point of indecision?

'From the Very First Coming Down . . .' (December 1927); 'The Letter'

In his collected editions Auden chose this poem to commence his early poetry (following 'Paid on Both Sides'). It was written at Oxford; he later identified it with Bill McElwee, who could not respond erotically and seldom wrote letters, and with whom, during the Christmas vacation of the previous year, he had undertaken a trip to Austria. When he wrote it, however, he had started a new friendship with Gabriel Carritt, another Old Sedberghian undergraduate who was undissuadably heterosexual. As with the previous poem, it suggests a northern landscape of steep-sided valleys, sudden fierce weather and sheep-pens sturdy enough to shelter by (therefore stone-built); here the setting is probably the countryside around Threlkeld and his parents' cottage at Wescoe in the northern Lake District (where it would be plausible for Auden to have received letters). Another similarity lies in the sonnet-like division of mood and tone between a longer first and shorter second part, and in the theme of non-communication which, in different ways, each shares: this poem opens evoking an intimate presence which turns out to be an absence. Finally, like 'Who Stands . . .', it incorporated images and lines recycled from earlier abandoned efforts (for which, see Bucknell's edition of *Juvenilia* (2003)).

The differences, however, are also marked: this is written in full-rhymed tetrameter couplets whose terse (over)control perhaps implies matters suppressed or left unsaid; and whereas the previous poem concerned irresoluteness, here an unwelcome decision has been made, announced by letter to the 'I' suddenly revealed at line 5. This poem's 'you' is no 'stranger' but a friend, not indecisively poised at a watershed but come down into 'a new valley' where it seems he will, separately, remain. The momentum established by the poem's opening – we do not encounter a comma until the end of line 3 – is stopped dead by the emphatic caesura after 'remain', which enacts their separation reinforced by time as well as place ('to-day', as the next word, infers a chasm between now and then), visually emphasised for the reader by lines 4 and 5 starting respectively with 'You' and 'I'. The introduction of the first person – another difference from 'Who Stands . . .', with its rhetoric of distancing – is immediately followed by a strong early line caesura: emphasising this speaker's isolation, amplified as abject victimhood in the depiction of his 'crouching' beneath the dual onslaughts of weather and unreciprocated love. Like the windblown bird he would 'cry out against the storm', for the poem at this stage is pervaded by knowledge of the letter he will shortly receive, but he refrains from Lear-like posturing, and untidy emotions born of thwarted longing compose themselves towards the acidic primness of the second part. This is accomplished by reviewing the year during which their relationship has unfolded, and inferring that just as season succeeds season – although summer oddly precedes spring in his retrospect – so love has its cycle; he even sees an omen of his current state in the 'solitary truck, the last/Of shunting in the Autumn' (as if shunting were a seasonal activity!). The signs were all there, in effect, and now this letter arrives in fulfilment of the prophecy: the section has started with 'the very first coming down' and ends with the dull thud of 'not to come'.

The poem has in various ways enacted interruption to the smooth sequence of feeling: in four lines 'sun' turns to 'storm', just as the disappointing letter chills the genial warmth of his evening fireside; then the poem's division separates two halves of a rhyming couplet, and the second part starts with a series of elegantly negative formulations, amid which is concealed the protesting reiteration 'no, no, no' (in lines which are an elaborate periphrasis for 'getting the brush-off is not the end of the world'). But since this is a poem about suppressing feeling, the outrage latent in 'deceived' is quickly finessed into the false composure of 'decent', and the affected world-weariness audible in the first part ('shall see, shall pass') comes to his half-rescue in the acceptance of seasonal change ('Different or with a different love'), as the poet envisages future collaboration with the world of timorous reticence and stony smile. The conspiratorial 'country god' possibly alludes to ancient boundary-markers representing Hermes (god of messages) with an erect phallus: a limit reached and an erection turned to stone – 'not to come' – is very much what this poem is 'about', and of course Auden was here doubly afflicted, by 'the love that dare not speak its name' and the love that dared not do its deed. Even the phallic god has been reduced to a role of furtive innuendo, nodding and smiling but 'Always afraid to say more than it meant' (thus the poem's longest line ironically concerns repressed utterance). Twenty years later, on Fire Island, Auden told a British visitor that 'Americans always say more than they mean, just as the English always say less': this early poem possibly foretold why he would leave (Maurice Cranston, interview with Auden published in *John O'London's Weekly*, 6 February 1948).

'Control of the Passes . . .' (January 1928); 'The Secret Agent'

Auden's composing notebook from this period shows how different from its initial conception this poem finally became, even though the last four lines underwent relatively little alteration (the notebook was published in facsimile (Lawlor 1989); changes are recorded in *Juv*). In the very first version, what are now lines 3 and 4 preceded lines 1 and 2, thus opening with the spy's entrapment, and the district was 'fresh' rather than 'new'; Auden quickly saw the better way to start his poem, and indicated transposition with an arrow. His first two attempts were ten lines long; but the third version much more closely resembled its final form which, as two groups of four lines and one of six, is that of an unrhymed sonnet, where the octave's anxious purposefulness is replaced in the sestet by a mood of disengagement – perhaps implying the speaker has run away like the water heard nocturnally, or is imprisoned. This version was still havering between 'fresh' and new' (preferring the former), and tried other small variations which were then rejected. Its major difference lay in the introduction of what now comprises lines 5–9, and the first part of line 10; unlike some of the material lifted from abandoned poems and interpolated into 'The Watershed' and 'The Letter', this seems to have been newly composed. Fuller (1998: 15) has pointed out that the poem's last line, 'Parting easily who were never joined', derives from the Old English poem *Wulf and Eadwacer* (which Auden later quoted in *A Certain World*), 'the monologue of a captive woman to her outlawed lover (she is on one island, he on another)'. All three poems so far examined, published in Spender's 1928 pamphlet, thus deal with themes of separation and broken or ineffectual contact: between the 'stranger' and 'this land' he surveys; between the recipient of the letter and its writer; and between secret agent and those for whom he works – the 'they' who may also end up shooting him – as well as the phantasmal lover he dreams of, from whom he will so easily and imminently be parted.

The stranger, the 'I' and the spy are all thwarted in their desires for emotional reciprocation, and their poems also share a northern English geography, such as would figure prominently in 'Paid on Both Sides'. This third version's new material emphasised the geographical aspect by specifying the name 'Greenhearth' – probably intending 'Greenhurth', a Teesdale lead-mining locality upstream from Cauldron Snout; 'Greenhearth' had previously occurred in two significant early poems (see *Juv*: 72n). Like 'Cashwell', 'Greenhearth' is suggestively obscure, disrupting any smooth transition between saying and meaning; such references seem complex in effect and intention: they partly presume a reader's knowingness, a state coercively encoded in line 13's 'of course', which in turn indicates a pervasive atmosphere of secrets understood or withheld ('Who will get it? Surely *you* will, Gentle Reader'). But John Buchan's fiction rather than Joseph Conrad's informs this poem, whose agent decodes his surroundings and predicts disaster (as the 'I' read the signs in the previous poem, and anticipating the Airman's sense of threat in *The Orators*); as in *The Thirty-Nine Steps* (1914), familiar landscapes conceal danger, and time is running out.

A 1950s poem by Thom Gunn called 'Carnal Knowledge' has as refrain 'I know you know I know you know I know' (varied as 'You know I know. . .'); which indicates disabling recessions of self-consciousness, feints within feints perhaps also involved in this Auden poem, so alert to who knows what. Concerning a man whose homosexuality comes between him and the woman he's in bed with, 'Carnal Knowledge' is doubly relevant to the landscape of this agent, whose secret may be identical, and whose situation is described in *doubles entendres*: the 'passes' desirably controlled may lead into the body; he has found himself 'seduced with the old tricks' ('fresh', if retained, would have reinforced such innuendo), and he does not seem to be getting 'it' – except, perhaps, finally he gets it in the neck, shot either as spy or deserter. Bozorth places this poem in the biographical context of Auden's 'frustrated homosexual desire' for McElwee and Carritt, but emphasises that subordinating the poetry to this narrative is still to misread it, for 'it is crucial to the signifying operations of Auden's early poems that we be able to read them "innocently", as having nothing to do with homosexuality': what links the world of espionage and the world of the closet is their recourse to 'plausible deniability' (2001: 33, 19).

Bozorth argues that the conspiratorial atmosphere of the poem and its particular deployment of Auden's northern landscape were decisively influenced by the Isherwood–Upward 'Mortmere' stories he was reading in manuscript at this period: too frankly obscene to be publishable unexpurgated, these constituted a kind of *samizdat* (and exclusively esoteric) intertext, subversive outrages known only to initiates. Auden's characteristic landscape was powerfully symbolic (as in 'From Scars Where Kestrels Hover', January 1929), switching easily from appearance to suggestiveness, implying knowledge of carnality as well as mountains of the mind; and if in part he employed it to dramatise a sense of homosexual exclusion, and later turned it to theological uses, he also used what he termed his 'Great Good Place' – which denoted an actual region – as a kind of touchstone of authenticity, which he both did and did not wish to share more widely. A.S.T. Fisher, a friend during his first year at Christ Church (the one who saw him reduced to tears by his mother), recalled that Auden seemed rather put out on learning that he, too, was familiar with the remoter reaches of Alston Moor.

'It Was Easter as I Walked in the Public Gardens' (April–October 1929); '1929'

The four poems assembled by Auden into this, his most ambitious non-dramatic work before *The Orators*, were composed after he had left Oxford; the first two in Berlin, the third at Wescoe and the fourth in London, where he was seeking work. Although driven by the significant changes in his life that followed graduation, they move beyond the psychodramas implicit in previous examples, attempting a broader engagement with the world of thoughts rather than sensations. As Fuller (1998) notes, Auden had the habit of writing a poem at Easter, and this Christian festival, together with the evocation of 'public gardens' rather than untamed landscapes reflecting turbulent subjective states, point up differences: the sequence is less concerned with helpless entrapment or frustrated repetition of 'love's worn circuit' (an image suggesting a gin-horse) than with the challenge presented by new life, both individually and collectively.

The sequence is not, however, routinely life-affirming: its sense of positive forces also alerts it to the negative. Easter may represent, as the first section has it, 'Season when lovers and writers find/An altering speech for altering things'

(*EA*: 37; Auden was now having to speak German), but this swelling optimism is immediately checked by a 'solitary man' weeping on his park bench, 'Helpless and ugly as an embryo chicken' – an image both visually effective and suggestive of new life ill-equipped for survival. The journal which Auden kept at this crucial period of his life, which is extant (a few extracts are published in *EA*), identifies this unhappy man as John Layard: the same friend whose persistent analysis of his own failure, later referred to, led to a botched attempt at suicide that subsequently involved Auden – in whose journal the phrase 'embryo chicken' somewhat coolly described his appearance at this juncture. Despite introducing his friend to the ideas of Homer Lane, Layard (who miraculously survived) could not convert those teachings into adequate control of his own life; his condition here reminds Auden, amidst his own burgeoning self-possession, of those excluded from success.

This is very much an autobiographical poem (based, according to Mendelson, on a verse-letter written the same month to Isherwood); but it does not depend on our knowing the name of the weeping man, nor the precise identities of Kurt Groote or Gerhart Meyer (friends Auden had made in Berlin's homosexual subculture: Meyer he first met on Easter Sunday), who emblematise happiness and strength. The foreignness of their names is significant; for in Germany Auden experimented with and confirmed his sexual identity, in a manner which would have been impossible in England (his Berlin period has been outlined by Page (1998), who speculates that Easter 1929 marked the point when Auden recognised his homosexuality was not a condition which could be 'cured'). In addition to this sexual liberation, the journal shows Auden to have been thinking furiously, in ways also visible in his poem's expounding ideas about individual development and family relations that engage principally with those of Freud and D.H. Lawrence (Mendelson (1981) also sets forth the importance of Trigant Burrows' 1927 book, *The Social Basis of Consciousness*).

The four sections suggest the four seasons, evoked without imposing any rigid scheme of identification. There is throughout an awareness of the forces which make for death and those affirming life; thus the first poem counters Auden's spring optimism with the thought of Layard, itself balanced by thoughts of his German friends; its final part, lifted from an Oxford poem about McElwee (hence the gowns and bicycles), perhaps serves to remind him of his own earlier unhappinesses, whilst affirming the 'necessary error' of making a choice. This need for change is picked up in the second section, stylistically strongly marked by the influence of Gertrude Stein, with present participles indicating a world of process. Candidly self-identifying as a 'homesick foreigner' – the German setting is underscored by place names – the ducks he looks at offer a model of unselfconsciousness, humanly inaccessible but contrasting with his voluble 'friend', whose overexcited talk of the class war implied by Berlin's contemporary political unrest provokes his deliberately callous response. The poet is more concerned with the stages of the self than of society, from which he seeks a 'hill-top' elevation, the better to ponder the sources of self-division that lead to alienation from the body and a death-wish. But as in the first poem his optimistic mood was chastened, so here his deterministic pessimism is persuaded to rejoice and he to embrace his life by a sense of cosmic unity that suggestively prefigures his 'vision of Agape' in 'Out on the Lawn . . .':

> In me so absolute unity of evening
> And field and distance was in me for peace,
> Was over me in feeling without forgetting
> Those ducks' indifference, that friend's hysteria,
> Without wishing and with forgiving,
> To love my life, not as other,
> Not as bird's life, not as child's,
> 'Cannot', I said, 'being no child now nor a bird'.
> (*EA*: 38–9)

This last line was recycled from an abandoned 1925 poem.

The third section, written back in England three months later (having just ended his engagement), opens with a railway journey to the family cottage at Wescoe; anyone who has looked at telegraph wires from a moving train will appreciate Auden's description here. Although there is a continuity of being in time, implied in his journey's interconnecting start and finish, the constructed authoritarian self, checking timetables and summoning food in the restaurant car, apparently conceals a 'frightened soul' whose return home may signify a faltering resolve. 'This life of sheep and hay' may no longer be his, but has a cosseting allure, despite imperatives to move beyond it; Auden's Berlin journal had had much to say to himself about the mother–son relationship, which re-poses for him now the difficult question of the ways in which that originating love conditions (or infects) successive versions. This section, then, repeats the pattern of predecessors, in which (positive) forward impulse encounters (negative) inertia – thus giving additional point to the telegraph-wire image previously noted. But the poet, who has gone for a walk into a nearby wood (Far Wescoe's topography is accurately evoked), startled from his reverie by the screech of a jay, is reminded not to desist from progress towards his soul's 'independent delight' (a somewhat Yeatsian formulation), and to embrace the seasonal and personal changes that implies. The memorable 'frozen buzzard' came from an earlier poem, acting here as augury of the winter that must be endured as part of the necessary cycle of change. Fuller (1998) notes that the dense prose-like musings about love, at the section's middle, derive from Chekhov, and its final line from J.W. Dunne's *An Experiment with Time* (1927).

The final section, written two months later (after which, Mendelson shows, Auden adjusted the previous poem), inverts the thematic pattern of the first: whereas that had begun in affirmation and encountered negation, this starts by imagining potent forces of decay, but ends envisaging the enemy's defeat. Opening with the threatening admonition 'It is time for the destruction of error' (*EA*: 40), its declamatoriness marks a tonal difference from the previous three: where those were notable for frequent omission of definite articles, this displays the deicticism which Cunningham sees as a marked feature of the Audenesque's attitude of coercive definition. Attention here is diverted from the self and its progress, towards an ailing society where madness, industrial sordor, mould and insidious poisoning imply ways in which draconian authority bends individuals to its will:

> To destroy the efflorescence of the flesh,
> The intricate play of the mind, to enforce

> Conformity with the orthodox bone,
> With organised fear, the articulated skeleton.

The denunciatory energy is surprising, given his previous impatience with a friend's 'hysteria' about street-fighting in Berlin; but although there was much hypocrisy to unmask in England on the threshold of the 1930s, the grounds for discontent may be as personal as political, relating to difficulties of maintaining the self liberated in Germany, in the more repressive mother-country where he now sought employment: if this was home, why had he bothered to be homesick?

The 'you' addressed in the final part he later identified with Robert Medley, who had set him on the path of poetry at Gresham's; in 1947 Auden compiled a list naming the most important sexual passions of his life, putting Medley's name first, dated 1922 (see *LA*: 266). By 1929, however, Medley was involved with Rupert Doone and unavailable to Auden as a partner; which is why their love is described as transcending the sexually automated 'admiring excitement of union'. Having thus outlasted the physically passional possessive stage, this relationship implies knowledge of the phases of death necessary to life's continuance: biblically, the seed needs to die in order to sprout (with a nod, too, to the title of the homosexual Gide's autobiography, *Si le grain ne meurt*), as do old selves and infatuations. These are embodied in the complicated imagery closing the poem: the 'hard bitch' and 'riding-master' who stiffen underground may encode Auden's distaste for what in his 1960s journal he termed the 'sadistic aggression' of penetrative sex, as well as grotesquely parodying the heterosexuality to which he had nearly conformed. The underwater bridegroom is more complex, since (as in Eliot) death by water can transfigure, Christ is sometimes conceived as a bridegroom, and the scene has a surreal peaceful beauty. Fuller sees this as another rejected selfhood, connected with Auden's fruitless passion for McElwee (by now about to be married) – the subject of an early poem, 'Narcissus', which is echoed in the first section. Thus it denotes the narcissism in which Auden's self-love, masquerading as attachment to McElwee, might have drowned him in desexualised suspended animation (he mortified his flesh by undergoing a period of total chastity during this 'relationship', which – unlike that with Medley – remained unconsummated). Bucknell gives a literary source in Hans Andersen's *The Ice Maiden*, linking it to Auden's acceptance that he would not become a bridegroom, but also describing this closing image as 'mysterious and serene' (*AS* III: 201–2). It may be that the lake in which the entrancing figure lolls, still visible, needed to be 'deep', because he tempts with the most dangerously seductive kind of inertia: an unnecessary error it was essential that Auden destroy.

In 'The Spur', Yeats asks any reader prudishly shocked by his late poetry of 'lust and rage' what else an old man has to 'spur [him] into song'. The same might be said about a young man's poetry, and the biographically inflected reading offered here acknowledges the fact; in writing an extended poem about himself, Auden was also clearly breaking with the doctrine of impersonality as preached by Modernism. To recall that this ambitious sequence was the work of a 22-year-old, is to be struck both by the prodigality of Auden's talent and by the rapidity of its progress: for whilst it deals with material related to that of 'From the Very First Coming Down', the advance beyond a personalised response, into a more structured consideration of what such things mean in a wider context, is notable. As the sequence is about the need to break out of old cycles of behaviour in meeting the challenges of new growth (and is readable as such, in ignorance of any specific biographical or intellectual contexts), so the kind of poem this is broke new ground for him.

'Consider This and In Our Time' (March 1930); 'Consider'

If it were possible to write a 'coming out' poem in 1929, then the previous one might have been it; but, as Bozorth (2001) indicates, the particular conclusions Auden reached obliged him to dissimulation, at the same time that they constituted the grounds for a personally implicated critique of English society and the kind of life it fostered. If '1929' is a type of crisis-poem, the significance of the year was personal rather than historical: *we* may associate 1929 with the stock-market crash in late October; but earlier political events convulsing Berlin during his months there did not engross Auden's journal, and were reflected in his poetry only as a friend's tiresome jabber (Smith, it should be noted, argues vigorously for the direct relevance of the political background to the entire sequence (1985: 46–51)). The 'error' whose necessary destruction '1929' announced was really Auden's own; yet the tone and some imagery of that final section, together with the whole sequence's greater outward-lookingness, indicated an engagement with the wider world that is aggressively reflected in the stance and subject of 'Consider This': whose further qualification 'and in our time' seems to insist on its contemporary focus. That he later omitted the lines from 'Financier . . .' to '. . . playing fives' probably signified Auden's subsequent dissatisfaction with the corrosively scattershot disrespect they directed upon bankers, clergymen, dons, self-gratifying nurses and hearty outdoor types; as noted below, the effect is to enforce a more generalised denunciation.

Auden might as well have left them in, because they were wholly congruent with the mystifying animus generating other lists in this poem, whose dominantly imperative mode bespeaks an evident determination to command attention. In its bravura opening, hawk or helmeted airman (the first suggesting the second's potential predatoriness) look down upon a body of evidence running the gamut from discarded cigarette stub to mountain peak commodified by 'plate-glass windows of the Sport Hotel' – a thumbnail evocation of 1930s 'international' architecture:

> Join there the insufficient units
> Dangerous, easy, in furs, in uniform
> And constellated at reserved tables
> Supplied with feelings by an efficient band
> Relayed elsewhere to farmers and their dogs
> Sitting in kitchens in the stormy fens.
> (*EA*: 46)

The vertiginous alteration of perspective and location – from sky to Alpine hotel to fenland farmhouses (the plural presumptuously instituting generic rather than specific identity) – gives little time to draw breath and pose the question: of what is all this the evidence? Are we supposed to dislike these privileged, apparently unfeeling people, the insufficiency of whose units may be cue for (our?) attack? (Still, those units are 'dangerous': better hold off.) Should we deplore the social inequalities separating their pampered luxury from lives led in houses with only one warm room, where the great chain of deferential being terminates in dogs?

That my responses have been so interrogatory indicates, Smith (1985) has suggested, the extent to which this poem destabilises its reader's position: set up as detached observer and even potential detective, one finds oneself somehow implicated in an unspecified crime, co-opted by the rhetoric into unforeseen positions, both active and passive. Fuller (1998) notes the relevance of Hardy and Lawrence to the opening imagery, but these alterations of perspective and serio-comic logical illogicality also perhaps suggest the world of Alice, shape-shifter who suddenly becomes The Accused. Smith describes the 'powerful transformations' to which the poem's readers are subjected:

> Like money, we are always passing on, and yet always fixed in the same position, projected passively at the receiving end of a series of commands that attribute to us the power and authority that the speaker himself seems to possess. . . . As speaker and addressee at once, the subject here partakes of the duplicity of the text, simultaneously culprit and judge.
> (1985: 45–6)

The position is made no more comfortable by our transit from the first part's cinematographic mode to the second, which suddenly drops us into the past ('Long ago . . .'), proceeds through a present emblematised by disused harbours, ruined factories, neglected orchards – similar to the synoptic landscapes of 'Get There If You Can . . .', his next poem – to a future where seditiously induced panic will trigger mass neurosis and complete social breakdown, virtually turning people into rubbish.

As if all this were not bad enough, the 'supreme Antagonist' who appears to be at the root of it, having long ago defeated Auden's boyhood heroes the 'mining captains' (metal-mine managers: the Cornish, Somerset and Pennine fields denote the probable historical succession of British lead-mining), and who in the present acts in nasty parody of Christ choosing disciples by the Sea of Galilee – only to put them to infernal uses – this Antagonist has a tendency, *via* the insistently vocative 'you', to merge into *us*, each Gentle Reader. We could sidestep this inference, by imagining that we overhear the denunciation of some insidiously powerful entity, prophet of decay and terminal deterioration, whose dispiriting message amounts to, 'You are all going to drop to naked pieces in damp graves' (Caliban's later imagery). But such evasion may not help, for even if happily convinced we are not like the financier and those other types admonished in the final part, we, like them, are surely going to die; and unless we can be certain of not being 'seekers after happiness' – much more difficult to do after Auden's revision – it is later than *we* think, as well. The poem troublingly alerts us to the signs of evil, exposes the conspiracy and what its effect will be – but tells us we are powerless to prevent it, implies that we are 'in our time' up to the neck. The 1930s world, with its bang-up-to-date plate glass, wireless communication and arterial roads, is the devil's territory, rotten to the core: Auden would return to the specious attractiveness of modernity in 'Letter to Lord Byron' (Part II; see *EA*: 175).

The poem's relation to its own reader can fairly be described as antagonistic. The high-pressure rhetoric – whose syntactical elisions speed us along as simultaneously they obscure meaning – compels attention; and having initially conscripted us as distanced onlookers, disconcertingly implicates us in the role of blustering, panicky objector, for whom no outcome is foreseeable but a failed abscondence leading either to disintegrative mania or semi-vegetative inertia (I'll take the second, thanks). The strategies of address here are similar to those encountered in 'Who Stands . . .', but more mercurial in their succession, more generally threatening and also, importantly, more actually comic in their effect. There is a pungent diagnosis, but no apparent remedy – except, perhaps, for that indicated in a prose comment from the previous year, which evokes potential forgiveness, but in other respects exactly resembles the poem's ending:

> He cannot forgive himself; therefore he cannot forgive others. This man, the prey to fugues, irregular breathing, and alternate ascendencies (*sic*), after some haunted migratory years, disintegrates on an instant in the explosion of mania, or lapses for ever into a classic fatigue.
>
> (*Plays*: 461)

This is indebted, Fuller (1998) shows, to McDougall's *An Outline of Abnormal Psychology* (1926); but the poem's implication is that 'abnormal psychologies' are, writ large in social structures, all that is on offer. It is as if in '1929' Auden had embraced the self he must become, and therefore began to externalise his anger towards the society he felt newly entitled to criticise for gangrenous hypocrisies further exposed in 'Consider This . . .'. Yet for all the energy driving its declamatory analysis, the poem moves us from a position of imperious surveillance to one of abject ineffectuality. In this, it resembles 'Who Stands . . .', except that there an onlooker stood rebuked by the purposive self-containment of scenes highlighting his own inadequacy; here, the world surveyed is manifestly inadequate, yet even a surveyor fortified by self-assurance foresees no cure, his compelling analysis dissolves in the *diminuendo* of the close – perhaps because its imperatives denoted ultimate complicity with the very power relations criticised. The dissatisfaction speaks loud and clear, but what does such sound and fury accomplish? The way forward may be indicated by its comic resemblance to a speeded-up film whose cartoonish characters finally explode or collapse: this would lead on to the strategies of *The Orators*. Boly, who evolves sophisticated models of the writer–text–reader relationship, locates the poem's voice as 'that of an aspiring Hyde Park orator, inexperienced as a public speaker though well-versed in visionary conventions' (1991: 140).

'Out on the Lawn I Lie in Bed' (June 1933); 'A Summer Night' 'Look, Stranger, at this Island Now' (November 1935); 'On This Island'

If *The Orators* and his abandoned epic ('In the Year of my Youth . . .') were kinds of 'English Study' Auden turned away from, this was not because he was no longer interested in studying England; what changed, however, were the modes and tones in which he undertook it. The chorus opening *The Dog Beneath the Skin* (1935) evoked England with a certain affection ('The Summer Holds . . .'), even if much of the detail derived from Collett; its vision of a declining and inauthenticised country shares some of the features of 'Consider This . . .' ('I see barns falling, fences broken,/Pasture not ploughland, weeds not wheat' *et seq.*, *EA*: 282; see also imagery of industrial decline in 'O Love, the interest itself . . .', *EA*: 119); however, this chorus also seems oddly regretful about the decline of the Great House: 'if this be Leftism,' Cunningham justly comments, 'it is a Leftism charged with old Deserted Village nostalgias' (1988: 235). Auden's poetry of the period did not altogether lose its tone of apocalypse nor its awareness of social suffering – 'These years have seen a boom in sorrow' (*EA*: 142) – but there was also a sense of possible community, and of the partially redemptive powers of love: which in the short lyric 'That Night When Joy Began' (*EA*: 113) is strong enough to convert an entire landscape from enemy territory into homeland. The sense of community was in part derived from the schools in which he was now teaching; at the Downs School in particular he was happy, and in 1933 he wrote there a poem whose atmosphere of magical calm was evoked in the title.

This poem offers an interesting case of authorial retrospection, not only in the alterations subsequently wrought, but also – and unusually for Auden, who seldom glossed his own work – in what he revealed indirectly thirty years later, in a foreword for a 1964 book on Protestant mystics. There, he defined one type of mystical experience as 'The Vision of Agape', which involves a sensed group identity; in illustration he cited an unpublished account for whose authenticity he vouched. This described 'a fine summer night in June 1933' when 'I' was sitting on a lawn with three colleagues 'when quite suddenly and unexpectedly, . . . I felt myself invaded by a power which, though I consented to it, was irresistible and certainly not mine. For the first time in my life I knew exactly – because, thanks to the power, I was doing it – what it means to love one's neighbour as oneself'. This aura – felt by the others – gradually decreased, and took a couple of days to vanish completely; but 'among the various factors which several years later brought me back to the Christian faith in which I had been brought up, the memory of this experience and asking myself what it could mean was one of the most crucial, though, at the time it occurred, I thought I had done with Christianity for good' (*F&A*: 69, 70); Auden dissimulated his authorship of this account, so made no connection to 'A Summer Night'. His poem, dedicated to the school's headmaster, originally consisted of sixteen six-line stanzas (aabccb) in which a tetrameter couplet is followed by a shorter trimeter line; later, he chose to omit the fifth, tenth, eleventh and twelfth stanzas. Fuller (1998) notes that the stanza form derived from Christopher Smart; to my ear, the shorter line acts as a sort of brake on the preceding couplet, whilst its rhyme serves to unify the inherently schismatic stanza: subtly evoking by sound the interplay of contrary forces which occurs at the level of sense.

Different as its tone and movement are from poems previously considered, this shares with them an atmosphere of foreboding ('Soon through the dykes of our content/The crumpling flood will force a rent'), and a sense of necessary destruction: for here, as in '1929', future growth – imaged as the first-appearing shoots of wheat – requires 'death of the grain, our death'. First published in *The Listener* as

'Summer Night', set in June, and evoking a dreamy nocturnal outdoors, it hints at an association with Shakespeare's comedy of transformation: for like *Midsummer Night's Dream*, it suggests an atmosphere of altered states, with day and night merging, sleep taking place outdoors. It too concerns a magic circle ('in a ring/ . . . Enchanted'), and a suspension of reality in which things lose their wonted attributes:

> The lion griefs loped from the shade
> And on our knees their muzzles laid,
> And Death put down his book.

This imagery, as if animating figures from an emblem book, points both the strangeness and the conscious archaism of the poem, but as in Shakespeare's play, there is also a sense of the fragility of this equilibrium and the proximity of its opposite. The poem's dreamy stargazing contrastively evokes the moon's downward vision; and what she sees is larger than the garden-bound perspective which, agreeable as it is, lacks 'gravity' or seriousness: as Auden would later observe, 'the earthly paradise is a beautiful place but nothing of serious importance can occur in it' (*DH*: 340). This point in space was exclusive, within 'creepered walls' of well-established privilege, but the point in time, sufficiently extended, had much to imply of what schoolpersons did not care to know about the broader world. The previous autumn had seen a hunger march descend on London, whose figures of 'wretchedness' now gather ominously beyond the walls, reproaching purely localised acts of charity and embodying the difference between physical and 'metaphysical' distress. The moon looks equitably down on churches and power stations (Battersea was being constructed at this time), on Europe as well as England, and so might have observed Dachau concentration camp, operational since March following Hitler's accession to power in late January. The world was full of 'violence' and doubtful acts, many of them bearing upon 'Our freedom in this English house', the threat to which had been underestimated by the controversial vote of 'this House' at the Oxford Union never to 'fight for its King and its Country' (February; Auden was reportedly appalled when that same month the Nazis cynically used the burning of the Reichstag as a pretext to suppress civil liberties; see Fuller 1998: 170). The stanzas later omitted enforce the connections with current events, forecasting a decisive difference between those who dream and those who do, and diagnosing sickness-unto-death in the English traditions of thought and feeling which have nurtured the speaker and his kind.

His oasis of summer happiness cannot endure, nor should: later, in 'New Year Letter' (III) Auden would describe the Jungian *temenos* (sacred precinct) where can be glimpsed 'The field of Being where he may/Unconscious of Becoming, play/With the Eternal Innocence' (*NYL*: 47); but to stay there creates 'Hell', and although in this Colwall garden he may taste Edenic 'Being', 'Becoming' urgently beckons. The poem dramatises evolutionary progress when in stanza 14 stranded lower life-forms uncomprehendingly hear man the metalworker; its imagery of inundation – Noah's, but also the Nile's fertilising flood ensuring the new harvest – indicates regenerative destruction, analogised to parents' contented displacement by their children (the note of festive comedy rather than *King Lear*!). By then, it seems, the strong will have inherited the earth, and the poem dares to hope that there will continue to be a place for its own values in this new dispensation – though there is just a hint here of the weedy swot asking to join in rough boys' games. The difficulty of establishing the referent for the 'it' of the final stanza (actually, 'this for which we dread to lose/Our privacy' – a deferral later altered) suggests the difficulty Auden had in effecting his conclusion; which seems metaphysically distressed, a pious hope that the enduringly humane will outlast the tigers of destruction (the closing imagery was recycled from his epithalamion written in 1930: see *Plays*: 486).

The poem attempts to reconcile harmony with discord, the impulse towards reclusive privacy (which it knows it feels, because this is where art is made) with the imperative for social and political engagement (which it feels it should feel); it carries most conviction when evoking the first, and tries to imagine *how* the germinal community in this enchanted circle might extend its values beyond the school-grounds, or could survive irruption by that excluded world. The results are poetically rather than intellectually persuasive, because the kind of neighbourliness felt in the garden is less convincingly projected as political agency, even though the poem implies a politics of love. The transformative forcefield of this group relation is so strongly registered, as to seem semi-plausible as a principle for solving problems of international division – which, for neither first nor last time, Auden relates to generalised psychopathy: the 'murderer' externalises his own self-hatred by his crime; could he be freed from his mirror by a truly communal relation, all might be well. Or not: the 'tigress' still embodies threat, and seems less pacifiable than those lions, earlier, no matter what forgiveness is on offer; the close finesses a solution of transcendent charity which is difficult to justify outside the religious context Auden later provided. A poem he would shortly write, 'Here on the Cropped Grass . . .', was to be less sanguine in its analysis of the transformative power of love in England's green and pleasant land: 'England to our meditations seemed/The perfect setting:/But now it has no innocence at all' (*EA*: 142).

'Out on the Lawn. . .' described a tempting insularity; 'Look, Stranger . . .' observes a real island: the Isle of Wight, representing England. This poem was composed when Auden was working in documentary film, and had been intended for that use; when first published it bore the title 'Seaside'. Fuller notes its 'sense of rediscovered Englishness' (1998: 152), which he compares to the contemporary *Dogskin*; here too Collett is echoed. Written in late autumn, it evokes the summer; its injunction to look at this island *now* establishes the immediate present, although it finishes anticipating future retrospection; this opening resembles the instruction to 'consider . . . in our time', just as the 'stranger' instructed so to look is reminiscent of the one at the watershed (with whom I assume continuity of gender); but here he is enjoined to abstain from action rather than take it, and these imperatives are much more concessive than those were: significantly, they vanish after the first line of the second stanza, as the sense of personality bleeds from the poem in its act of rapt attentiveness. There is a generosity of response that justifies Fuller's use of the adjective 'rhapsodic', though he also shrewdly notes 'the "delight" turning to instant nostalgia' (p. 153) – a slackening of immediacy perhaps reflected in the final stanza's looser rhymes and emphatically unemphatic last word.

This poem, also, leads into temptation: it tempts us to read it in the manner of seductive pastoral, as justifying the desire for quiescence interrogated in 'Out on the Lawn . . .', and which in the chorus of *Dogskin* is associated with a compliant English village, whose location we can choose 'Wherever your heart directs you most longingly to look; you are loving towards it' (*EA*: 282). It seems as if *this* stranger, unlike his predecessor, longingly looks on a location where his love *can* find reflection; but despite the poem's skilfully wooing effects of assonance and alliteration, we should perhaps less easily lose sight of his estrangement: for he moves from island to its edge to the ocean (thence to his memory), and what he has principally looked at is the sea – where he can never live, and where the gull lives only precariously. Perhaps this stranger, like his forerunner, wants to commodify the scene in the safety of memory; in doing so, does he not too easily slip into the offered Edenic presumption that all this is 'for [his] delight'? After all, sea-sounds offer chaotic violence as well as soothing somnolence – as in the curt 'pluck . . . knock . . . suck' of the second stanza, whose energies resist the imposed shape (brilliantly captured in the agitated piano accompaniment of Britten's setting). He surely has to do more than 'pause' at the cliff edge, for to go further would be to plunge into an element catastrophically not his own ('The sea,' Auden later declared, 'is that state of barbaric vagueness and disorder out of which civilization has emerged. . . . It is so little of a friendly symbol that the first thing which the author of the Book of Revelations notices in his vision of the new heaven and earth at the end of time is that "*there was no more sea*" ', *EF*: 6–7; after their month in Dover in 1937, Isherwood noted that 'Auden loathed . . . the sea – for the sea, besides being deplorably wet and sloppy, is formless' – quoted by Parker (2004: 355n)). Those distant ships, fulfilling errands paradoxically both 'urgent' and 'voluntary', imply a world where compulsion can operate, just as the innocently sauntering clouds may presage a storm gathering. Here again, it seems to me the antitype is Wordsworth: 'I gazed, and gazed, but little thought/What wealth the show to me had brought' starts a process in which the operation of memory will renew and peacefully deepen the originary pleasurable stimulus; but in Auden's poem, whilst there is a strong intimation that the 'full view' may 'indeed' – a rather ominous word – become clearer in retrospect, it is likely to be more darkly complex than the sunny immediacy in which the poem began; more shadowed, like the clouds.

'Lay Your Sleeping Head, My Love' (January 1937); 'Lullaby'

'Lullaby' (for ease of reference) was one of the last poems composed before Auden left for Spain in January 1937; he copied it out for Britten when they met for farewells. Written as his affair with the much-younger Yates came to an end, its trochaic measures enact the dying fall of a relationship whose true nature had to be kept secret, but whose inequalities are implicit as the conscious speaker gazes upon his sleeping, silent partner. The poem's originality lies, Mendelson (1981) suggests, in itself being a confession of faithlessness rather than complaining of another's; and this playing against convention operates at most levels, as it insistently does not say quite what we expected it would: the first stanza tellingly rhymes 'love' with 'grave', 'ephemeral' with 'beautiful', in an utterance which combines enormous particularised tenderness with hardheaded intimations of the way things generally work. Insistent, also, in its insertion of these human realities into the facts of time, its vocabulary of universals, rather than affirming Love's everlastingness, asserts the reverse: 'Certainty, fidelity / On the stroke of midnight pass'. Cinderella's moment of truth was when her ordinary self was reinstated; so it is here: these chimes at midnight point the relentlessness of passage through the few hours between bedtime and daybreak – that contracted period during which the beloved will be deemed 'entirely' beautiful.

Each stanza consists of one sentence. The second opens, apparently, with the kind of expansive lie commonly encountered in love lyrics; its import, however, seems not to be that soul (abstract) and body (physical) are inherently without limits, but that the boundary between them is frequently and surprisingly crossed: by lovers mistaking the 'ordinary swoon' of orgasm for evidence of 'Universal love and hope', and by hermits whose 'abstract insight' induces self-mortification, a perverse type of 'sensual ecstasy'. The superiority the speaker might claim is that, unlike those, he is undeceived; in the third stanza he seems on the brink of lying when, having forecast the ominous future, 'but from this night' *might* introduce his assurance of unfading devotion. Yet it is better understood not as a promise of what will happen hereafter ('from this night on'), but as a re-intensification of focus on the passing instant: 'let me miss nothing from this night happening now'. This is underlined by the final stanza's opening assertion, 'Beauty, midnight, vision dies' – whose singular verb enforces sequence, not simultaneity: almost before our eyes *that* night becomes *this* disentrancing day, and the street – where dawn wind replaces lover's arm – beckons his ex-beloved out into a 'mortal world' which has to be 'enough', since it is what there is. The closing invocation extraordinarily hopes that

> Noons of dryness see you fed
> By the involuntary powers,
> Nights of insult let you pass
> Watched by every human love.

The first stanza suggestively rhymed 'lie' with 'me', and here again dissonant imagery and open rhymes ('enough'/'love'; 'powers'/'pass') hint at insufficiency: in a state of dryness *water* is more needful than food, and 'involuntary powers' seem unreliable substitutes for willed assistance – the anticipated absence of which on the speaker's part is glaring (Mendelson notes his hope that 'some vaguer source' will provide what he will not (1981: 233)). The complex final image seems to suggest that with any luck the ex-beloved, apparently envisaged on the streets, will manage to avoid getting beaten up – although in his onward passage scrutiny by 'every human love' may not exclude sneering or predatory kinds of appraisal.

In contrast to 'Out on the Lawn . . .' this is a poem of disenchantment. Its antitype might be Drayton's sonnet 'Since there's no help, come let us kiss and part', extravagantly affirming love's extinction only, at the end, to hope for its continuance ('From death to life, thou might'st him yet recover'); in contrast, 'Lullaby' addresses language of continuing affection to an unhearing partner, to indicate inevitable sundering: mean streets replace the bed's safe haven. It is part of the poem's covert aggression towards generic precursors that its final 'love' denotes no transcendent generality, but individualised examples, rather as if the words 'type of' preceded 'human' (Bozorth insists that the poem cannot be read as if 'the conditions under which heterosexual and homosexual love are experienced are the same' (2001: 192)). A further provocation may consist in recalling that Christ biblically endured 'noons of dryness' and 'nights of insult'; which parallel might indicate the extent of desertion and betrayal this dreamer should expect. The title subsequently given was deceptive: a sleeping person needs no lullaby, and here actually receives a poem about rude awakening, more appropriately titled 'The Less Loving One'. 'I have written a wicked book, but feel spotless as the lamb,' confided Melville on finishing *Moby-Dick*; the other poem Auden gave Britten, 'It's Farewell to the Drawing-room's Civilised Cry', employed tub-thumping metre to voice the persona of a genial maniac, whose mission is to defeat the devil by exterminating humanity. In 1965, however (when Auden contemplated dropping 'Lullaby' from his Collected Poems), he wrote 'Since' (*CWW*), whose 'you' was also Yates: in unobtrusive affirmation that beauty, midnight, vision live.

'Spain' (April 1937); 'Spain 1937'
'In Time of War' (1938)
'September 1, 1939'

In his 'Letter to Lord Byron' (1936) Auden had offered an apparently straightforward presentation of his poetic self and its relation to history, even as he acknowledged – at the beginning of Part V – that current events were taking a turn for the worse. That deteriorating world-picture dominates these poems, each of which is concerned with wars: one in which he tried to take part, one he went to see, and one he half-avoided. They also necessarily involve issues of an individual's responsibilities, as defined by historical events; 'Lullaby' and other poems about love (e.g., 'As I Walked Out One Evening') emphasised how that experience occurs in and is qualified by time; each of these poems places the event of war within a historical perspective which also enfolds writer and reader. Only the sonnet sequence rising out of his Chinese trip would survive into his finally defined canon; in 1964 he described the other two as 'trash' which he was ashamed to have written.

'Spain' was the first poem written after his return thence in March; it was published by Fabers as a pamphlet in May, and it is this version (in *SP*) to which I refer, enthusiastically received by Day-Lewis and the *Daily Worker* reviewer, less so by Cyril Connolly (who preferred 'Lay Your Sleeping Head . . .' for being 'utterly without political purpose'; Haffenden 1983: 239); its sentiments regarding 'necessary' murder were criticised by George Orwell in December 1938, and were changed when it was reduced to twenty-three stanzas in *Another Time* (retitled 'Spain 1937' – as if to emphasise its historical contingency). It was composed back at the Wescoe cottage where, before setting off, he had gone to get into training, as he wrote to Dodds: there was a contrast between that Auden, departing amid (undesired) publicity, and the man who inconclusively returned. 'Spain' nevertheless seems to define an arena in which action was urgent and its nature clear, despite being composed by one whose own experiences there had undermined such certainties. It can be seen as the culmination of the apocalyptic menace predicted in his earlier works, for rather than indicating something ominous in the future, it describes a present that requires urgent attention: 'To-day the struggle'. It also differs in that their apocalypse was presented as essentially an English affair, whereas here the scene is Spain; thus this poem, like others from this period, opposes a sense of Europe to a more insular Englishness.

As first published, the poem consisted of twenty-six four-line stanzas, in which the three-stress third line interrupts an otherwise five-stress sequence. Fuller (1998) has suggested the symmetrical structure of the original version, whose central two stanzas culminate in the line, 'I am your choice, I am your decision. Yes, I am Spain'. The poem is well-constructed oratory, in which the modulating repetition of key-phrases marshals the rhetoric and prevents the accumulative diversity of its images from diffusing the argument's march: 'Yesterday . . . But to-day . . . To-morrow . . . But to-day . . . To-day' are the resonant markers of the opening and closing stages – where the final stanza offers a terse summary and challenging conclusion, in which the participial forms predominating in the poem's opening and closing sequences ('whispers' is the first finite verb) are displaced by an emphatic flurry of finite and modal verbs, insisting on agency. The poem's power also derives from the quirky compellingness of its illustrative lists, which offer a semi-playful *obbligato* accompanying the logical development. The opening describes the intellectual and technological phases by which present-day civilisation has been achieved; the logic appears to be that such improving inventions, these various levels of biological and social organisation, amount to an 'argument from design' now requiring urgent proof, since history seems in danger of regressing. Very broadly put, the poem's first half dramatises this case: 'Surely there must be some meaning to history, paralleling progress in life; but please let's see the designer's hand'. This petition is made to 'the life' (stanzas 10, 12), which is best understood as Life manifesting itself in each individual's circumstances, and which repudiates any controlling role: 'I am whatever you do'. There are no divine or historical determinisms dictating people's actions; so if we do not like what is happening in Spain in 1937, the question becomes what do we intend doing about it.

Each life, thus, is constituted by whatever choices or decisions it makes: there is no possibility here of the visionary inaction with which the 'stranger' contemplated his island; and the poem's second half is concerned to demonstrate *why* History is now and Spain – to anticipate Eliot's formula from *Little Gidding* (which poem David Trotter sees as partly answering the final challenge of 'Spain'). It starts with reference to the foreign volunteers who enlisted in the International Brigades, often reaching Spain under their own steam: there were enough of these to confirm that the conflict was seen at the time as a crucially important battle for Europe's soul; most were pro-Republican. Mendelson rightly observes that their effectiveness in exemplifying conscious choice is impaired by imagery suggesting they have responded instinctually or unthinkingly, like windblown seeds; but perhaps Auden wished to imply the kind of non-individualistic communitarianism that led foreigners to risk themselves in another country's civil war. When, as if from space, Spain is visualised as an 'arid square . . . nipped off from hot/ Africa, soldered so crudely to inventive Europe', where 'our thoughts have bodies', there is a hint that its geographical mediation between (instinctual) Africa and (intellectual) Europe potentially offers an ideal balance; the Spanish Civil War is here represented as our own psychopathologies writ large, with bad impulses producing destruction, and good impulses, healing and comradeliness – scorned as 'daydream laxity' by Hecht, who saw horrors in the Second World War and scoffs that '(f)ighting a war is not joining a brotherhood of like-minded friends, and "hours of friendship" do not make a fighting force' (1993: 128). The possibilities envisaged for 'to-morrow' resemble a set of derisive newsreel glimpses of lives frivolously unconstrained by the imperative that, now, reasserts its focus on the present's 'struggle', and what that entails: risks of death, involvement in killing, boredom, energy wasted and 'makeshift consolations' of the combatant's existence.

Since Auden was a non-combatant absented from the scene of conflict, these comments may best be read as his tribute to those still there; perhaps also as an attempt not to insulate himself from moral complicity, nor to pretend that murders were not committed by those on 'his' side: as much is suggested by the penultimate stanza's last word 'hurting', joltingly not the anticipated 'parting' – an effect to be echoed in the poem's ending. The last stanza re-emphasises our constraint by necessary choice, shared neither by stars nor animals; this is 'our' world, not in any sense of Adamic birthright but, post-Edenically, as the place in which difficult decisions *must* be made, and may not be deferred. 'History to the defeated/May say Alas but cannot help nor pardon': Auden later claimed this equates goodness with success, but it is self-evidently untrue that the victorious are always good, even if 'the defeated' are frequently consigned to historical irrelevance (as he would note; see *WHACP*: 788). The crux lies with that explosive last word – so closely resembling the word expected at the previous stanza's end, so unlike the formulaically alliterative 'help or hinder' expected here (there we foreheard 'p. . .' but got 'h. . .' instead; here we forehear 'h. . .' but get 'p. . .'). 'Pardon' unexpectedly extends the poem, because it cannot refer to 'the defeated', for whom it would be a despicably irrelevant alternative to 'help': its logical object must be others. History, inscribing an unalterable past, can do no more than wring her hands; the defeated will have gone down, but at least *they* tried; her record, however, will not necessarily exonerate those who might have shaped a better outcome, but did nothing. Thus the close enforces what it is to act in time, in both senses of the phrase; and its challenge is to the reader.

Such a poem runs the risk of not surviving its occasion (as was perhaps tacitly admitted by the altered title), or of being later seen as a mistaken construction of it; but in running that risk 'Spain' was at least being true to itself. It was a powerful piece of rhetoric, for which Auden later despised it (proceeds from its sale, however, helped buy medical supplies; Bryant (1997: chapter 4) sets 'Spain' in the context of other contemporary responses by writers and film-makers); but although his sympathies were with the Republican cause which as he feared became 'the defeated', the poem was no recruiting-ballad; for all its air of urgency, 'Spain' tells nobody what to do, but does affirm a crisis of choice – such as was expressed in the broadside circulated that June, to which he was cosignatory: 'Are you for, or against, Franco and Fascism? For it is impossible any longer to take no side' (*P* I: 730; for Auden's statement of his own position, see p. 388). Although he abhorred what Franco represented, this poem is less against political repression than against political abstention or evasion of commitment; 'Spain' was a political act, by which Auden wished to help shift the climate of opinion against governmental policy of non-intervention: his unsuccess in this would lead to subsequent assertions of poetry's practical ineffectiveness. Smith describes the poem as 'a direct polemic and practical contribution to a continuing struggle, in which Auden acknowledged his place as a partisan' (1987: 155); Mendelson (1981) and McDiarmid (1990) discuss the developing importance of ideas of 'pardon' or 'forgiveness' in Auden's writing.

His set of twenty-seven sonnets in *Journey to a War* showed him making a different kind of response to conflict. He used the form with facility, introducing many creative variations in rhyme-scheme and line-length; its discipline prevented him from reproducing the button-holing polemic of 'Spain'. Fuller observes that 'the core stylistic effects of the sequence are quite often achieved without straying much beyond the currently fashionable Basic English', although he also discerns 'Rilkean obliquities' and describes the sequence as 'Auden's *Essay on Man*, a seriously secular theodicy' (1998: 235); Smith argues that '[b]y taking the personalized, self-regarding lover of the sonnet sequence, and dispersing him into the multitude of collective subjects who make a history, Auden deconstructs the political and literary traditions of bourgeois individualism' (1985: 110). Both 'Spain' and 'In Time of War' adduce a long historical perspective, leading to a focus upon a present state of affairs; but the latter uses the Sino-Japanese war more generally: not a crystallising moment of historical clarity, but part of a dismaying continuity.

The historical synopsis – a favourite device of Auden's – occupies the first twelve sonnets: I and II show creation and the subsequent expulsion from Eden; the self-consciousness this brings leads to the alienation of the subject from his world through the intermediation of language (III); the next sonnets show representative types, suggestive of phases of historical progress: the peasant smallholder (IV); the roving swordsman (V); the soothsayer or philosopher (VI); the poet (VII); and urban man (VIII). Each seems to end in some kind of false relation (except VI, who begins there, but learns that he is part of, not exceptionally above, common humanity); this pattern holds true for IX, where by persisting merely as ourselves we fail to bring the honoured dead back to life in our own being; and in X, where the institutionalisation of Christ's teaching in hierarchical church structures perverts the radical egalitarianism of Christian fellowship. Using the tale of Jove and Ganymede, XI describes a false relationship between an interfering God and his creature, who must be left to choose but finds evil fascinating; XII (from 1936) ends this series by describing a world in which the triumph of reason in the defeat of superstition means merely that the banished powers reinstall themselves as psychotic or neurotic disorders.

In the light of the foregoing, the injunction to praise with which sonnet XIII begins seems difficult to comply with, notwithstanding its sweeping alexandrines; and, having indicated the unhappiness of eras, the poem acknowledges this in a crucial line: 'History opposes its grief to our buoyant song'. This marks the move towards the specific location of this war, as the close sees both the West and the East offering no answers; for 'The quick new West is false; and prodigious, but wrong/This passive flower-like people' (imagery which encodes some contentious Orientalisms). At the centre of the sequence, XIV suddenly brings us up to date and place: 'Yes, we are going to suffer, now' – suggesting a participant vulnerability not evident in 'Spain' (where 'struggle' was a noun rather than a verb), and underlining that immediacy of evil startlingly evoked by XVI, whose close, morally, zeroes in on its target:

And maps can really point to places
Where life is evil now:
Nanking; Dachau.

The Japanese dive-bombers (XV) revise Auden's glamorously sinister helmeted airman; they fly machines whose progressive technology contradicts the destructive uses to which it is turned. But the poet is ground-based, associating with the nameless victims of these onslaughts: 'We live here. We lie in the present's unopened/Sorrow; its limits are what we are' (XX); faced with this perception, the buoyant songs to which, in XXII, the bystanding nations listened while brutality triumphed successively in Austria, China and Spain, are models of a dreadful artistic wrongness – which leads into the evocation of Rilke, the true artist, whose correct devotion to his calling forms the counterbalancing sestet of XXIII. Ten sonnets earlier he had been echoed, and his (anonymous) reappearance marks the turn towards what positives can be mustered, in this panorama of contemporary violence. The fact of his not being named leads into XXIV, which balances the famous dead of IX by focusing on those enabling, uncelebrated precursors distinguished only by the capacity for love which, rather than fame, is effectively transmitted to the present; this is no passive state, but a fellow-feeling that in XXV (where the city in question is Shanghai) teaches us 'to pity and rebel'. XXVI argues that 'the little workshop of love' is the only attribute of humanity which, unlike all the evidence accrued in the first twelve sonnets, is an enduring positive; but again, this offers no quiescent solution, for the final sonnet reaffirms the landscape of choice in which we live, repudiating any Edenic state and insisting on the mountains that, in Auden's moral geography, suggest the rigorous North rather than lotus-eating South.

This is not, as in 'Spain', a choice leading to intervention; rather, it concerns understanding the nature of reality, and accepting the responsibility not to try to change the world, but to change oneself as prerequisite; writing about Rilke's example in August 1939, Auden declared it 'not a denial of the importance of political action, but rather the realization that if the writer is not to harm both others and himself, he must consider, and very much more humbly and patiently than he has been doing, what kind of person he is, and what may be his real function' (*P* II: 27). 'September 1, 1939' is as strong on love, but less strong on choice; the date of its title was that on which Germany's invasion of Poland made European war inevitable – although not formally declared until 3 September. All the dreaded cards had been predicting this evil day for several years; now it had come and Auden, in New York, shaped his responses; unlike 'Spain', where the writer's geographical and ethical positions were disguised, he places his own predicament at the heart of the poem; his model in this was Yeats's 'Easter, 1916', whose three-stressed line he adopts, and whose first word was also 'I'. Just as Yeats was outside Ireland when the Easter Rising occurred, so Auden was displaced from Europe, and had to consider what his separation might mean for a poem concerned with events in a different continent and time-zone: for whereas his earlier poem urged the need to choose while there was still time, by 'September 1, 1939' it is already too late. Clever hopes, now dead, spawn anger and fear that may be no less concerned than those were with evading the unmentionable.

Having made his impressive debut in Eliot's *Criterion* in January 1930, Auden was well-qualified to write the decade's epitaph and duly did so, applying to it the terms 'low' and 'dishonest' from which not many then or now would demur. Yet this poem could not be characteristic of much of his 1930s writing, since he had in his elegy for Yeats and 'The Prolific and the Devourer' abjured any notion – such as seemed to animate 'Spain' – that poetry could make a political difference. In a letter of 1967 he would, however, describe 'September 1, 1939' as the most dishonest poem he had ever written: so issues of honesty inhabit both the depths and the surface of this poem; and whilst it eschews the latent demagoguery of 'Spain', its own initial pose of uncertainty and fearfulness is no less a rhetorical strategy. If, as has been suggested, its opening echoes Dashiell Hammett's *The Thin Man* (though Ogden Nash is as plausible a source), then the hard-boiled persona becomes another pose the poem toys with, but rejects almost immediately; for there are instabilities in this 'I', whose relation to any 'we' is shifting: he claims to be uncertain yet reads us a history lesson; he thinks he may be as error-prone as any man-in-the-street, yet feels he ought to preach at him, in the relation 'I and the public'. Each irregularly rhymed stanza forms a complete sentence whose syntax, extended over eleven lines, invariably deploys the elbow-grabbing colon to sustain itself.

As in 'Spain', history has thrown up a situation which cannot be ignored; yet if the poet denounces the dying decade's delusions, he seems to have nursed some of his own – not least, that of having a quiet drink in this dive (by definition a 'low' place), without having to obsess about war and such offensive matters. Smith (1985) has noted how the poem has much to do with knowing and speaking, and the subject's uncertain construction within these acts – whose effectiveness is called into question by their failure to prevent what everyone foresaw happening. Yet again, in the second stanza we encounter Auden's psychopathological theory of history, wherein Germany's Lutheran inheritance, Hitler's upbringing at Linz and the Treaty of Versailles could all be offered in evidence; but what is the point of 'accurate scholarship' painstakingly construing these causes and effects, when its conclusions can be summarised in any school playground? Again, in the third stanza, exiled Thucydides (the Athenian historian whose account of its war against Sparta outlined the downfall of his society) has already written a template for these times:

> The enlightenment driven away,
> The habit-forming pain,
> Mismanagement and grief:
> We must suffer them all again.

But foreknowledge has not helped, and it may be that these classical allusions are merely part of the irrelevant educational baggage self-exiled Auden has brought to cosmopolitan New York, city of the future and the Common Man. Yet, in stanza four, this city too seems merely an evasion, another delusory island whose neutrality cannot disguise the accusing and guilty face in the mirror; in the next stanza this mirror, behind the bar, reflects the childish escapisms by which the customers evade the true nature of their childishness.

Although notionally self-included in the 'we' whose failings are being analysed, the speaker begins to sound a bit of a know-all, as he dissects windy politicians and our own self-centred fantasies. In June 1940 Auden wrote to Dodds that he had been looking into Nijinsky's published diary (covering the period of his developing madness). There he found the following: 'Some politicans are hypocrites like Diaghilev, who does not want universal love, but to be loved alone. I want universal love' (quoted in Fuller 1998: 291). Compared to Thucydides this was rather an obscure source, but the distinction drawn here becomes structural as, contemplating 'dense commuters' pouring from the subway and 'helpless governors' equally stuck in a clockwork morality, the next stanza rises to a triply interrogative crescendo, whereby it somewhat awkwardly appears that the poet is about to claim that *he* can confer release, reach the deaf, and speak for the dumb. As originally composed, a stanza intervened between these resonant questions and their apparent answer by the voice that he has (see *Early A*: 327n): this makes even clearer that they rhetorically imply the answer 'nobody'. He still claims that his voice, oddly enough, might undo – well, what exactly *is* a 'folded lie', and how do we visualise its undoing? It would make some sense as a newspaper, accompanying those airwaves overburdened with messages of anger and fear circulating above the skyscrapers; but you 'undo' a knot, the classic image of a crux or conundrum. This lie in fact is double, and in this stanza the dichotomy set up by the Nijinsky allusion, and represented in the preceding stanza by commuters and governors, is resolved by mediation. The opposition is between personalised and collectivised visions of humanity: the commuter restricts his moral horizons to wife and work, Authority sublimates erotic drive in phallic cityscapes; the first lies that there is no such thing as the state, the second, that there is no such thing as the individual. Placing their lies side by side the poem encourages us to see that, converted into positive rather than negative statements, each would be true, and reconcilable with the other: 'We must love one another or die' enforces the mutual interdependence of self and society.

Problem solved, then – yes, but the War . . .: this is the awkward 'or die' bit of that formula. In 'August for the People . . .' (stanza 6), Auden had already cast a corrosive retrospect upon an earlier fantasy that 'love' could act as universal solvent for historical difficulty; in 'September 1, 1939', war's re-obtrusion in its final stanza is acutely problematical, subverting the self-contentment of that absolutist mantra and disagreeably confuting its inference that love is all there is: there remains still-unmentionable death. Auden later tried to mend this line by changing 'or' to 'and', in a curiously overliteral interpretation; yet he may not have been wrong to sense that the sentiment was 'afflicted with an incurable dishonesty'. For what is expressed is a totalitarianism of love, notionally balanced by the alternative, 'or die': but nobody would prefer *that*, would s/he? It was evasive in proposing a choice that is not a real one; but more profoundly evasive in declining the perception that many people – enthusiastic Nazis and happy Fascists the world over – were in various ways preferring death, busily bringing it about in places like Nanking and Dachau. The close presents a stupefied, vulnerable world (reminiscent of some Great War poster in which defenceless Belgium cowers before 'the Bosch'); the winking city lights, however, indicate points of awareness – though quite what use these isolated Just with their ironic signals are going to be, is a far-from-rhetorical question. 'To sit still and pray seems selfish and unheroic', continued Auden in his remarks about Rilke, 'but it may be the wisest and most helpful course': there were many at the time who doubted this; and the closing imagery has just a hint of the 'little candle glowing in the night', from the mawkish childhood hymn. The possible bathos may encode an apologetic self-awareness; the speaker acknowledges negative impulses, but hopes that his 'flame' will be affirmative; yet despite the claim for commonality formulated in 'like them' and 'the same', the community envisaged seems to be that of the ironising (Forsterian) few rather than the insensible many: those who are *not* about to die salute us. Smith argues that 'it is precisely its honesty in catching the duplicity and bad faith that makes it a fine and powerful poem, revealing more than the guy at the bar will ever know' (1985: 31).

These three poems are all concerned with the world beyond England. 'Spain' urges intervention; the word 'ironic' near the close of 'September 1, 1939' indicates its reserved position; 'In Time of War' seems under no illusions regarding the usefulness of irony or love; unlike the others, this war had no acknowledged claim on Auden, and possibly for that very reason his responses seem more measured: as if in confirmation of Goethe's dictum that 'The acting man is always without conscience; no one has conscience but the observing man'.

Musée des Beaux Arts (December 1938)
The Shield of Achilles (October 1952) (*SA*)

Connections or disconnections between observation and conscience are at the heart of these two poems, which like others previously considered involve looking. Here, however, the objects of attention are not landscapes or islands, but examples of artistry raising questions about our possible relations to the truths displayed, about linkages between art and action.

After his return from China, Auden spent more time abroad than in England; 'Musée des Beaux Arts' was written in Brussels at a time when he had already decided to leave for America; he wrote several poems this December, including sonnets on named writers (Rimbaud, Housman) and on artist-figures ('The Novelist', 'The Composer'). 'Musée . . .', prompted by paintings in the city's collections, is in rhyming lines of variable length whose persistent enjambment enacts life's tendency to overspill art's containment; as well as meditating this, it continues some of the concerns of 'In Time of War', in specifically addressing art's response to suffering. Fuller (1998) sees its proportions as suggestive of a sonnet, and also discusses which pictures Auden had in mind; these evidently impressed him by the authority with which they relativised reality by showing life's indifferent continuance round the edges of major events, thus reinforcing insights about haphazardness itemised in his radio-broadcast (January, 1939) on the Chinese conflict:

> War is bombing an already-disused arsenal, missing it and killing a few old women. War is lying in a stable with a gangrenous leg. War is drinking hot water in a barn and worrying about one's wife. War is a handful of lost and terrified men in the mountains, shooting at something moving in the undergrowth.
>
> (*P* I: 490)

In 'Musée . . .', two of the pictures cited have religious subject-matter (martyrdom and the Nativity), and the uninterested children, like the animals fortuitously there, imply a context dissenting from the principal focus; the picture Auden names, its subject classical rather than religious, takes this tendency to an extreme, because pictorially it ludicrously minimises Icarus's calamity. This poem is not difficult to understand; what is more complex is what to make of what it tells us. The Old Masters are presented as figures of omniscience, 'never wrong' about the nature of suffering (even though they show the world to be one where absolutes do not govern): thus the poem might seem to affirm the timeless greatness of Art. But if what they are always right about is the world's extension beyond any given frame of reference, then the sanctified museum-hush within which their paintings hang itself begs the question of its relation to the noisier, unexalted world outside.

Where 'Spain' urged decisiveness, 'Musée . . .' might appear to offer an excuse for doing nothing (because this is the way things happen); yet what are we to make of the ploughman who may have heard and the ship that, more culpably, 'must' have seen – yet refuses (having, unlike the sun, a choice in the matter) to alter course? How close is its wilful unconcern to the contemplative stasis induced by looking at these pictures, where choice is perpetually deferred? If we doubt that the poem's motto could possibly be, 'We must ignore one another and survive', this instigates a more rigorous probing of the wisdom it transmits, which bears on Marx's differentiation between merely interpreting the world, and changing it. Obduracy towards other people's disasters had been demonstrated by Britain's abandonment of Czechoslovakia, two months before Auden wrote his poem; much of Europe resembled a museum stuffed with an expensive past that – like the emblems of Englishness itemised in 'Summer Night' – had no wish to live and was not worth fighting for (and would soon be ransacked). Rather than endorsing inaction, however, 'Musée . . .' may wonder whether history can pardon those who have not helped; it also may inquire whether this museum might be another kind of island or delusionary sanctuary. Auden later asserted that it would be wrong to attempt a poem about Auschwitz or the Crucifixion, and possibly the question arises of the extent to which these wise Old Masters *aestheticise* the suffering they portray. Two memorable sonnets in his Chinese sequence (XVI, XIX) dwelt on the very particularised bloodshed resulting from abstract considerations of generals or politicians; 'Musée . . .' appears to reverse that, moving from specific event to a generalised attitude; but in fact the poem, like the pictures, and like Keats's Grecian urn, offers a provocative enigma rather than a resolved philosophy. 'Poetry', he would shortly suggest in a note to 'New Year Letter', 'might be defined as the clear expression of mixed feelings. The Poetic mood is never indicative' (*NYL*: 119).

'The Shield of Achilles', Mendelson observes, was instantaneously welcomed for its 'sturdy, unobjectionable sentiments against violence and war' (*LA*: 375); but, as he and others note, the case is more complex. In 'Fleet Visit' (1951), also classically allusive, Auden's playful seriousness had converted docked battleships into triumphs of abstract design (ironically, the cultural export of American Abstract Expressionism would turn out to have been a CIA-funded move in the Cold War); here, however, the aesthetic is conscripted for military use, and the well-wrought shield inaugurates a chain of reactions reaching out to include our own response, as readers, to the poem itself. It refers to the *Iliad* (book 18), when Thetis commissions a set of armour for her son; but whereas Homer's elaborately described shield was two-toned ('Two cities radiant on the shield appear,/The image one of peace, and one of war', in Pope's version), in Auden it is unrelievedly bleak in its depiction – although his poem maintains a contrast in the two different stanza-forms employed to represent what Thetis hopes to see, and what the shield shows. Her expectations of scenes variously celebrating civic life (as in the Homeric original) are thrice dashed by successive revelations of a world in which all bonds of neighbourliness are obliterated: conformity displaces individuality, power supplants justice, and feral self-interest alone survives, in settings uniformly denatured. This shield has something in common with Paul Nash's Great War landscapes of destruction and could, like one of them, be ironically titled 'We Are Making a New World'.

A shield, however, is not an offensive weapon, and Homer's scenes from the radiant city of peace perhaps denoted values that might deserve defending; the absence of these from Auden is subversive, excluding anything worth fighting for: this poem seems to reinstal that 'despair' forbidden by the first part of 'Memorial for the City' (1949), similarly focused on desolation. Its structure opposes Grecian-Urnish expectations to inhospitable scenes from modern life; yet the *artifact* uncompromisingly shows things as they are (the rhyme royal stanzas depict process, movement and even – impossibly for a shield – inner states: which Lucy McDiarmid argues as implying art's limitations; see Criticism, **p. 130**), whilst its observer yearns for an enduring classical continuity to shelter behind. The repeated first line describes a 'she' who gazes over a male shoulder, at a set of desolate scenes perhaps suggesting patriarchy taken to extremes – as in that Auschwitz where Primo Levi heard a guard shout, 'Here, there is no "why?"!' Only in the final stanza, named as 'Hephaestos' and 'Thetis', do they acquire characteristics; their mythological names simultaneously identify and distance, relegating them to a classical past from which this shield gleams balefully, offering itself as a text she does not care to read concerning the implacable world of 'because'. Perhaps, like the gentlefolk of 'A Summer Night', she would rather overlook connections between her freedom and violences enacted elsewhere: after all, a shield is principally intended for viewing by the enemy. The sequence of seeing includes us – we look over *her* shoulder – but so do questions of responsibility: what sort of mother arms her son, what sort of son rejoices in such a shield, or in the epithet 'man-slaying'? Is she – and behind her, us – dismayed by the armourer's truthfulness, or indiscretion? Like the poem it appears in, this artistically wrought shield is designed by a master craftsman (whose limp suggests the artist's Freudian wound); yet the words 'artful', 'crafty' or 'designing' all denote untrustworthiness, and his skill perhaps exposes a world with which it is, nonetheless, complicit: for although it unflinchingly describes an uncongenial reality, the shield forms part of the processes by which that is maintained, and armoured flesh believes the myth of invulnerability – as did Achilles. 'There is no document of civilisation which is not at the same time a document of barbarism,' declared Walter Benjamin; we are left alone with our day.

In Memory of W.B. Yeats (February 1939)
The Sea and the Mirror (August 1942–February 1944) (*FTB*)

Each of these shows Auden's evolving debate with himself about the role of poetry in the modern world, through engagement with an illustrious precursor. His elegy for Yeats commemorated, as well, the wintry weather gripping New York when he and Isherwood disembarked on 26 January, as news came that Franco had taken Barcelona and effectively sealed victory in the civil war. Two days later Yeats died in France, and Auden started work on his first poem written in America, where it was published in the *New Republic* in March – appearing in England that April in an enlarged version. The much-more-than 'slightly unusual' coincidence of these significant public events with a decisive personal transition forms the background to his poem, which Smith has seen as Auden's 'Oedipal dialogue' with the dead precursor: 'is this elegy not also a bid for the poetic succession?' (*AS* III: 158; Smith's essay in *AS* III (pp. 155–63) proposes possible Yeatsian intertexts). Auden also wrote an obituary essay, in the form of a mock trial, published that spring in *Partisan Review*, in which he made some parallel points:

> For art is a product of history, not a cause. Unlike some other products, technical inventions for example, it does not re-enter history as an effective agent. . . . The case for the prosecution rests on the fallacious belief that art ever makes anything happen. . . . But there is one field in which the poet is a man of action, the field of language, and it is precisely in this that the greatness of the deceased is most obviously shown. However false or undemocratic his ideas, his diction shows a continuous evolution towards . . . the true democratic style.
>
> (*P* II: 7)

Something of the ambivalence towards Yeats that Auden later expressed to Spender is audible in both poem and prose of 1939, where there is a dual impulse to praise and to bury: the first section emphasises his physical transition from life to death, in imagery classically allusive (the division of Yeats's corpus amongst his admirers echoes the dismemberment of Orpheus by enthusiastic maenads), but also reflects current events in Barcelona. This conjunction of conventional and contemporary imagery – the stilled (frozen) but persistent stream of poetry alongside the instrumental modern world, its stockmarkets and executives – is a structural device in the poem, which shows how the writer's removal from this transitory world confers a timelessness which adds authority to his surviving writing, and purges it of merely venial faults which Time will pardon because (an assertion Auden later expunged) it 'Worships language'. What will fall away are the temporal sillinesses, what will remain is the well-written; but even as the elegy honours Yeats, its associating him with Kipling and Claudel suggests there were aspects of his life requiring pardon, relating to his 'undemocratic' politics. This also illuminates those problematically wise 'Old Masters' of 'Musée . . .', who may in their lifetimes have been 'silly' but, surviving through their art (Time also worships painting), are transfigured in our subsequent conceptions of them. The poet invoked in the final section may be Yeats – its tone and metre echo 'Under

Ben Bulben' (V), first published in Irish newspapers on 3 February 1939 – but may also be Auden, or any successor: assigning him a 'voice' that persuades rather than constrains concludes the poem's imagery of mouths and utterance. The resonant imperatives here, however, hardly exemplify an 'unconstraining voice': in effect, the poem orders its poet not to give orders; yet conceding choice to the reader respects freedom, and in a climate of murderous probabilities affirmed what Robert Lowell, in 'For the Union Dead', termed 'man's lovely,/peculiar power to choose life and die'. The last two stanzas' paradoxes suggest that poetry can only exercise its possible powers by not pretending to impossible ones (e.g., of historical agency); to choose the life of poetry is to die to the life of the executive. The poem's final word echoes the opening of sonnet XIII of his Chinese sequence, in a context every bit as alert to what obstructs an impulse to 'praise'.

The first long poem Auden wrote in America, 'New Year Letter', was evidently autobiographical, and in that respect could be seen to update his previous letter, to Lord Byron; the second, 'For the Time Being', was written in the context of two acutely personal events which inflected his handling of the Christmas story. 'The Sea and the Mirror', despite taking for its subject Shakespeare's play, also mapped the personal contexts of Auden's life onto that apparently impersonal commentary; thus in a 1944 letter to Isherwood he identified Kallman with both Caliban and Ariel (see *LA*: 231n). In addition, the play offered a means by which he could elaborate his thoughts about the responsibilities and temptations of the artist, as well as on the nature of freedom: the poem begins after the play has ended, by which stage Ariel has been set free; yet Prospero's first words to him are an imperative, even if the order is framed as a request. Ariel perhaps learns that part of freedom involves acknowledgement of obligation; still there at the poem's end – for he speaks its final verses – it is doubtful he will ever leave: a note to 'New Year Letter' cited Engels's definition of 'freedom' as the 'consciousness of necessity' (*NYL*: 81), and as Auden's 1948 lecture on 'Poetry and Freedom' declared: 'The freedom which is asserted by the choice of the rules makes the game important' (*P* II: 489).

An enchanted island, such as contains *The Tempest*, figured for Auden as a symbol of artistic withdrawal from an unruly world and what Caliban calls its 'unrectored chaos'; another note asserted that '(w)orks of art really are closed societies' (*NYL*: 83). Fuller (1998) observes that he inherited from nineteenth-century commentaries an allegorical interpretation of this play, which also read it as the Bard's crowning statement and farewell to his art; when Auden returned to *The Tempest* in 1954, he described 'Shakespeare's last play' as 'a disquieting work', because in it 'both the repentance of the guilty and the pardon of the injured seem more formal than real' (*DH*: 128). Shakespeare was not, however, the exclusive patron saint; since arriving in America Auden had been studying another writer, a model of literary self-consciousness and craftsmanship, but for whom ethical rather than aesthetic consequences were paramount: this was the Henry James of whom in 1944 he wrote that he 'was not, like Mallarmé or Yeats, an esthete (*sic*), but, like Pascal, one to whom, however infinitely various its circumstances, the interest itself of human life was always the single dreadful choice it offers, with no "second chance", of either salvation or damnation' (*P* II: 243). It was the voice of James which, after false starts (see Fuller (1998)), enabled him to bring this poem to conclusion; and although Shakespeare's late plays offer comedic affirmations of possible second chances (lost children rediscovered, Hermione's statue coming back to life, Prospero outgrowing his revengeful sorcery), it may be that the Calvinistic note Auden emphasised in James repudiates, in his poem, the fresh start anticipated by Shakespeare. It was also congruent with Kierkegaard, in whose thought Auden had also immersed himself, and for whom – he explained in a 1944 review – man was 'a conscious being who at every moment must choose of his own free will one out of an infinite number of possibilities which he foresees. Moreover, each choice is irrevocable. . . . Hence his anxiety, for he can neither guarantee nor undo the consequence of any choice he makes' (*P* II: 214).

'The Sea and the Mirror' is a dramatised reading of the play, extending and subverting its proffered resolution: this Prospero is one whose forgiveness and renunciation of omnipotence may be nullified by Antonio's refusal to accept either. Thus the poem offers a potential model for engagement with itself: Boly has asserted that reading Auden 'is partly a matter of outwitting a dominant voice (in effect, outwitting oneself as the conjuror of that voice) by patiently tracing its repressive stratagems' (1991: x); the question in respect of Prospero is whether he can in fact achieve an unconstraining rather than a dominant voice. Here, all the play's *dramatis personae* have speaking parts (excepting the figures in Prospero's masque); it starts with a 'Preface' and ends with a 'Postscript', enclosing three sections. These are: Prospero's address to Ariel, written in Auden's system of syllabics but including three songs; 'The Supporting Cast', commenced by self-excluding Antonio, variations on whose closing refrain with its rhyme-words 'my own' and 'alone' interlink the other items and end the section; and, in distinction from their *sotto voce* utterances, 'Caliban to the Audience' – the longest section, re-establishing theatricality with a magniloquent prose oration in the highly mannered late style of James (who on his disastrous foray into theatre was cat-called when, inadvisedly, he responded to the audience's calls for 'Author!'). This *tour-de-force* Auden sometimes nominated as his favourite poem; its comically convoluted orotundity resonantly caps the less ostentatious but still remarkable technical achievements of the previous section, whose various forms encompass terza rima, sonnet (in alexandrines), ballade (whose intricacies are, improbably, given to Stephano), sestina and villanelle: just as in *The Tempest* Shakespeare exploited to the full contemporary stage-effects. The artistic display of the entire performance is, paradoxically, driven by the desire to establish and affirm the limits of art; Mendelson has argued that '(t)he poem is designed to educate and disenchant through a progressive sequence of disillusionments' (*LA*: 225), and Caliban's perception of the 'perfected Work which is not ours', the 'Wholly Other Life' of which the play is an inadequate reflection, leads to anticipation of a 'restored relation' to the world art did not make and cannot alter.

The poem does not endorse its epigraph from Emily Brontë, affirming the empire of imagination: rather, it acknowledges that while art can be defined as 'the most difficult game conceivable to man', its realm (aesthetics) is distinct from the fundamentally serious arena of 'The Ethical', whose activity 'always remains work, . . . which can never be done perfectly and so give us aesthetic satisfaction' (all from *NYL*: 89). Like the commuters in 'September 1, 1939', Prospero wishes to re-inhabit the ethical life, his wish springing from a weariness with art's perfectibility which is itself the mirror-image of the impulse fuelling his magic, 'the power to enchant/That comes from disillusion'. That perfected world, whose presiding spirit is Ariel, excludes the reality of death: to this extent the mirror that – in Hamlet's words – art holds up to nature is falsifying. Prospero's speech suggests that the sea represents what is inimical to human values, and the mirror, that which is exclusively a function of them: to refer to the headings on the chart Auden gave his Swarthmore students, the sea is 'Power without Purpose', the mirror's two-dimensionality implies 'Knowledge without Power' (*LA*: 240), the art that can arrange anything but change nothing. What lies between is 'Existential Being', from within which Prospero envisages himself as later undertaking the Kiekegaardian leap of faith (sailing out alone over seventy thousand fathoms). For Kierkegaard, as Auden noted in 1944, the Religious is the means by which to move beyond ultimately disabling extremes of both Aesthetic and Ethical responses: 'The power by which, without blinding himself to his anxiety, [Man] is nevertheless able to choose, is religious faith: without that faith, he must either despair, i.e. be unable to act, or become an idolater, i.e. invent an illusion of absolute certainty out of the individual passion of his immediate moods (the Esthetic) or the universal abstractions of his intellect (the Ethical). Such an endeavor is, however, doomed to failure' (*P* II: 214).

Prospero, then, wants to re-enter the world of Becoming, but there are obstacles; not, as he supposes, ineducable Caliban who has naughtily displayed his dildo to Miranda and who so surprisingly bursts into florid unstoppable speech: he, the servant refusing dismissal, is the body (or disobedient phallus) with which cohabitation is inevitable; Auden later described *The Tempest* as 'a manichean work, not because it shows the relation of Nature to Spirit as one of conflict and hostility, which in fallen man it is, but because it puts the blame upon Nature and makes the Spirit innocent' (*DH*: 130). As Caliban observes, however, 'the one exception, the sum no magic of His can ever transmute, is the indifferent zero' (*SP*: 162); silence is less amenable than speech, and Antonio, self-identified as 'Creation's O' – like unspeaking Iago, like Lucifer who will not serve or like Goethe's Mephistopheles, spirit of nay-saying – by standing beyond the circle of reconciliations renders potentially futile his brother's renunciations of power: 'Your need to love shall never know/Me'. Antonio implies that Prospero could no more brook a challenge to his universalising charity than he could formerly endure resistance to his magic; although he wants to return to a world of ordinary relationships these cannot be imposed as he chooses, in a dictatorship compelling others to enlightenment, but are mutually constitutive and involve each party: to that extent he will always be defined by his relations with the brother who, to his declaration 'We must love one another or die' has in effect responded, 'I would rather die'. Lacking the power to disown his omnipotence, Prospero remains potentially trapped, unable to acknowledge the nature of his connection to Antonio; in this, he falls short of Ariel's closing perception that he (Ariel) is merely the 'shadow' of Caliban's 'lameness'. Auden's terminology here derived from Jung, *via* Layard, and is explained by Mendelson: 'The Lame Shadow was Auden's name for the ideal figure that the wounded ego seeks in the world of the Alter Ego. . . . The imaginary ideal is a shadow because its existence is merely an emanation from ourselves, a figure who is everything we are not, one whose powers compensate for our weakness. But the shadow is lame because it has no strength of its own and exists only through our weakness' (*LA*: 95n).

Shakespeare's play is in turn reflected in Auden's poem, whose final word, its assertion of 'I', is an echo.

'In Praise of Limestone' (May 1948) (*N*)
'Amor Loci' (July 1965) (*CWW*)

Where Achilles' shield would show denatured and inhuman settings, 'In Praise of Limestone', also concerned with mothers and sons, had celebrated a landscape suffused with the sense of humanity. This was the first poem written after Auden's arrival in Italy with Kallman (having briefly visited England), on the trip which inaugurated their sequence of summers henceforth spent in Europe. He wrote from Florence to Elizabeth Mayer that he 'hadn't realized till I came how like Italy is to my "Mutterland", the Pennines. Am in fact starting on a poem . . ., the theme of which is that rock creates the only truly human landscape i.e. where politics, art etc. remain on a modest ungrandiose scale' (Berg Collection). In his 1971 Freud Memorial Lecture (reprinted in *AS* III), Auden placed it in a sequence of poems deriving from his lead-mining passion, whose other examples were the earlier evocation of Alston Moor in 'New Year Letter', and the later 'Amor Loci': like them, it offers a *paysage moralisé* in which an actual landscape suggests analogies for the human body and for human love, and a model for understanding human experience. Consisting of three unequal sections of what Edna Longley defines as 'loose syllabic elegiacs', in this as also by persistent enjambment 'In Praise of Limestone' suggests form's dissolution, into formlessness or informality. This is a poem of semi-homecoming, inspired by Auden's return to Europe – whose difference from America (where his poetry had been preoccupied with time) is signalled by its evocation as a region of 'short distances and definite places'. A rediscovered sense of location emerges, in details culled lovingly from *The Changing Face of England* (in a passage later included in *CW* (216–18) where Collett mentions specific geographical features from northern England familiar to Auden); these, however – as in the later 'Not in Baedeker' – are assembled into a composite scene mingling Italian and English features: thus, 'gennel' is a northern English dialect usage (more often 'ginnel') indicating an alleyway; whereas the need to find a village square's shady side at noon suggests Mediterranean customs and climate.

Auden also noted in his Freud lecture that 'the limestone landscape was important to me as a connecting link between . . . the northern guilt culture I grew up in, and the shame-culture of the Mediterranean countries, to which I was now exposed for the first time' (*AS* III: 193); the greater openness of this sunnier environment is embodied, literally, in the carefree self-display of the naked youth, whose 'dildo' (later altered) denotes the erection proudly shown to his permissively indulgent Mother – behaviour inconceivably transgressive in other climes and cultures. It is a 'dildo', as the first in a series of constructions progressing naturally to architecture and horticulture, which become his more elaborated means of attention-seeking; and perhaps also to imply that even the most seemingly natural human state involves artifice. Here, then, is no castrating Father to contend with, and in his lecture Auden initially related the guilt–shame contrast to that between Protestant and Catholic approaches: the 'Mother', therefore, associates with the Madonna.

If Auden had visited the Uffizi galleries during his stay in Florence when writing this poem, he could well have seen the famous 'Doni Tondo', Michelangelo's only oil painting: an unusual grouping of the Holy Family (Mary kneels, face averted towards the Child whom Joseph hands from behind her right shoulder). Horizontally in the background of this circular composition is an 'athletic group of male nudes leaning louchely against a continuous band of jagged rock' (as described by James Hall, *Guardian Review*, 18 December 2004, p. 17); the most prominently casual of these, albeit unaroused, might have suggested Auden's 'son' lounging brazenly against his rock. This is speculation (although Hecht, too, cites this picture as a visual parallel for the poem's commingling of religious and sensual elements); but Michelangelo's bright-lit conjunction of holy theme and self-celebrating flesh implies an attitude foresworn by northerly asceticism: and having witnessed celebrations of Forio's Saint Restituta at the end of May 1949, Auden told Mrs Mayer how cross he was with Luther, for denying such festivities to Protestantism. His poem, however, is not about major historical schisms, even though these happen in its hinterland (as Lawrence Lipking notes, contributing to a 'Symposium' on the poem in *AS* III, the Italy in which Auden found himself in 1948 had within recent memory aligned with Hitler). Its tone is concessive: the first word is 'if', and subsequent imperatives to 'mark', hear' and 'examine' have more an air of invitation; its refusal to make a Major Statement matches the unextremism of the landscape it celebrates. In illustrations which Mendelson relates to Toynbee's *Study of History*, the kinds of sensibility attracted by 'immoderate' environments – of loftily ascetic granite, flat plains amenable to military endeavour, or oceanic estrangement – soon quit unemphatic limestone in order to pursue extremer visions (whose truthfulness is not disputed). At the heart of the poem, notes Fuller, is 'praise of moderation' (1998: 407), and the sudden vocative intimacy of 'my dear' combines with an admission that not even limestone can simulate that Eden 'From which original address / Man faulted into consciousness' (*NYL*: 55):

> this land is not the sweet home that it looks,
> Nor its peace the historical calm of a site
> Where something was settled once and for all

As the land of change rather than fixity, however, it offers a salutary lesson, especially relevant to a writer about to change his mode of life; it rebukes the certain certainties of poets too attached to abstraction, as well as scientists' over-absorption in the unimmediate (Wallace Stevens was the primary target, although 'the poet' is also a generic figure who, cocksure that reality is reducible to mind, reverses the immodest youth with his too, too solid flesh). Limestone also rebukes our own search for transcendence in the appetite for music, whose bodilessness we, like Walter Pater, incline to think the purest art form. For, metamorphosing into marble which is shaped into the statuary adorning classical gardens, by such modifications of its matter limestone implies that – as the poem modulates through more 'if's into echoes of the Apostles' Creed – through the forgiveness of sins and the resurrection of the body the *flesh* may recover what Yeats called 'radical innocence'. Until then, however, our immortality depends on being fully mortal; the epigraph from 'Memorial for the City' (1949) – whose darker evocations of European history offered an antiphonal note, in *Nones* – is relevant: 'In the self-same point that our soul is made sensual, in the self-same point is the City of God ordained to him from without beginning' (Juliana of Norwich, *N*: 34). 'In Praise of Limestone' ends embracing human love which exists despite faults, not in their absence; and at its close, celebrating interactions of water with rock, verbs of sensory perception supplant verbs of cerebration ('know', 'imagine'), with timeless perfection envisioned as a dissolving landscape in which is overheard the agency of change:

Dear, I know nothing of
Either, but when I try to imagine a faultless love
Or the life to come, what I hear is the murmur
Of underground streams, what I see is a limestone landscape.

If his first response to Italy embraced it as a land good to the newcomer, ten years later 'Good-bye to the Mezzogiorno' embodied the look of a stranger, who cannot call it home: 'there yawns a gulf/Embraces cannot bridge. If we try/To "go southern", we spoil in no time' (*HtC*: 81). Italy survives only in the Latin title of 'Amor Loci'; in his Freud lecture Auden described this as another attempt to write directly about his 'original sacred landscape', with which he here asserts proprietorial intimacy: as already noted, he associated this with Rookhope, in Weardale; its northernness offers a much bleaker sense of the imperfections of human love. Unlike the inhabited world of 'In Praise of Limestone' (over-inhabited, in '. . . Mezzogiorno'), its spare syllabics underline an obsessive fascination with human absence; he could draw its lonely map by heart, and contrasts that cartographical knowledge with his unrepentant ignorance about former inhabitants (cf. 'I doubt if he'd ever made friends with a Weardale or Alston lead-miner', see Works, **p. 69**), evidenced only in the crumblingly impressive remnants of their feats of industry:

Here and there a tough chimney
still towers over
dejected masonry, moss,
decomposed machines,
with no one about,

In his lecture, Auden argued that 'mining is the one human activity that is by nature mortal. Steam-engines may render stage-coaches obsolete, but this cannot be foreseen. But when a mine is opened, everyone knows already, that however rich it may turn out to be, sooner or later it will become exhausted, and be abandoned' (*AS* III: 187). The poem's 'Jew Limestone' (which Donald Davie mistook for an anti-semitic note) is the proper name of that stratum below which it was unproductive to seek ore; as such, it is a kind of bedrock level where, for this poem, all the ladders start. Such unprofitable scenery offers nothing to gratify industrialist, sybarite, nor wilderness-addict; unwanted by them, however, it focuses intense desire on the part of a poet who, not for the first time (see 'The Prophets'), enumerates the interpretative phases of his relationship, by which he moves from conceiving it as an Eden, a New Jerusalem (terms previously explored in 'Vespers'), to this final understanding of its value, as symbol for a love persisting through neglect (Kierkegaard's 'aesthetic', 'ethical' and 'religious' stages may also be suggested).

If 'In Praise of Limestone' became a love poem addressing Kallman and anticipating a re-founded happiness, this disenchanted, solitary utterance seems to categorise him as a 'frivolous worldling' (the singular noun apparently refers to someone in particular); its anticipation is not of any 'life to come' but the death to come. A resolutely unfashionable poem, 'Amor Loci' evokes an enduring Christian 'Love' – denoted by its capital – to which Auden had found himself able to return, just as the Pennine landscape remained stoically in place for him to reinterpret, its limestone now a symbol of persistence rather than dissolution. The title (meaning 'love of place') uses a 'dead' language to imply both the effacements of time and the survival of truth; the absence of any specific place-name suggests that what is significant is the response, rather than place itself. Unlike 'The Watershed', also linked with Rookhope, this is an undramatic poem uncoercively asserting inwardness with place, rather than exclusion from it.

'Horae Canonicae' (1949–1954) (*SA*)
'Bucolics' (1952–1953) (*SA*)
'Thanksgiving for a Habitat' (1958–1964) (*AtH*)

Mendelson suggests that the years between 1948 and 1963 were overall the most settled and contented in Auden's entire life. If his American period was notable for its four long poems, his European period (for he wrote most of his poetry during the months in Forio and Kirchstetten) saw him return to shorter forms, made longer when he assembled thematically linked elements into extended sequences. These can be seen as more hospitable structures from a reader's point of view, and the voice ushering us around the scenery in 'Bucolics' or the house in 'Thanksgiving . . .' (whose individual poems are, significantly, dedicated to various friends) is urbanely unintimidating, despite its intermittently abstruse vocabulary. As early as 'Spain', Auden had foreseen that pyrotechnic poets would fascinate only the immature, and later, praising limestone, mildly deprecated the kind of tenor who ruins his voice in crowd-pleasing ostentation; the poet he had determined to become was one whose brilliance did not compel a reader's submission, but was more a matter of fact than a matter of display, there to be discovered by those who looked. Unlike Prospero's, such works are not extensions of a power to charm.

'Horae Canonicae' is, as its name suggests, concerned with time; its use of the formal observances into which the monastic day was divided (reducing these to seven by omitting Matins) had an appropriateness for one whose personal routine was notoriously rigid. The canonical hours had interested him from the mid-1940s, and first conceptions of this subject in his notebooks (reproduced in *LA*: 311–13) were ambitiously and complicatedly schematic; but during the lengthy evolution of the poem he moved away from grand designings towards a more intensely focused meditation, which nonetheless reflected his 1947 notion of writing 'a series of secular poems based on the Offices' (quoted in *LA*: 312): Smith argues that it is 'one of the most insistently political of all Auden's poems'

(1985: 186), and Mendelson sees it as a 'Cold War poem, haunted by secular and religious apocalypse' (*LA*: 337). By consecrating a particular segment of each day to commemorate the events of Good Friday, the Offices both assert its timeless relevance and align ordinary ongoing time with extra-temporality; Mendelson judges this as 'the most ambitious and successful of Auden's encyclopedic poems, works in which he tried to integrate patterns of world history and local personal detail' (*LA*: 332). Although 'Prime' was the first-written, the sequence was not composed in order: 'Nones' was written next, and the final poem, 'Lauds', dated from 1952 (dates are given in *Selected Poems* and in Fuller (1998)); the first two were more metrically intricate than their successors.

The first word of 'Prime' – 'simultaneously' – suggests the double time-scale. It is 6.00 am, and the return to consciousness-of-externality, as opposed to the undisciplined inwardness of dreaming, is analogised to the creation of the world: a paradise that is no sooner gained than it is, in full self-consciousness, lost (cleverly enacted in the enjambment and internal rhymes of the third stanza). The poem is written in alternating lines of nine and seven syllables, with contiguous vowels counting monosyllabically; its structure expands the instant of awakening into a threefold process of coming into being and entering the world of time and memory, where living will involve dying. At this hour Christ was mocked, and each awakening involves the mockery of glimpsing an innocent world immediately foregone in the resumption of our 'historical share of care'.

The hangman and judge with which 'Terce' open allude to the hour of Christ's condemnation by his judges, and its closing allusion to Good Friday – secularised as the banal self-interests of a world anticipating its weekend – points to the religious dimension, without deflecting questions about human responsibility for what happens when, for the sake of a quiet life, none opposes injustice. 'Sext', midday, is the hour of the Crucifixion; tripartite like the preceding poems, its distichs ambiguously celebrate three exemplars of humanity: those who pursue a practical vocation, those with an appetite for power, and those who join the crowd. Each contributes towards the collective: the first by that absorption in task which, moving beyond immediacies of need, enabled primitive technologies and the rudimentary social state; the second, by that itch to discover order or impose it which created a vision of rightness, necessary for the elaborations of any metropolis; the third, by surrendering individuality to the group identity – in his 1948 lecture Auden defined a crowd as 'a collection of people whose common bond is that they are together' (*P* II: 492). Yet the second commands, the first enacts, and the third approvingly spectates the atrocity; a sting in the tail especially mordant in the case of the crowd, whose superiority to social insects precisely depends on its ability to choose evil: as it does here, worshipping 'the Prince of this world' (Satan).

For as 'Nones' asserts, it is only in the possibility of that choice, compressed into the chance rhyming of 'will' with 'kill', that moral identity exists; a God who compelled mankind to goodness would merely impose a totalitarianism of love: Prospero could only really prove the seriousness of his intent, by letting Caliban rape Miranda and endure the consequences of his deed. It is such an aftershock that this central poem probes, in the siesta hush after death has occurred, when the crowd has re-atomised into its amnesiac irresponsible components, nonetheless aware of something irrevocably done, something irreparably broken, which establishes a tension between the death's terrible uniqueness and endlessly replicatable routines of everyday: like clockwork, shops will re-open and the bus set off, giving 'time/To misrepresent, excuse, deny'. 'To know my deed, 'twere best not know myself', says Macbeth; but knowing the first is the only way to know the second: as 'Nones' asserts, 'its meaning/Waits for our lives', and the setting in a contemporary Italy only recently emergent from its ugly Fascist past adds point. There is no revelation; there is the victim's destroyed body and a sense of alteration, leading to panicky evasions in dream-flight ending in confrontation with a 'Double' who may, as Mendelson (1999) and Fuller (1998) suggest, derive from James's story 'The Private Life', but whose studied inattention also suggests an interrogator's opening gambit. But if in such dreams begin responsibilities, in sleep – that abatement of the will denied to the Macbeths – the body's self-healing occurs, and what was uniquely mutilated earlier is collectively restored (again the Mediterranean siesta makes sense of sleeping at this hour).

In a fine discussion of 'Nones' (*LA*: 341–7), Mendelson suggests ways in which the seven stanzas of this central poem each relate to another in the (not-yet-fully-written) sequence. The creatures evoked at the close exemplify, not recoverable innocence – not even the shy deer – but, he suggests, those kinds of uninvolved spectatorship which, alongside human malignity, have enabled the murder to take place. There is no refuge in returning to nature, any more than in burgherly immersion in the safety of home (end of stanza 5): for just as Antonio's dissent inescapably organises Prospero's response around itself, so the fact of this victim makes complicit the entirety of creation. While this parallels the Christian rearrangement of all time into BC and AD, the issue is less one of strict theology than of ethics: that the point at which an individual comprehends the nature of his/her relationship to the actuality of evil, is the point at which moral life becomes possible.

The two antitypes presented in 'Vespers' are not, separately, at that stage, but together might inhabit it; each is concerned with his own tactic of evasion, by dreaming respectively of Arcadia or the New Jerusalem, the artistic retrospect or the socially progressive vision. This poem is written in prose perhaps suggestive of the Psalms; its hour is 6.00 pm or dusk when, the Arcadian poet claims, figures of Adam reclining by Eve are evoked in contours of the hill behind the city, and when people manifest their true selves rather than a social construct, as the city briefly goes into abeyance. Thus the Arcadian and his Utopian counterpart confront each other without dissimulating mutual antipathy, in sentences marked by strong divisive colons (as in older English poetry); Auden wrote of the 'characterological gulf' between the two types (*DH*: 409). This momentary intersection of their paths is amusingly illustrated in terms of their opposing tastes and prejudices, but for an instant they unwillingly glimpse, as well, their symmetrical relation to a necessary victim, whose immolation founds alike arcadian (Abel's murder in Eden), utopian (Remus's killing by Romulus, building Rome) and democratic states: 'For without a cement of blood (it must be human, it must be innocent) no secular wall will safely stand'. Alluding to ancient builders' use of oxblood as a binding agent for mortar, this image does not rehearse a superstition but outlines the sacrifice of innocence as precondition for any human community.

'Compline', whose hour is 9.00 pm, consists of four sixteen-line stanzas, written in syllabic verse marked by strong internal rhymings; each is a single sentence which, not unlike Molly Bloom's soliloquy at the end of *Ulysses*, enacts the garrulous unspooling of the mind towards sleep. It matches 'Prime' in its renunciation of the consciousness there initiated, its re-embracing of the dreams there quitted; and where that came into guilt this renounces or evades it, amnesiac concerning the hours when the Crucifixion occurred. Each day dies in sleep, in Hopkins's phrase, prefiguring death's 'total absence' in which the body permanently eludes consciousness. 'After such knowledge, what forgiveness?', as Eliot's Gerontion asks; but the final stanza's question about salvation – which it democratically refuses to think likelier for poets than for those working in television – is less rhetorically closed. It modulates into a prayer that the hereafter in which self and deed are equally known, and what happened between noon and three is lucidly confronted, will enable the forgiven self – which in the second stanza had been separate from the stars – to join in the celestial dance: in which the eucharist is no longer symbolic but, engagingly, an actual 'picnic'. The deliberate avoidance, here, of a seriously Christian tone differentiates this poem from Eliot's *Quartets*, which superficially it resembles in some aspects, just as the final poem 'Lauds', about daybreak, differentiates this cycle from that of *Ulysses*, which ended in deep night (where *Finnegans Wake* takes place). Its form derives from a Spanish *cossante*, and although, greeting the new day, it suggests resurrection rather than – as in 'Prime' – reinstigation of loss, it celebrates equally temporal actuality and transcendent possibility. While the repetitious structure indicates patterns of recurrence, the tone is light, and returning consciousness unburdensome: the dripping mill-wheel (human industry) and the singing birds (spontaneous nature) alike enjoy renewal, and the refrain '*In solitude, for company*' indicates a possible harmony of discords, an accommodation between individual and society. Thus, while its emphasis on worship indicates an ultimate salvation 'not in time's covenant' (*Little Gidding*), it also finds the mortal world enough because, in microcosm, the sequence has enacted a coming into moral being which is the basis for fully human life. Smith acutely adduces the formula from 'Spain 1937' about conscious acceptance of guilt in the fact of murder, to explain the perception reached (which is perhaps what Thetis shies away from, in commissioning armour for her son yet rejecting the implications of doing so):

> 'Horae Canonicae' then is not finally a blasphemous religious poem about 'Good Friday' but a secular poem about 'our dear old bag of democracy'. It uses the Christian fable as a vehicle, not because it does not credit it – it clearly does – but because the very meaning of that crucifixion . . . is that Christ offered himself to be used, to become the sacrificial vehicle of meanings other than himself. . .
>
> (1985: 186)

'Bucolics' was started later than 'Horae Canonicae', although finished earlier as a sequence; the first poem in *The Shield of Achilles*, its seven parts were balanced by those of 'Horae Canonicae' at the end. The title's allusion to the pastoral tradition in poetry might indicate a concern with nature or place rather than culture or history; but Fuller quotes Auden's sleeve-note definition, from a recording, that their common theme is 'the relation of man as a history-making person to nature' (1998: 443), and Smith asserts that 'History . . . infiltrates them all'

(1985: 186). The first poem in the sequence, 'Winds', was in fact the last-written, and the only one not to deal with a geographical feature. Each poem bears a personal dedication, although Mendelson argues that 'Lakes' (for Isaiah Berlin) implies a critique of Berlin's thinking; and notwithstanding the overall title, only the last poem, 'Streams', presents a setting that provokes any wish to linger – itself in part the consequence of a pleasant dream.

This is no sequence of pastoral amenability, therefore, and 'history' functions as an agent of separation from such possibility. 'Winds', dedicated (by his real name) to the poet St John Perse, appropriately evokes the wind of inspiration; but it deals also with God's breathing life into Adam, the pentecostal wind, and less elevated winds emitted by the body in whistling or – Mendelson suggests – farting. This is another poem in which Auden goes back to the beginning of life; but the journey is one through layers of violence to the 'First Dad', whose 'watch' may suggest an association with Kronos, devourer of his own children and, in turn, supplanted by Zeus. Here too 'metropolis', its solidity opposed to the insolid winds, is founded on blood, even if its later citizens include aimiable parties who measure the weather (Auden's father had a rain-gauge). The poem closes by implying that the wind of inspiration requires the visible world for its subject.

'Woods' returns to regular rhyme and metre, perhaps suggesting how in modern industrialised society woods have lost their primitive awesomeness in more routine enclosure; we enter them for the picnics or even love-making that affect to be reunion with nature, but actually the gulf is absolute, and this poem comically sees trees in terms of what they might be turned into: coffins or paper. More seriously, it asserts that a modernised world which neglects to care for its woods reveals a state of terminal decline; the priggishness of the formulaic last line may, as in Frost's poetry, make us wonder whether we should credit it or not. 'Mountains', set out in six stanzas with regular intermittent rhyme, is – notwithstanding its affectionate nostalgia for Penrith station where he used to catch the train for Wescoe – laden with comical spleen against mountaineers, mountain types and mountains themselves: not even the difficulties they present to military strategists can endear them to him. Moving from the Lake District to an alpine setting (in deference to its Austrian dedicatee), the poem acknowledges their usefulness as places of refuge, but implies that inbreeding is the norm for such sequestered societies, and notes mountains' attractiveness to vampires. Its bristling prejudice continues into the last stanza, where a Technicolor Alpine Family fantasy is judged worthy of five minutes' attention – a concession instantly withdrawn in the reflection that even that might be too long. This levelling comedy is, in itself, opposed to the sublimity habitually associated with the subject, and to some degree rehearses the dislike for 'mountain-bores' expressed in 'Letter to Lord Byron' (although mountains were important in *The Ascent of F6*, dedicated to his mountaineering brother, John). The manifest injustice of the attitudes struck, the rebarbative sophistication displayed, emphatically remind us that all responses to nature are culturally produced, like these prejudicial conceptualisations: in the mountains, there you feel unfree.

It then turns out that 'Lakes' aren't much better (just in case we were thinking the previous poem's allusion to the Lake District augured well). If mountains immoderately repudiate human inhabitation, lakes are, perhaps, all too amenable, and the peacefulness they enclose may be a shade too 'comfy' for our own good, encouraging a perversely militant possessiveness intent on repelling intruders: the 'man-traps' are no more admirable here than was the gamekeeper forcing retreat at the end of the 1930s poem 'Who Will Endure . . .'; both enforce the selfishness of privilege. A lake colludes with dreams that nature is humanly intended; the multiplicitous terms we can apply to it resemble so many labels establishing unjustifiable proprietorship; this clever poem dedicated to an Oxford philosopher is quietly aware of self-protective societies and their excluding codes: Every Mortal Jack and Jill Not Welcome Here. In 'Islands' the idea of a lake as an inside-out island reinforces the point, as it lists the kinds of use to which islands have been put or the type of person attracted there, none of which is greatly encouraging: even the supposedly democratic nudity of the holiday beach encodes hierarchical relationships. This small poem lists small worlds and, at its close, implies the small-mindedness resulting.

'Plains', like its two predecessors, has nine stanzas, but unlike 'Islands' its lines are long and prosaic – as befits its subject, which offers yet another uncongenial terrain. Geologically, plains are what is left after more dramatic processes have taken place, leaving this flattened residue of 'mere substance': clay that takes any shape the potter chooses, and gravel that collaborates in concrete's anonymity. Politically, this is a landscape of compliance, whose inhabitants are at the mercy of unpropitiable Nature and a State to whose apparatus no obstacles are presented; good for a battlefield, its featurelessness acquires character from history, not geography. The poet imagines plainsmen as consumed by fantasies of impotent hatred, but then confesses that plains provide the desert places for his own nightmares of desolation and impotence, which shows that he should fear himself rather than that setting. From this perception he moves to an understanding that any landscape we spectate is the product of our relation to it, and that, unpoetic as flat plains may be, like this poem they have the merit of giving what Wallace Stevens called the plain sense of things (the last line alludes to the famous opening dictum of Wittgenstein's *Tractatus*: 'The world is everything that is the case').

This unexalted poem is the means by which we reach 'Streams', written in eighteen quatrains with a complicated hybrid internal rhyme-scheme (explained in Fuller (1998)), but always rhyming the second line's final syllable with the last line's penult. Winds are everywhere, and therefore nowhere in particular; woods, mountains, lakes, islands and plains are always in the same place; a stream combines attributes of both by being changeably constant. It is, as well, composed of life-essential water, whose flowing interconnection of different landscapes, preserved integrity (despite the uses to which it can be put) and frontierlessness all offer potent symbolism for the universal fraternity evoked by Gaston Paris, lecturing on poetry in his besieged city. From that image of universal love and hope, the poem immediately moves to a particular and recent personal memory of an actual location. Previous poems dealt with generic places, and where names occurred these were mythical (Arcady, Babel) or illustrative (Lake District, Michigan, Baikal); only 'Penrith' and 'Zurich' suggested locations of personal significance, intruding an unfeigned desire and specific nostalgia at odds with the opinionated poem in which they occurred. Now, suddenly, three proper names denoting an exact Pennine spot contrast with the generalising address of earlier poems; and rather than talking about nightmares, the poet tells us of a particular dream, a baroque theophany combining elements of Lewis Carroll with dream-poets from

Langland onward, from whose love-dance he wakens to a sense of grateful belonging. It is an attachment to the human that this 'holy' place has consecrated, just as water is celebrated for its association with humanity, here instigating a momentary confluence between actual and visionary worlds.

Smith (1985: 192) argues that this eirenic tone is achieved at the expense of an historical forgetfulness; and in 'Ode to Gaea', written soon afterwards, Auden from his plane window registered a different assessment of earth and its places. The sense of being 'at home' is, however, the dominant if not uninterrogated note of his final sequence, 'Thanksgiving for a Habitat'. Consisting of twelve poems (plus 'Postscripts'), the first two offer general considerations about architecture and home-owning, while each subsequent poem concerns a particular room. 'Prologue: The Birth of Architecture' was dedicated to a little-known architect; written in syllabics (which Mendelson suggests offered Auden a way to use form and shape that did not imply archaism), it perspectivises time according to heart-beat rather than carbon-dating, suggesting that beyond a certain distance all history is equally remote; it finds the roots of architecture – as distinct from hives or nests of social insects, which are not projected before being built – in human embracement of possibility, summarised in the last word, 'if'. The sequence's title poem amusingly collapses time by momentarily imagining the interments of ancient emperors transposed to a contemporary setting, going on to propose that a home is an idealised extension of the body, and considering how fashions and self-conceptions change. The poet's modest *imperium* is the house and grounds in Kirchstetten, where he is unlikely to meet all his putative subjects; but just because he may not like them (e.g., spiders), he does not have the right to destroy them. The mention of Hitler touches on the consciousness that prevents the poem or the sequence being complacent: his first and only home inspires Auden's gratitude, but it might (the poem was written shortly before the Cuban missile crisis) be instantaneously vaporised, or, more conventionally, invaded. Thus the choices celebrated in the last two stanzas are not absolute, but conditional.

The first room to be considered is Auden's workroom; the poem is dedicated to the memory of MacNeice, fellow-poet whose classicism is registered in the dactylic foot ending each alternate line. Auden uses the occasion to meditate upon the craft and the times they shared, in a relaxed intimacy of vocative address; quietly, it celebrates poetry as 'this unpopular art which cannot be turned into/ background noise for study/or hung as a status trophy by rising executives' (an opposition first mooted in his earlier elegy for an Irish poet), and insists on poetry's right to be unimposing. Here, too, even in the *sanctum sanctorum*, the world beyond is present: the historical Carolingian boundary suggests more recent ones (Auden's house was a moderate drive from what was then an Iron Curtain border), and Stalin and Hitler leave an indelible stain on past and future. Auden added a 'Postscript' consisting of epigrammatic short poems, but concluding with a longer self-reproaching piece, whose stepped line visually enacts the schism between two viewpoints; its argument is that while a poet might hope to be excused a reprehensible life because out of it grew good poetry, the missed and preferable alternative might have been better poetry grown out of a better life.

The next two poems, respectively celebrating cellar and attic, offer them initially as opposed realms: the first dark food-storage, full of primitive awe and associations, a realm to test masculine courage; the second full of bric-a-brac unsystematically kept and associated with the feminine. This pair of poems makes clearer the house's analogousness to the body, with the cellar suggesting fleshly needs and dreads, and the attic the mind's associativeness, the imagination. Their dedication to a husband and wife implies the necessary marriage between these elements; and although encoding the gender differentiation ('Up There' has exclusively feminine line-endings), the pairing also breaks it down: 'Down There' has predominantly feminine endings, and the closing image of 'Up There' is of an imaginative boy. Callan (1983) has suggested that these titles relate to the vocabulary of existentialist theologians, whose ideas had been controversially deployed in Bishop John Robinson's *Honest to God* (1963); one theme of this was that traditional notions of God as 'up there' or 'out there' should be replaced by a concept of God situated 'down there', in the ground of being.

The poem celebrating the lavatory (its title is an Edwardian euphemism), dedicated to Isherwood, deflates pomposity: the act of artistic making is analogised to that of defecation, in a jokily sub-Freudian reading which refuses to let Ariel forget about Caliban. 'Encomium Balnei' starts off by insulting the English, as may be appropriate in a poem imitating the stepped line and absent punctuation of William Carlos Williams; the bathroom is celebrated for its cleansing rituals, but also for its pampering of the body, its indulgence of the flesh. This occurs, too, in the kitchen; where six long stanzas, rhyming the short lines, extend the Americanist emphasis by noting the 'American' kitchen's installation in Austria (a kind of *urbs in rure*); it also marks the transition, in the sequence, from rooms of the house dedicated to private or unseen functions, to those connected with hospitality and the social life; and notwithstanding Brecht's aggressive title it celebrates the modern appliances which enable cooking to become an act of creation rather than labour, whilst (like the lavatory at the other end of the process) satisfying fundamental needs by which all are united; yet the world of threat and aggression is acknowledged in the final stanza.

'For Friends Only', written in stanzas alternating lines of seven and five words, evokes the expectant emptiness of the guest-room, its sociability underscored by the dedication to a married couple (who, however, found it stuffy in summer, and secretly resorted to those 'orderly woods' for love-making). After its low-key register, 'Tonight at Seven-Thirty' sets off the fireworks of verbal and formal display: six regular stanzas with fourteen rhymed lines of a varying length, that impose a distinctive pattern on the page and contain *recherché* words such as 'flosculent' and 'dapatical'. Although sharing the need for nourishment with all living things, humanity alone has made the act into a social rite whose elaborate courtesies prioritise the claims of others, celebrating 'Nature's bounty' and 'grace of Spirit'. The closing evocation of silence harks back to the description of speech as a 'shadow' which echoes the more truthful 'silent light', in the MacNeice elegy. 'The Cave of Nakedness', about the bedroom, is a discursive poem which, although opening with Don Juan, immediately dissociates nakedness from sexual activity; love-making, like dreams, is part of what happens at night that is essentially incommunicable to outsiders. Sleep, here, is renewal, only touched by a momentarily darker envisaging of death, police-states, and the torments of insomnia; the evocation of which offers a ground of contrast for the grateful awakening at the close (followed by a postcript of short poems). The final poem, 'The Common Life', dedicated to Kallman, observes the living room; the most communal area in the house, yet one which also expresses shared and unshared aspects of their lives: the place where their solitudes companionably meet, just as the small windows offer a view but preserve privacy. The poem ponders the twenty-four years of their relationship, and acknowledges in understatement the 'criminal noise' of History, which has spared them, unlike so many others; that they are 'cater-cousins' rather than lovers is part of the more difficult, less ostentatious and appetitive love-as-forbearance, that the poem's close defines. The last word of the sequence is 'truth', but it affirms 'love': not any universal love and hope self-deceivingly offered as a cure-all, but attachment enduring through time, noted in deliberately unresonant formulation. Aware as they are of the long perspectives of history and its criminal noise, as of the fact that 'this land is not the sweet home that it looks', these poems nevertheless celebrate situatedness: in time, in place and in body. Like so much of the later poetry, they acknowledge the commonplace aspects of life; unlike the early Auden, they may be challenging in their unchallengingness, teasing us into thought by the unnecessariness of their being: whilst also affirming that, seriously playful, they were meant to be.

3

Criticism

Critical contours: Auden and his readers

There has never been critical consensus about Auden, nor is there likely to be; there was probably most agreement over the promise of the early work, which then divided into those who found it fulfilled by what came later, and those who did not. The very terms in which this contrast is set up, however, presuppose a difference rather than a continuity, and the critical installation of a schism in Auden's career comes near to being a truth universally acknowledged – not much displaced by Michael Wood's suggestion, in his review of *Later Auden* (*London Review of Books*, 10 June 1999), that the qualitative question becomes urgent after 1948 rather than 1939. The peculiar authority of the earlier date illustrates ways in which what may be accidents of Auden's career have received purposive amplification from historical coincidence: for just as his first significant publication in Eliot's *Criterion* occurred in January 1930, so his departure for America exactly nine years later (ironically coinciding with *Criterion*'s last issue), in a year of crisis for British history, is resonant. Myth-making does not squander such coordinates; the earliest book-length study of Auden, by Hoggart (1951), treated the 'American' poetry separately from what had gone before, and even though Mendelson's *Early Auden* (1981) emphasises the dissatisfactions with England which repeatedly impelled Auden abroad during the 1930s, the point of division (reinforced by content and title of his invaluable edition *English Auden*) remains that at which he embarked for America. This schismatic Auden was reflected in Carpenter's biography (1981), alongside the fact of his devoting less attention to the later years (Parker (2004) observes the same structural division in his biography of Isherwood). Barbara Everett (1986), reviewing both Mendelson and Carpenter ('Auden Askew', reprinted in *Poets in Their Time*), drew attention to the 'enormous importance' such patterning gives 'to the imputed division in Auden's career (. . .) as though the move to America were not only the most important thing that happened to him but as though it were important precisely because in some form it expressed his deepest wishes' (1986: 215–16); yet even she cannot avoid registering the act as crucial to subsequent readings of the career: 'For Auden to leave England at that time had a kind of terrible gracelessness from which the poet's reputation has never really recovered' (1986: 218). She continues – in an essay well worth seeking out – to assert the importance, in

Auden, of the unwilled or accidental; and it is perhaps necessary, in order to grasp how the reputation may have been distorted by the pressure of history, to imagine what the assessment of Auden's emigration would have been, had there been no war, or if it had occurred long enough afterward not to excite any imputation that he had left in order to avoid it.

This issue relating to the life is accompanied by one almost as profound relating to the art, and concerning Auden's revisions of published work. The two have in common that they potentially involve notions of betrayal: if by emigrating Auden seemed to evade the dangerous flood of history, so in changing or expunging poems he was attempting to alter the record, and falsify the work's relation to its historical moment; or else he was violating its organic integrity. The first implied a kind of Stalinist adjustment – and in 1948 Auden did comment on another poet's alteration of a poem in terms of details 'liquidated' or 'deported to another stanza' (*P* II: 349) – and the second, a repudiation of Romantic notions of the poem as a living system. Both criticisms were reflected in Joseph Warren Beach's *The Making of the Auden Canon* (1957), where he noted the 'surprising adjustability of Auden's work written from the point of view of a given ideology to the requirements of a quite different ideology involving a different point of view' (1957: 96), and darkly hinted that the issue of integrity was at stake; later, he criticised Auden for manifesting 'a curious notion of the creative process' which involved conceiving it 'not as something organic involving living tissues with their appropriate functions, but rather as the arrangement of words in patterns' (1957: 226). This book was the first systematic exploration of Auden's changes, but enshrined within it were humanist and New Critical orthodoxies with which Auden's practice was demonstrably irreconcilable, repudiating as it did notions of the poem as something which once finished was detached from history, in a realm of transcendent Art. He acknowledged in a lecture ('Robert Frost', in *DH*) that, even if a poet had written a 'Prospero' poem embodying wisdom rather than an 'Ariel' poem embodying delight, in the eyes of subsequent readers it might well switch identity from one to the other: for he saw poetry as inescapably involved in time, no matter how seductive notions of its timelessness might on occasions be. This poetic opposition of 'Ariel' to 'Prospero', as John Bayley pointed out, is overneat; but Auden was right to say that poems are not fixed entities, but sites of interpretative change and contention: in his elegy for Yeats he had seen how the city vacated by the dead self is figuratively invaded by insurgent readers; Yeats's accomplishment of his corpse leaves his corpus to be divided amongst his admirers, who will – in imagery almost sacrilegious in its import – consume, digest and 'modify' it.

The Oedipal implications of this process were clear to Auden, who once commented only semi-flippantly that Randall Jarrell had written a vehemently critical review out of disappointed love for him, and who knew what was at stake when readers felt themselves betrayed by a favourite writer. His crime in Beach's eyes lay in failure to be the kind of poet Beach felt he ought to have been: which did not, as perhaps it might have done, lead Beach to revisit his own assumptions. If at the beginning of his career Auden received some benefit from *coterie* boosting, later he could be punished in as partisan a manner – as, for example, in the unrelenting hostility of the *Scrutiny* clique, whose leader F.R. Leavis, reviewing its achievement in 1962, asserted with self-satisfaction as audible as it was premature that 'Thirty years after we put the case against Auden it passes as a commonplace . . . . Quietly, by tacit consent, his spell of glory has lapsed' (1963: 16, 17). The kind of animus that could be directed against Auden, based on his personal failure to conform to an unquestioned template – which in *Scrutiny*'s case was likely to require heterosexuality as part of its watchword attitude of 'maturity' – could be met and mirrored by those arguing *for* him, sometimes overcommitted to repudiating the case for the prosecution. Thus, in response to a view influentially expressed by poets such as Jarrell and Larkin, that Auden's work deteriorated in America, Mendelson's commitment to the contrary leads him (Everett (1986) argues) to strain to produce a poetry which is improved by the revisions visited upon it, and, likewise, a poet whose improvement after expatriation can be charted as part of a consistently evolving approach to life and art. John Bayley also writes within a humanist tradition when in his 1969 review of *City Without Walls*, he seems to pre-digest the likely criticisms (another reviewer remarked that Auden had become 'rather unfashionable these days'), to instate the idea of Auden as exemplifying the sort of civilised, unegotistical liveliness that might make him an ideal companion on a long journey:

> W.H. Auden is the rarest kind of poet in a post-romantic age: interested not in himself but in the plural aspects and manifestations of the world which he turns into his art; interested in people and animals as in ideas and landscapes, rivers, buildings, metres, histories, coigns and quirks. In his poetry, as in Renaissance rhetoric and the diagrams of Vitruvian man, the human being can take on the impersonal contours of nature or art without ceasing to be human. . . . All this is rare in an age in which even reportage can become a kind of self-caress.
>
> (Haffenden 1983: 456)

Bayley's is a sensitive response, but may illustrate the tendency, common in assessments of writers whose work we admire, of assuming them to be wisely coherent as people, in order to discover the same attributes in their art. In respect of Auden, Everett pungently argues this to be a distortion:

> The poet's life, like most people's, was clearly full of things which he was 'incapable of dealing with': but it was his gift to harness that incapacity, . . . and it is this that militates, too, against that deliberative, purposive and successful quality which Carpenter and Mendelson tend to endow it with. . . . [H]e is the genius of the makeshift, the virtuoso of contingency, and to perfect his achievement is to endanger his essential character.
>
> (1986: 228–9)

No less than the positions it disputes, however, this moves from presumptions about the life to find them reflected in the art.

If Auden had become 'unfashionable' by the late 1960s – and it was certainly the case that in that era a volume from him did not have the *éclat* of new work by Larkin, Hughes, Ginsberg, Berryman, Lowell or (posthumously) Plath – this contrast with his 1930s importance and noise reflected a situation he had himself brought about. At this period he drafted (but did not send) a letter to Naomi Mitchison, who in a *Festschrift* for his sixtieth birthday had reproached him for deleting cherished poems and for no longer producing 'memorable' work: 'If, by memorability, you mean a poem like "Sept 1st 1939", I pray to God that I shall never be memorable again' (quoted in Carpenter 1981: 418). By this stage, Auden was defining an ideal reader as someone attuned to his unobtrusive if rarefied feats of metric ('Every poet has his dream reader: mine keeps a look out for curious prosodic fauna'; quoted in Haffenden 1983: 55); but in a 1966 review Christopher Ricks – whose close attentiveness to text Auden praised – whilst acknowledging 'the expertise of an old maestro', had pithily expressed his sense of the problem posed: 'Disarming is the word for *About the House*. What is harder to pinpoint is the moment at which such a word has to be said accusingly rather than thankfully' (Haffenden 1983: 434). Although implying concessive acceptance, 'disarming' is a word that also presupposes a potential antagonism or armed encounter between writer and reader; and whilst the early Auden might seem more to exemplify such relations, Ricks clearly found the learnedly 'avuncular' later poet provocative, just as a not-entirely-unaggressive exasperation underlay Auden's response to Mitchison, above. In the dialogic 'Epilogue' of *The Orators*, 'reader', fearful of transgression, is opposed to 'rider' (writer) who in the closing stanza mocks his timid stasis as he leaves him there; later Auden continued to leave readers behind, by arranging his *oeuvre* alphabetically and jettisoning their old favourites: in each, manifesting a continuing desire not to conform to expectation.

In respect of the career these operate as tactics of estrangement, enlarging more localised attempts to counter the predatory interestedness brought to the reading of a poem (whereby the poet 'becomes' his admirers) by subordinating the reader as an entity created to textual specification. 'The Watershed', for example, predetermines its reader as one whose prejudices will exclude him/her from the landscape – or poem – inspected, whilst simultaneously and coercively s/he is situated as a fascinated aspirant. Leaving the reader 'there' – pacified, immobilised or in some other way objectified by the text – is one aspect of the game as played by an Auden poem; of which Ricks's consciousness of being disarmed, of having a militant interpretative awareness short-circuited by its own sense of superfluousness to the poetic occasion, is another: in each case, the 'reader' becomes a dramatised or performative function of the text, rather than (as s/he might intend) the other way round. This perhaps seems a rebarbative description of the process; but even if Frank Kermode, reviewing *Epistle to a Godson* (1972), spoke of Auden having in his later work grown 'quieter, more explicit, more conversational' (Haffenden 1983: 470), the obtrusively unusual words Kermode listed posed a challenge of sorts to Auden's readership. Many, however, felt underchallenged; in her *Irish Times* review Edna Longley bemoaned the 'mellow garrulity' inhabiting 'uncorseted alcaics which barely nudge into shape the flow of chat and reminiscence' (Haffenden 1983: 51); but reviewing the same volume, Clive James, working within an essentially humanist framework, outlined the moral imperative that underlay the nature of the poet's development:

> The greatest modern verse technician, Auden long ago ran out of metrical rules needing more than a moment's effort to conform to.

> Technically, his later manner – which involves setting up a felt rhythmic progress inside an arbitrary syllabic convention – is really a way of restoring to the medium some of the resistance his virtuosity earlier wiped out. This technical mortification is closely allied with [an] ethical stand.
>
> (Haffenden 1983: 474)

Readers as well were mortified by the loss or clumsy alteration of favourite poems, yet James's brief but compelling account of the career argued that it was the very prodigality of Auden's poetic gift that provoked in its possessor the urge to rein it in: 'Part of Auden's genius was to know the necessity of chastening his talent, ensuring that his poetry would be something more enduring than mere magic' (1983: 479).

If Auden was alert to the dangers of being the creature of his talent, he became equally alert to the dangers of becoming the creature of his readership. In *Modern Poetry* (1938), MacNeice had looked back on the poets of the 1932 anthology *New Signatures* and defined their difference from Yeats and Eliot in terms of their being 'emotionally partisan': 'The whole poetry, on the other hand, of Auden, Spender, and Day Lewis implies that they have desires and hatreds of their own and, further, that they think some things *ought* to be desired and others hated'. This was quoted by George Orwell in the title essay of *Inside the Whale* (1962 [1940]: 30), where he acknowledged that 'for the middle and late thirties, Auden, Spender & Co. *are* "the movement", just as Joyce, Eliot & Co. were for the twenties' (1962 [1940]: 32). But it was precisely that (delusory) appearance of programmatic cohesion and leaderly purposiveness that encouraged a camp-following which, when two of the leaders refused to lead any longer, expressed its disappointment; also in 1940, Connolly's remark in *Horizon* about the significance of Auden's ('our best poet') and Isherwood's ('our most promising novelist') move to America, concealed some razorblades within the bouquet, claiming also that they 'did not suffer from lack of recognition in England, where they received a publicity which they did everything to encourage' (quoted in Parker 2004: 458). Such a comment illustrated the perils of 'stardom' or charismatic visibility, with its unspoken contract between adoring and adorer; consciousness of which underlay Auden's later investigations of the bad magic of art, and his comments about the unforgivingness of disappointed readers.

Perception of Auden as the poet of the 1930s was becoming naturalised as early as 1940; and only five years later Jarrell, outlining 'The Stages of Auden's Ideology' in a *Partisan Review* essay, installed an interpretative model which Boly has more recently argued as possibly 'the most influential criticism ever written about Auden. Its idea of a three-step development, from personal, to social, and then back to personal (religious) concerns, has furnished a framework that both Auden's defenders and detractors have been obliged to accept' (1991: 40). The detractors, in this view, are chiefly constituted by those registering the disappointment of the unfulfilled expectations of the 1930s 'movement'; the defenders Boly divides into 'polemicists' and 'humanists'. The former 'maintain that Auden did indeed have a prophetic message', although when pushed to its definition they 'resort to vague locutions about Auden's sense of disintegrating civilization and Malrauxesque violence' (1991: 42–3); the latter shift that message 'from the treacherous plains of history to the more congenial sanctum of psychology. For the humanists, Auden is the upholder of individual rights and personal freedom against the insidious encroachments of mass culture and its mechanized bureaucracies' (1991: 43). Implicit in this, however, Boly suggests, is an ideal of 'a free and autonomous individual, set apart from social currents and detached from ideological frays' which 'runs counter to Auden's insistence that human beings are historical entities' (1991: 44).

Criticism of Auden does not exist in clearly delineated successive strata, but the theoretically inflected approaches taken by Boly himself, by Smith, by Rainer Emig and by Bozorth naturally reflect the academy's embracing of critical theory in the last quarter of the twentieth century, as well as the evolution of theoretical subsets which, for example, has resulted in the historicisation of Auden as a writerly phenomenon, or focus on the specific consequences of his sexual orientation for the production and reception of his work. It could be argued, however, that none of these entirely escapes the making of an Auden in its own image or conformable to the critic's interpretative predisposition, even when the antagonistic ground of that engagement remains evident. Mendelson (1999) suggests that it is characteristic of Auden's poetry to unsettle fixed positions, repudiating dogma but nurturing our negative capability: it discomfits equally the 'aesthetically tolerant' reader and her 'morally censorious' opposite; whereas for someone prepared to question such convictions, 'Auden's poems offer responses that combine the consoling triumph of form with the disturbing uncertainties of freedom' (*LA*: xxii).

An obituary of the poet Anthony Hecht in a recent *Auden Newsletter* (no. 25, January 2005) defined his 'idiosyncratic' critical study of Auden as 'an argument with an admired master as [much as it was] an exposition of the older poet's work'. This section has already touched upon the ways in which an Auden poem can constitute what Wallace Stevens called an 'element of antagonisms', where poet and reader come into contention through the medium of the text. Boly (1991), who has undertaken the most systematic exploration of the dynamics of this encounter, suggests that despite the coercive appearance of many Auden poems, the provocation to argumentative dissent (embodied in such a book as Hecht's) is actually their fundamental aim: albeit that the reader is potentially cast as a subservient Caliban, his revolt against the Prosperian dictates of the text is the most productive of responses. Boly contends that Auden 'saw reading as an activity that takes place in a cultural arena, where murderously opposed interests compete for status and power' (1991: ix): which is a slightly lurid way of stressing adversarial strategies implicit within the reader–writer relationship, whereby the reader's responsibility is not to enact deformative compliances textually prefabricated for his/her role, but to discover what voluble erasures or speaking silences betray the unvoiced message. Be not affeared, he urges, the text is full of noises:

> Through a series of remarkable textual experiments, then, Auden explored the possibility that in the course of achieving its repression of an audience, the presiding voice of a discourse unwittingly, helplessly, enacted a series of betraying syntactic gestures. These perfomed cues,

> the unvoiced but gesticulating aspect of a discourse, provide the otherwise silent inscriptions of a text with both a provocation and a point of convergence. For it is only through such neglected gestures, the forgotten body of an utterance, that the responses of a text, the impulses forbidden or denied by its usurping disciplines, are called upon to speak.
>
> (1991: 9)

Whilst Boly's argument above could be criticised for embodying what might roguishly be called 'The Unintentional Fallacy', its deconstructionist manoeuvres challengingly remove the encounter with a poem from a reductively humanist arena.

Whatever the quarrelsome nature of Hecht's (1993) book on Auden the 'admired master', it underlines one factor that has played its part in the older writer's survival; another is the fact that if Auden has been justly described as a 'poet's poet', he has proved to be a 'reader's poet' as well. This is suggested by the surprising regularity with which, in the twenty-first century, direct allusions to the work are encountered in the broadsheet press, not invariably in pieces whose primary focus is literary (writing in the *New Yorker* in 1996, Nicholas Jenkins noted that Auden's reputation now 'carried him beyond the confines of the merely "literary" audience'). His breadth of appeal may in part be because of the not-overwhelmingly-apposite use of 'Stop All the Clocks' in the hit film *Four Weddings and a Funeral*, but is also and more significantly because of qualities in his poetry that at best make it, when not complicatedly or playfully intriguing, rewardingly engaging and approachable – in ways whose good and bad aspects were encoded in Ricks's 'disarming'. Overall, and in its different aspects, Auden's poetry offers continuous material for thought, continuous provocation, and an unequalled range of technical expertise: all of which has led to the sustained interest and respect – even if disputatiously expressed – that underlies the frequency with which fellow-poets, of his own and subsequent generations, have chosen to address his work in their critical prose (in addition, of course, to the various poems dedicated to or written about or alluding to Auden). Those will be considered later (see Criticism, **p. 136**), as part of my examination of the criticism of Auden under thematised headings; I want to close this survey by noting Marsha Bryant's observation that nowadays 'the signifier "Auden" exceeds both the person and his texts' (1997: 4), which she supports by showing how 'Spain' and the Yeats elegy were cited as part of journalistic responses to the civil wars in former Yugoslavia (as was 'September 1, 1939'; also cited after the terrorist destruction of New York's twin towers). She refers to the double function of such poems, which 'shape cultural memories of the thirties, and . . . provide strategies for coming to terms with contemporary social conflicts' (1997: 5); which emphasises how 'the signifier "Auden" ' resonates beyond the 1930s, partly as a result of his being so identified with the period: 'a cultural figure', as she puts it, 'that has become synonymous with this vexing decade' (1997: 4). The strength of this association, which can be traced back to that decade itself, provides the first heading under which I consider the criticism.

Critical perspectives

Inventing Auden and the 1930s

'A decade, a movement, a group of writers: the '30s is now one of literary history's most stable and flourishing concepts', declared Cunningham in his wide-ranging study *British Writers of the Thirties* (1988: 14). In a 1970 interview Spender claimed that editors and anthologisers, rather than the poets themselves, had been responsible for stamping the decade with a particular identity: 'Geoffrey Grigson and Michael Roberts – and, later, John Lehman with *New Signatures*. They were the people who invented the 1930s. It really wasn't us' (Carter 1984: 53). The perceived centrality of Auden to the period was certainly signalled by the title of Francis Scarfe's study *Auden and After: The Liberation of Poetry 1930–1941* (1942), and its delineation of a finite epoch continued to strike chords: jointly reviewing the collected poems of MacNeice and Auden in 1967, Graham Hough declared that both 'were formed irrevocably by the thirties', but acknowledged that the same was true for him as well ('a history which we all share'); he deplored, therefore, the 'maddening' experience of acquiring 'a new edition and find[ing] old familiars missing, others altered and mutilated' (Carter 1984: 120, 119, 123). Thus a relationship the reviewer thought he shared with Auden had been fractured by aggressive authorial revisions; this involved geography – Hough contrasted the 'essentially English' early work with, later, 'a certain tenuousness in his relation with the physical and sensuous world', judging that '[a]fter he left for America there is hardly a sign that he derived any nourishment whatever from the world around him' (1984: 126) – but, more importantly, it comprised a joint experience of history, which such changes disrupted.

If Spender disclaimed 'the 1930s' as largely the invention of literary entrepreneurs, it was nonetheless true that self-inventing poets who were simultaneously inventing their readers featured prominently at the time, as well as in retrospect. Bernard Bergonzi, seeking in *Reading the Thirties* (1978) to account for Auden's spokesmanship for that era, proposed a confluence of interests:

> If Auden was widely and rapidly imitated, at least in his most evidently imitable stylistic and structural devices, it was, I believe, because there was a general readiness to look at the world in Auden's categories. At a time of world economic depression there was something reassuring in Auden's calm demonstration, mediated as much by style as by content, that reality was intelligible, and could be studied like a map or a catalogue, or seen in temporal terms as an inexorable historical process. Hence the instant appeal of the classificatory vision, the reliance on definite articles and precise and unexpected adjectives, which placed and limited their subjects.
>
> (1998: 196–7)

Cunningham extended this beyond Auden, defining '(t)he period's widespread deicticism' as 'undoubtedly an effort to assert authority, knowledge, command of experience', summed up as its 'effort to achieve an authoritative air by dint of deictics' (1988: 10). He, too, noted the importance of adjectives as 'a major component of the Audenesque. And since adjectives describe what and how things are and seem, a command over adjectives is a command over experience and the knowledge of things' (1988: 193). This epistemological confidence offered a contrast with the uncertainty about or lofty disdain towards the world of current events, evident in the previous high Modernist generation, and can to that degree be seen as a strategic posture by which successors defined their own empowering difference: 'Finding things to say goodbye to had been a more or less full-time occupation for many writers since the end of the First World War. But Auden and his contemporaries were also looking for things to say hello to. They required their readers to spot both decadence and signs of the birth of a new social order'.

That a style of writing can be used to position or invent its reader as well as its writer was argued by David Trotter in *The Making of the Reader* (1984), from which the foregoing quotation comes (p. 118). This study of 'Language and Subjectivity in Modern American, English and Irish Poets' spreads its net beyond Auden, but offers acute analysis of the ways in which particular employment of the definite article, characteristic of 'the Audenesque', became a means by which readerly complicity was ensured. Commenting on the categorical lists found in 'Journal of an Airman', Trotter asserts:

> In each case the definite article does all the work. It seems to suggest that middle-class faces look like something specific – a fucked hen, a favourite puss – but relies on the reader to complete the identification, to bring to mind a particular face which might be thought to resemble a fucked hen or a favourite puss. That is precisely what Auden's readers did, taking on themselves the responsibility for interpretation. . . . The definite article . . . has no semantic content and does not position the individual or sub-class it refers to. Auden exploited not only its specificity, but also its neutrality: a neutrality which allows the reader more scope for interpretation than a demonstrative [*e.g.*, 'this' or 'that'] would, assuring him that he can identify the item in question from his own experience.
>
> (1984: 114)

In such a way, the compliant reader achieves insidership with a text that, by inciting prejudicial identifications of its 'Enemy', equally implied a category of outsiders; so that, as Spender noted, '(o)ne's own little set draws closer together', on which Trotter enlarges: 'Auden's definite articles encouraged his own little set, and the larger "set" which grew out of it, to supply information which only it could supply, and thus draw closer together. They were making a readership' (1984: 115). This particular process, by which a rhetorical strategy – the Audenesque – was conceived in response to political circumstances, is one which Trotter limits to the 1930s:

> When Auden left for America in 1939, he abandoned a major subject of his poetry – Europe under the threat of fascism and war – and an audience which could be expected to register the nuances of that subject. The proportion of definite articles in his poems dropped steadily from this

> point onwards. He also rewrote much of the work he had produced during the thirties, erasing wherever possible the definite articles. In the 'Foreword' to *Collected Shorter Poems 1927–1957* he described his earlier preference for those items as a 'disease'. He was in effect dismantling a particular rhetoric, sealing off the places in a poem where the reader had been invited to step forward and become known by distancing himself from what he alone could identify. It was an important disavowal from an important writer.
>
> (1984: 134)

Such a way of putting it rather begs the question whether Auden continued to be 'important' when separated from that subject and that audience; his centrality to the epoch and inhabitation of its modes is axiomatic for Cunningham, who asserts that '(t)he name of Auden became a touchstone of the period' and that 'the influence of Auden on his time was extreme' (1988: 19, 20). Yet that kind of importance has about it, it appears, something spurious or dislikable; Cunningham sees the abandonment of the Audenesque not as a strategic choice, but as a consequence of its exposure as ethically inadequate to the task set for it – index as it was, he argues, to a 'monstrously inhumane aloofness' (1988: 394) in its author. This aloofness he asserts as 'Auden's continual failing' (1988: 423), glaringly revealed by the Spanish conflict from which Cunningham sees him 'slink[ing] quietly away' (1988: 461); but not before his prose piece 'Impressions of Valencia' had shown that its author was 'a monstrously unfeeling childish joke-machine', incapable of responding adequately even to a picture of a dead baby: 'The failure of the Audenesque in "Impressions of Valencia" [is] at one with Auden's failure to become more than a Spanish tripper and his "Spain" 's disconcerted aloofness' (1988: 448). There is a strong implication here that Auden had all too much in common with his low, dishonest decade.

Nevertheless, the identification – whether pejorative or otherwise – between Auden and the 1930s has been decisive, and particularly in his availability to mirror the political concerns of the times: an approach which tends to situate him as the *primus inter pares* of a group of like-minded writers. Such a perception was part of the contemporary literary journalism or Roy Campbell's 'Spauden' and 'MacSpaunday'; but it has been persistently seen in more recent criticism, with the most influential example being Samuel Hynes's 1976 book *The Auden Generation: Literature and Politics in England in the 1930s*. Its subtitle implies that the decade saw an association between the literary and the political which demarcates it from the 1920s, and one of the characteristics Hynes offers to justify such demarcation is the epoch's self-consciousness, whereby writers seem continually to be caught in the act of evolving their identities *as* 1930s writers. Thus he notes that Michael Roberts in a 1934 article claimed that the figure of 'the returning hero, the man who knows his own mind' in work by Auden, Charles Madge and Spender was 'the antithesis of Eliot's Prufrock'; commenting that 'it is part of the generation's growing sense of itself that it should see this break from the past, and from Eliot's example, in absolute and heroic terms' (1976: 150, 151). Although there was a sense of a group, tow-headed Auden was its *éminence blonde*: citing various contemporary tributes, Hynes asserts that 'by 1933 Auden was a larger-than-life figure in a movement that was political in general intention, but was religious in tone, and literary in its manifestation' (1976: 111–12); his was the most influential example of the period's evolution of private mythologies – made shareable by their application as parables – as means for addressing political issues.

Following a precursive chapter charting 'The Generation's Beginnings', Hynes's book follows the sequence of history, taking each successive year as a container for its literary productions, broadly contextualised against the backdrop of current events, with 1939–40 offering a kind of postscript. Although sceptical of the kind of recollection that treats the decade as if, like tragedy, all events conduced to its inexorable conclusion, he assembles persuasive contemporary evidence for a broadly held perception of the increasingly ominous momentum of events, coinciding with a particular sense of identity or mission: 'From about 1930, prediction of war, and anxieties about war, begin to enter English writing, and more and more frequently as the decade passes; and at the same time the younger generation began to write about itself *as* a generation' (1976: 61). This, he suggests, was largely informed by a Marxian view of the 'historical dialectic', whereby high Modernist distrust of history (Eliot's 'immense panorama of futility and anarchy' or Joyce's 'nightmare') gives way before a determinism implying programmatic structure to the sequence of events; such a view gained ascendancy during the early and middle thirties, but was in decline amongst the *literati* from 1937. One criticism of Hynes's study is that its implicit identification of 'politics' with left-wing attitudes endorses that routine conservatism supposing itself uncontaminated by political ideology (disreputable attribute of leftists or the fascistic right); a critic such as Smith has been consistently anxious to remove the cloak of invisibility within which a predominating right-wing political agenda has hidden its operations. Nevertheless, Hynes valuably adduces some consistent literary preoccupations in his survey, showing how various elements of the thirties 'myth' fell into place: he notes obsessions with frontiers, with heroic mountaineers, with a move towards documentary forms of notation, which privileged the ordinary or random and reached a kind of apotheosis in the Mass Observation project. He argues for the authority of Auden's presidency over the times, evidenced in the ' "Auden Country", that parabolic landscape that so dominated poetic imagination in the 'thirties' (1976: 55), and shows how Auden's symbolic geography was as important as notions of history, and offered a powerful interpretative template for some crucial experiences of the decade:

> The nature of the generations's new experience can be described best in terms of one of their dominant metaphors – the figure of the journey over the border that Auden had invented in his early poems. When these young travellers crossed over from France into Spain, they passed from the known world of peace to the unknown world of war, from the world of symbolic actions (the rhetoric, the resolutions, the protests and rallies) to the world of actual fighting and dying. Memoirs of English volunteers make much of the strangeness and emotional intensity of this passage: on one side of the border the familiar lives of ordinary men, on the other soldiers, passes, bullets, and uncertainty – all the fearful things that Auden had told them would be there, if they ventured far enough from security.
> (1976: 244)

Cunningham's more encyclopaedic survey offers a different model from Hynes's 'truly orthodox one' (1988: 16), whereby Auden's conceded significance ('clearly, in the period itself Auden and his group were regarded by very many of their contemporaries as the central figures', 1988: 17) is ascribed more to the fact that he echoed and expressed the *Zeitgeist*, rather than that he originated and influenced its attitudes. Arguing against any gulf between 'literature' and 'society', Cunningham promises that 'all texts and contexts will be thought of here as tending to lose their separate identities, collapsing purposefully into each other and existing rather as what we might call (con)texts'; invoking post-Saussurian semiotics, he asserts that 'A period of history and its literature are, like a language, most realistically to be seen as a sign-system, or a set of sign-systems, of signifying practices, composing a structural and structured whole' (1988: 1). His impatience with the canonical view represented by Hynes is extended, in a boisterous opening chapter, to include purely deconstructionist approaches, which reduce texts to 'mere plays of signifiers' (1988: 3) and drown out the contingent noise of history, as if reading were akin to the silently dissociated contention of chess grandmasters. The authority of his subsequent account derives from the massive quantity of evidence Cunningham brings to bear; and whilst Auden remains an unignorable presence, he finds himself as often in the dock as on the witness stand. Thus, for example, Cunningham asserts that Auden's revisionary view of the swooping aviator, in the sonnet-sequence of *Journey to a War*, found him inhabiting a position many others had already reached; and, unlike Hynes's view of Auden's status as pre-interpreter of the experience of the Spanish Civil War, for Cunningham, as already intimated, that conflict offered an arena in which Auden fell lamentably short; near the end of his book he offers a view that would not have been out of place in *Scrutiny*:

> His 'Spain' is miserable precisely because Spain has turned out to be no holiday. His poem is tensed unhappily between holidays: yesterday's 'brochure of winter cruises' and tomorrow's 'walks by the lake' and 'bicycle races/Through the suburbs on summer evenings'. And this poet, like many another tripper, flinched away, lest he too become one of the 'poets exploding like bombs'. Auden returned home disillusioned after only a few weeks in Spain. Returned, what's more, to teach for the summer term of 1937 at the Downs School that he'd left in 1935 to join the GPO film unit. Auden's period as political activist was over, and he'd chosen to mark it by re-entry into schoolmastering, deserting the destructive for the youthful element.
>
> (1988: 447)

Cunningham's 1930s Auden thus has some resemblances to 'the Hero (who never appears at all)' of *The Orators*; the traductive tendency audible in the passage above was disputed by Michael O'Neill and Gareth Reeves in *Auden, MacNeice, Spender: The Thirties Poetry* (1992):

> Throughout 'Spain' Auden seems to hear himself in the act of utterance. When Valentine Cunningham rebukes Auden's article 'Impressions of Valencia' . . . and, by implication, 'Spain' for a 'slick management of

> words that wilfully rebuffs any human connection with what is being described' . . ., he fails to see that Auden's 'slickness' in both article and poem bears witness to his acutely uneasy awareness that writing – about any subject – involves the 'management of words'. By highlighting his own such 'management' in 'Spain' Auden attains a difficult integrity, giving self-indulgence the slip by a hair's breadth.
>
> (1992: 210)

Distinguishing their own approach from Hynes's ('judicious') and Cunningham's ('pyrotechnical'), they seek a much less sweeping overview of the period, more attentive to the individual works which are the origin of critical enquiry, whilst at the same time trying to avoid making them make too much sense: 'we lay emphasis on the poems as linguistic events that often derail paraphrase', also avoiding any New Critical well-wrought urnestness by treating poems as 'experiences just as much as structures' (1992: 3). Their book does not seek to rival in breadth of coverage Hynes's, still less Cunningham's: their limited focus is signalled by the exclusion of Day-Lewis from any sustained attention, and they are disinclined to view poems as historico-cultural evidence; but their close readings are productive engagements. Among other things they offer some interesting analysis of the nature of early Auden's debt to Laura Riding (1992: 25–31) – which her partner, Robert Graves, saw as tantamount to plagiarism – suggesting her influence is seen not just in his combination of short lines with abstract imagery, but also at a thematic level: 'Riding's influence on Auden was not simply stylistic. The argument, central to her poetry, that present action is stalled because identity is inherited, must have impressed itself on Auden, especially as one of her poems, "The Map of Places", expresses the idea in terms of maps and ships' (1992: 30).

Other studies of 1930s Auden have set him in the context of particular working relationships, narrowing their focus to a specific segment of time and a specific activity. As its title suggests, Donald Mitchell's *Britten and Auden in the Thirties: The Year 1936* (1981) examines the brief period when the impressionable young composer and the impressive, slightly older poet worked alongside each other in theatre and on sound-track, most celebratedly on Grierson's *The Night Mail* (a colleague recalled Auden resembling a half-witted Norwegian deckhand, on location shoots). Michael Sidnell's *Dances of Death: The Group Theatre of London in the Thirties* (1984) takes in Auden and then Isherwood's association with Rupert Doone's company (Britten was also involved, and also found himself at times exasperated by Doone's attitudes); the photographs of productions suggest a certain 'Am.-Dram.' quality to some of the staging, for the Group Theatre could not afford expensive sets and costumes, but Doone was attempting to displace a somnolent naturalist tradition in the English theatre. As with his work for the GPO film-unit, the requirements of collaborative work caused Auden to produce what seem, encountered out of that adventitious context, to have been always intended as enduring gems, such as the first chorus of *Dogskin*, or 'Look, Stranger, at This Island Now'.

The historical and ideological circumstances inclining Auden towards such collaborations (with MacNeice as well) are touched on by Marsha Bryant in *Auden and Documentary in the 1930s* (1997). Like Hynes, she places the documentary movement in the context of a privileging of unvarnished presentation and a fascination with proletarian lives that are both traceable to socialist realism derived from Marx; she argues that 'Auden's industrial landscapes reflect his culture's documentary excursions into the working-class communities of Britain's North' (1997: 9). The ideological content is what distinguishes such activities from that of Victorian humanitarians, such as Mayhew, who equally 'transgressed class lines to establish contact with the working classes' (1997: 19); she sees Auden's participation in documentary modes not only in the work he undertook with the film-unit, but also evident in the techniques of 'Spain', as in the methodology of books such as *Letters from Iceland* and *Journey to a War*, with their assemblage of discrete kinds of information and inclusion of photographs. Auden himself, however, upset Grierson by publicly doubting that upper-middle-class directors could ever really understand the working-class existences they filmed (in a review of a book on documentary film: see *EA*: 354), and Bryant sees *Journey to a War* exhausting the possibilities of a documentary mode inescapably entwined with a concept of 'Britishness', as well as with conflicted attitudes: 'To what extent can documentary bear effective witness to some social inequalites while participating in others? For Auden, a gay man writing and photographing against the grain of dominant documentary practice, this contradiction became insurmountable by the end of the thirties' (1997: 170). In her account, Auden's emigration coincided with his abandonment of a now-distrusted methodology: 'After *Journey to a War* Auden separated his writing from documentary representation, abandoning photo-textual collaborations and eyewitness accounts for his more abstract ruminations of the 1940s' (1997: 172); his principal artistic collaborations thereafter were the libretti he co-authored with Kallmann – a mode as far removed as can easily be envisaged from the documentary.

This in itself might endorse Auden's own tendency to dismiss his earlier work; and the Cold War atmosphere in which many books about him were written – often by American academics – was one in which a denigration of left-wing politics came easily to pen. Yet Frank Kermode, reviewing the period in *History and Value* (1988), justly declared that 'it is surely to the credit of the intellectual left, now somewhat despised for *naïveté*, that they were so moved, that they came to believe that they must do something about the whole system that in their view made poverty and war equally inevitable' (1988: 47). Such a system, Kermode reminds us, imposed the infamous 'means test' for unemployment relief (which was experienced as a punishment for thrift), paid carefully calculated disability pensions to 2.5 million ex-servicemen ('16 shillings for a whole right arm, 14 shillings for an arm missing below the elbow, and so on'; 1988: 46), and ensured that '88 per cent of the population had less than £250 a year' (1988: 47). This did, however, mean that the 12 per cent were separated by a deep divide, and Kermode suggests another intellectual model than Marxism was relevant: 'In fact intellectuals invented Mass Observation to find how the workers lived and behaved, much as if they were a "primitive" tribe and the Observers anthropologists willing to learn a new language in return for knowledge of an alien culture' (1988: 47). Despite that estrangement and the imperfections of the methodology, Kermode disagrees with Auden's later self-estimations, which he castigates as promulgating a myth far more iniquitous than that of the 1930s: 'Auden's more substantial contribution to the myth of his own early failure is his wilful and, as I believe, imperceptive renunciation of his own work, his implied denunciation of himself as liar, fraud, or dupe' (1988: 73).

Other kinds of revisionist criticism have disputed the retrospective attribution of an unjustifiable importance to Auden, by approaches like Hynes's and Bergonzi's. In chapter 2 of *W.H. Auden: Contexts for Poetry* (2002), Peter Firchow sets forth the limitations of an 'Auden generation' view and justifications for an 'Auden group' one. John Lucas edited an attempt at displacement in *The 1930s: A Challenge to Orthodoxy* (1978), and Adrian Caesar in *Dividing Lines: Poetry, Class and Ideology in the 1930s* (1991) also contended that the overestimation of Auden's centrality skewed a proper assessment of the decade. Of the second, Cunningham has commented that 'seeking to replace the Auden Generation orthodoxy by merely substituting for it Rattenbury's *Left Review* crowd is much dafter' (1988: 17), and however alert Caesar's study is to the impermeability of class boundaries, Janet Montefiore points out that his book reproduces another kind of distortion in its account of the period, by under-representing writing by women. Her *Men and Women Writers of the 1930s* (1996) sets out to offer a corrective, but it is more than a matter of trying to instal new names on the honours board: 'To revive the work of women writers while acknowledging the historical and cultural context in which they wrote implies also examining the ways in which the collective memories of the 1930s have been constructed. This job is both helped and complicated by the fact that much of the writing of and about the 1930s is a self-conscious literature of personal memory' (1996: 2). She is not concerned to diminish the importance of Auden (and offers interesting commentary on 'Paid on Both Sides', 1996: 85–7), although she notes that his work, like Spender's and Isherwood's, tends 'to represent women as projections of a male subject's fears and desires – devouring mothers, dried-up spinsters, vamps, and an occasional pure maiden' (1996: 22). She notes how the constructions of the era prevailing at the time, and reinforced by subsequent literary historians, have been mythically inhospitable to the idea of a woman writer; but she is concerned to do justice, not only to neglected sisters, but also to genres of writing which have fallen on critical hard times:

> The choice of 'Socialist realism' as the proper form for progressive writers at the 1934 Congress of Soviet Writers has been taken as an ideological whipping-boy by people who don't bother to read Marxist novels, because they already know that these must be either boringly naturalistic slices of proletarian life, or else even more boring glorifications of grain silos in Kiev. Yet the Popular Front alliance of Communist and liberal intellectuals that produced a rebirth of rich and lively European historical fiction had its counterpart in England, where the record of anti-Fascist novels is, in fact, surprisingly long and distinguished.
>
> (1996: 143)

Auden and others

Whilst the 1930s and its literary associations have been the most durably influential contexts within which Auden has been viewed, some critics have been concerned to explore his broader affiliations. Thus Lucy McDiarmid, in *Saving Civilization* (1984), offers a study of 'Yeats, Eliot, and Auden Between the Wars', using as basis for comparison 'the conflict all three felt between a civic urge to become *engagé* and an artistic need to remain disengaged . . . All three sought to save civilization through some form of communal identity based on inherited myths, legends, and religious truths' (1984: xi). This common concern she sees as more significant than any ideological differences between these 'major voices of three different literary generations' (1984: xii). Although admitting Auden's consistently more sceptical attitude, she charts resemblances between the three, seen through their different ideas about a 'small circle' imagined as an ideal community ('Summer Night' is the earliest example from Auden), and also in their recourse to Dante as representative of an era of systematised wholeness, alongside a myth of 'an auditory golden age', involving 'a prelapsarian oral era and a "fall" into print' (1984: 62). In Auden's case, this led to an emphasis on the 'living voice' – seen in the title of his *Poet's Tongue* anthology and its opening affirmation of poetry as 'memorable *speech*' (my emphasis) – but which was also accompanied (as in the title *The Orators*) by a balancing awareness of the voice of the demagogue. She helpfully sees Auden's forays into theatre as attempts to achieve immediacy of linguistic relation within a communal context; but, despite the longer timespan of her study, she reinforces the division between 1930s Auden and his later self by arguing that his renunciation of the theatre (most clearly seen when he turned Shakespeare's *Tempest* into a poem) accompanied a turning away from the living voice with which his work of that decade had been preoccupied:

> How far – and how consciously so – Auden had come from the thirties' poet who spoke of surrendering to the 'audible spoken word . . . as we do when talking to an intimate friend', when he writes, 'That is one of the wonderful things about the written word; it cannot speak until it is spoken to . . . thank God for books as an alternative to conversation'.
> (1984: 90)

Other critics have invoked the context of Yeats: Smith sees Auden undertaking 'Oedipal dialogues' with him, and Edward Callan, in *Auden: A Carnival of Intellect* (1983), suggests that 'much of the story of Auden's development as a poet after 1940 is also the story of his struggle to exorcise the persistent spirit of Yeats' (1983: 145). In 1972 Francois Duchêne even gestured towards Pound ('Only Ezra Pound comes anywhere near Auden in the mixed feelings he arouses. Such feelings have done a great deal to devalue Auden's reputation since its palmy days in the . . . Thirties', 1972: 9); but beyond his 1930s collaborators and contemporaries it is unsurprising to find that Eliot is the commonest comparator: not only was his the dominant influence in Modernist poetry, but the superficial contours of Auden's career, by which a challenging innovator turned away from early radicalism, switched nationalities and became an Anglo-Catholic, also echoed Eliot's. Scarfe's study had dwelt on Auden's indebtedness to Eliot, and later Duchêne expresses what was the received wisdom of his period when stating that 'it is presumptuous to set Auden's work on a par with Eliot's' (1932: 161); but in recent times more sympathetic appraisals of the former and less respectful appraisals of the latter have rendered questionable Eliot's pre-eminence. Unlike many, Auden was in thrall to Eliot's influence for a comparatively brief if formative period; where Eliot had gone to Baudelaire, Laforgue and the Elizabethans and Jacobeans to bypass the stultifying legacy of Victorian forbears, Auden's eclectic style-models included Eliot himself, supplemented by American women like Dickinson, Riding, even Stein; and his own means of evading Eliot's powerful example lay in reaching back to English poetic traditions pre-dating Eliot's 'undissociated' seventeenth century, to which he had been introduced at Oxford. Grigson, writing for Spender's *Tribute* (1975), recalled an early poem in which Auden visualised 'the blood-trail which had dripped from Grendel after his arm and shoulder had been ripped off by Beowulf'; it was as if the untidy Christ Church undergraduate 'had given imaginative place and "reality" to something exploited for the Examination Schols, yet rooted in English origins' (1975: 13–14). Chris Jones has recently argued that 'Auden's importance is that he is the first Saxonising poet to be widely accepted within the mainstream of British poetic tradition and to hand back to that tradition an Old English poetic which does not call great attention to itself' (Jones 2002: 167–8).

As its title suggests, Lachlan MacKinnon argues differently in *Eliot, Auden, Lowell: Aspects of the Baudelairean Inheritance* (1983), where he discusses the particular relation each has to 'the peculiarly modern problem of belief' (1983: 1). This 'problem' is partly answered by the kind of serious dandyism exemplified by the French poet: 'Art not as an end in itself; life as a quest for the transcendent which will offer self-knowledge; the poet as hero of that quest; the quest conceived principally in relation to the Christian religious and cultural traditions' (1983: 2–3). He sees important differences between Eliot and Auden, connected to the ways in which each configured for himself poetry's relation to the modern problem of belief; in Eliot's case this led to an *impasse*: '*Four Quartets* is Eliot's last major poem because it rests on validity rather than sincerity as a criterion. Sincerity is for the moment, validity is for all time. Another major work would have betrayed it as merely another pose' (1983: 47). The self-authentication involved in poetry-writing was always more crucial for Eliot than for Auden, whose belief in 'light verse' and conviction that poetry could never seriously rival religion committed him to a poetics of sincerity rather than validity: 'Auden renders each poem flawless: yet poetry is always, insistently, lesser than truth. Auden's dandyism protects and sustains his solitude in the presence of that truth' (1983: 92). Such attitudes underlay his lifelong productiveness: 'He achieved the continued poetry which Eliot could not by realising that his position was essentially comic. All significances point to God: they legitimise a fecundity of self-repetition' (1983: 92).

A consideration of Eliot's last poems leads to a closing chapter on 'Eliot and Auden' in Steve Ellis's *The English Eliot: Design, Language and Landscape in* Four Quartets (1991). Whilst reasserting Eliot's poetic significance during the 1930s, in which decade literary criticism has tended to prioritise Auden, he also extends the observation made by Everett and others, that a mark of Auden's stature is that his style can be seen to have influenced Eliot's:

> The major import to Eliot from Auden . . . was the abundant use of the definite article; indeed, this 1930s mannerism was favoured by

> many poets. There is, however, some confusion over who originated it; Bergonzi and [Rostrevor] Hamilton both see Eliot himself, in 'Ash-Wednesday', as the inventor, and point to lines like 'The vanished power of the usual reign' and 'The infirm glory of the positive hour' from the first part of that poem. In the collection brought out by Spender in 1928, however, Auden already has lines displaying the characteristic impersonality and rhythmic self-containment we associate with such a usage, as in 'The heel upon the finishing blade of grass'.
>
> (1991: 145)

Ellis gives other examples to support his case – and notes that Trotter, in the book already cited, also sees Auden having influenced Eliot. His larger argument is concerned to differentiate Eliot's notions of England from Auden's, despite surface similarities which he relates to Eliot's doctrine of classicism: 'the "classic" elements in Auden's work . . . which make for a formalism akin to Eliot's are in fact offset by what one might call abundant local detail and "ornamentation", these latter elements representing a resistance to the type of centrism displayed in the *Quartets*' (1991: 152). Nevertheless, noting the 'extraordinary allegiance in his work to both classic form and non-conformist detail' (1991: 162), Ellis hesitates 'to salute Auden as the voice of freeedom and plurality in opposition to the monologic emphases of Eliot. In spite of the individualistic components of Auden's picture, there remains an ambitious urge towards totality that seeks out some detached, omnipotent prospect whence all of England, History, or the World is magisterially surveyed'. Finally he sees them as mirror-images: 'Ultimately the all-inclusive England is but the reverse of the all-exclusive one; that which gives the work of these poets its immense power is in part . . . intellectually and politically specious' (1991: 164). As a comment on the ambiguities of early Auden this is supported by Nicholas Jenkins's assertion in 'Auden in America': 'For a while, whatever his professed Leftism, Auden offered his readers an intensely realised lyric version of English belonging, subtly but indelibly tinged with the aura of a potentially violent, regenerative nationalism. Wholeness and integration, to the young Auden, were at once philosophical, social and imaginative ideals. Correspondingly, his work of this period is filled with emblems of social totality and cognitive completeness' (*Cambridge Companion to W.H. Auden* ed. Smith 2004: 40 – hereafter cited as *CCWHA*). He sees this, however, as a phase which necessitated and was transcended by Auden's expatriation, arguing that nearly all critics 'have overlooked the depth and thoroughness of Auden's critique of that most modern marker of personal identity, nationality' (p. 44): a matter presumably to be rectified in his forthcoming book *The Island: W.H. Auden and the Making of a Post-National Poetry*.

Mendelson has argued that Auden, whilst respecting Eliot, often disputed the older poet's ethical and religious views (*LA*: 150n), and Hecht defines his attitude to Eliot as 'interestingly equivocal' (Hecht 1993: 196). Jenkins cites the poet Richard Eberhart in 1939 reporting Auden as having in conversation contrasted his own crossing of the Atlantic with Eliot's, who had sought 'a truly old world', whereas *he* came in search of 'new attitudes, a place for growth' (*CCWHA*: 45). If, following his lead, critics have tended to discriminate Auden from Eliot, grounds for comparison have also been advanced, as by John Bayley in his study

The Romantic Survival (1957), where he attributes to both an 'enormous self-consciousness', of which 'deprecation' in Eliot and 'irony' in Auden are the symptoms (1957: 144). But whereas Eliot's deprecation (summed up by *East Coker*'s self-dismissive 'That was a way of putting it – not very satisfactory') is effective antidote to the magic whose effects Auden invariably reproaches art for simulating, his own irony does not; and for Bayley this leaves the magical sources of Auden's poetic potency unexorcised. This in turn implies Romantic attitudes surviving in him; Bayley – whose suggestion was endorsed by Everett in her study of the poet – notes the significance of the childhood memories that surface in the work; and this point was also offered by MacKinnon as one reason for Auden's continuing productivity: 'This ability to remain fecund was underwritten by a renewed contact with the imaginative world of his childhood, now approached consciously rather than naively' (1983: 92). Received wisdom has tended to follow Auden's consistent discrimination of his own attitudes from Romantic idealism – especially as embodied in Shelley's intermixing of the spiritual with the political – as has been set forth by Alan Jacobs in *What Became of Wystan: Change and Continuity in Auden's Poetry* (1998: chapter 2). For Callan, too, '[Auden's] later American work expresses a conviction that Romanticism's deification of the imaginative original genius spawned the modern totalitarian dictator, whether of the left or of the right' (1983: 15); he prefers a different set of associates: 'Auden is more aptly classed in the company of Pope and Wren, whose names recall an age' (1983: 8). In *The Problem of Consciousness in Modern Poetry* (1992), Hugh Underhill notes Bayley's suggestion, but offers another line of connection: 'One way of seeing Auden (especially the later Auden) is as a twentieth-century example of the Horatian poet, essentially urban in sensibility, a category to which his friend and follower Louis MacNeice also belongs' (1992: 70). *What Became of Wystan* devotes a chapter to exploring Auden's Horatianism.

Early Auden – later Auden

Jacobs's (1998) title alludes to the question posed by Larkin's notoriously critical review; and any study of the entirety of Auden's career, or any sustained focus on the poetry written after his emigration, has to confront it. Although Mendelson can write dismissively about poems he does not admire, the underlying contention of *Later Auden* (1999) is that the poetry grew in stature, and that this can partly be related to the replacement of Auden's 1930s gesturally experimental ideologies by intellectual positions evolved rather than adopted, more cogently considered and more deeply inhabited. These new attitudes were connected with the Anglicanism to which the poet re-declared allegiance almost simultaneously as he withdrew it, apparently, from England; thus one way of describing the change was to view it as entailing replacement of his social or political concerns by religious ones. This has by some been seen as implying the loss of Auden's true subject; but Bozorth has described Auden as, alongside Eliot, 'one of the most important English-language religious poets of the last hundred years' (*CCWHA*: 175), so for others gain was also evident.

In his biography, Carpenter (1981) stressed the intellectual, rather than the spiritual, character of the poet's conversion; in 'Auden and religion', Gareth

Reeves comments that whilst this was congruent with the categorical cast of his thinking, it led towards the Kierkegaardian crux that 'rationality eventually involved the recognition that Christianity paradoxically requires the exhaustion of all reasonable explanations and a leap of faith into the unknown and unreasonable' (*CCWHA*: 189; this essay also includes an interesting discussion of 'Horae Canonicae'). Mendelson (1999) draws attention to a 'long, often magnificent prose piece' Auden wrote in 1970–1, which he cannibalised but never finalised, titled 'Work, Carnival and Prayer'; and this is given some prominence in Arthur Kirsch's study of *Auden's Christianity* (2005). Like Bozorth, Kirsch sees the 'extraordinary' fusion of 'erotic and religious imagery' in Auden's imagination, and also notes that his 'relentless exploration of the duality of the self was a function of his own particular temperament, but . . . also increasingly a form of religious meditation' (2005: 23–4, 158–9). Noting the resentment of Auden's expatriation evident in some English circles, he also suspects that a resentment of his Christianity equally produced an undervaluation of the later work:

> Auden's restraint of his vast lyric powers and his consequent disciplinary focus upon metrical virtuosity, as well as the revisions of his poems and canon, may also be understood as acts of religious humility, acknowledgments that poetry is not magical or sacred, and that like all things of this world it is a vanity. Auden's doubts about his art are Christian doubts, and the American Auden is emphatically a Christian Auden – which may be yet another, and often unacknowledged, reason for the depreciation of the achievement of his later poetry.
>
> (2005: 170)

That the religious Auden should not be seen as radically discontinuous with the 1930s writer was argued by Monroe Spears in *The Disenchanted Island* (1963), which was the first extended systematic analysis of the career and, despite being written during the poet's lifetime, remains of interest. The opening pages of Part III, 'Religion and Longer Poems', offers a helpful exposition of what is acknowledged as a 'shift in perspective' but not as a reversal: 'Auden's religious position is not a denial but a fulfillment of his earlier beliefs' (1963: 171). 'It is no accident', Spears continues, 'that his religious approach should be existential, for this type of religious philosophy starts from the same kind of psychological analysis that had formed the perduring basis of Auden's various attitudes and convictions' (1963: 172). Quoting extensively from Auden's untitled essay in *Canterbury Pilgrims* (ed. Pike, 1956) – in which he defined the preachings of Blake, Lawrence, Freud and Marx by which he had once been influenced as 'Christian heresies' – Spears sets forth the importance of Kierkegaard, 'whose influence is apparent in Auden's work far more often than that of any other writer' (1963: 177), even though Auden felt that Kierkegaard undervalued the importance of human corporeality. Whereas for Eliot Anglo-Catholicism sat alongside 'Royalism' and 'Classicism' as an attitude hierarchically driven, Spears emphasises Auden's ecumenical aspect: 'An Anglo-Catholic whose attitude is basically existentialist, he interprets the existential tradition with maximum catholicity' (1963: 177–8). Quoting from Auden's 1944 'Preface to Kierkegaard', he shows how his philosophical and religious beliefs involve what I would call historical 'situatedness' (in many ways the obverse of Eliot's contention in *Burnt Norton* that 'To be conscious is not to be in time'):

> In contrast to those philosophers who begin by considering the *objects* of human knowledge, essences and relations, the existential philosopher begins with man's immediate experience as a *subject*, i.e., as a being in *need*, an *interested* being whose existence is at stake.

Cognition, for these thinkers, is always a historical act, accompanied by hope and fear; not something performed by a timeless, disinterested 'I'. Existentialism, says Auden, is not a surrender to relativism, but an attempt to begin the search for a common truth by being honest about this subjectivity. The relation of the theological, psychological and political realms for the Christian existentialist he states thus:

> From this viewpoint, the basic human problem is man's anxiety in time; e.g., his present anxiety over himself in relation to his past and his parents (Freud), his present anxiety over himself in relation to his future and his neighbors (Marx), his present anxiety over himself in relation to eternity and God (Kierkegaard).
>
> (1963: 178)

For Lucy McDiarmid in *Auden's Apologies for Poetry* (1990), although the religious turn to Auden's thinking became clearly audible from the early 1940s, there had been predictive hints in earlier work, such as 'Summer Night' and even 'Paid on Both Sides'. What happened in America, however, was that his religion had decisive consequences for his theory of art: 'The significance for Auden's poetics was enormous. If all human activities were religiously grounded, no such activity (for instance, poetry) was itself expected to provide absolute truths. The notion that poetry could and ought to provide absolutes constituted the central position that Auden's poetics argued against for the rest of his life' (1990: 10). Thus her later discussion of 'The Shield of Achilles' sees its exposure of the limits of art as the major statement of his postwar aesthetics, where the subject turns out to be 'art's own inabilities'. Her argument here focuses on the third view of the shield:

> The lines . . . describe primarily what cannot be on the shield. It is certainly possible to show a ragged urchin alone in a weed-choked field and a bird in the sky above him: but how could a shield show 'axioms' in a child's mind, and how indeed could it show *what he has never heard of*? These notions exist in an abstract and hypothetical dimension that cannot be made pictorial; and so, the poem implies, the spiritual cannot be depicted in poetry or in any work of art. Just as dimensions are missing in the visual arts, a dimension is missing in language. Why describe in language . . . what cannot possibly be on the shield, if not to dramatize that the qualities he has never heard of, commitment and sympathy, can never be in a work of art?
>
> If art is not wish-fulfilment, as Thetis assumes, what is it? Auden in the 1950s would say, a means of disenchantment, through which our

> expectations for the absolute are answered with the contingent and derivative. If art's subject is always its own incapacities, then it will always disenchant those who come to it seeking the fulfillment of their wishes. The notion of disenchantment is built into an art that dramatizes what it cannot do.
>
> (1990: 130)

In *Auden's Poetry* (1969), Justin Replogle also stresses continuities underlying what he calls Auden's 'pattern of ideas', whereby his 'entire intellectual development' can be seen to occur within 'the tradition of post-Hegelian Germanic thought' (1969: 6), which encompasses thinkers as superficially diverse as Freud, Marx and Kierkegaard. At the beginning of his study he helpfully discusses the nature of Auden's debts to figures such as Lawrence and Groddeck, where again he finds connection: 'Groddeck's self-mocking discourse, in fact, is somewhat like Kierkegaard's, and the comedy of these two Germanic dialecticians surely plays its part in attracting a poet addicted throughout his life to horseplay and the burlesque, who would ultimately make comic self-mockery his habitual manner' (1969: 10–11). Replogle clearly sees Auden's progress as improvement, describing 'The Sea and the Mirror' as his 'first masterpiece' marking his 'greatest achievement – comedy. Soon after Caliban, nearly all Auden's poetry becomes comic' (1969: 149). This accompanies, in Replogle's view, an abandonment of poetry concerned with ideas – 'the poetry after 1951 is less *about* ideas than at any time in his career' (1969: 89) – nor even with the religion which had dominated his middle period: 'Though clearly descended from and rooted in religious beliefs, Auden's poetry after 1950 can be called almost completely secular again' (1969: 85). The tone of comic acceptance which Replogle hears in the late work is somewhat differently represented by McDiarmid, who reads it as a continuous exposure of poetry's inadequacy by one who had once hoped for too much:

> Ultimately, all Auden can do to indicate spiritual value is to talk about his own and poetry's inabilities. Every poem becomes an apology, undermining its own significance and alluding to the value it cannot contain. Barnaby [in 'The Ballad of Barnaby', 1968] could at least tumble before a holy icon responsive to his efforts, redeeming his frivolous art. Auden's later poetry anticipates no such redemption for itself: 'I dare not ask you if you bless the poets,' he coyly says to Clio, 'Nor do I see a reason why you should' . . . Clio can be invoked and praised, but she will never say, 'Well have you tumbled . . .'
>
> (1990: 12)

This, echoing Auden's own view of poetry as 'small beer', almost makes the later work sound like a retreat from earlier ambitions as he changed himself into a 'minor' poet. Frederick Buell's *W.H. Auden as a Social Poet* (1973) attempted to argue for a continuity of serious aspiration in Auden's writing, beyond what he regards as its speciously political manifestation in the 1930s. 'His concern with writing social verse did not cease' (1973: 7), but from the 1940s on Auden adopted a 'self-consciously apolitical standpoint', by means of which he became 'spokesman for a half-mythical group of right-minded, well-meaning, harried citizens of the modern bureaucratic, philistine age', united with them by a shared dislike of 'the "managers" who control such a society' (1973: 8). Buell's concern to demonstrate that the informing spirit of the 1930s survives into the later work, however, leads him to a concentration on that decade's work which somewhat undermines his case. Something similar is observable in Firchow (2002), whose discussion of Auden's 'contexts', whilst offering (for example) interesting consideration of the importance of Homer Lane as filtered by Layard, especially with regard to *The Orators* (2002: 106–16), rather runs out of steam once Auden has expatriated, as if disabled by a critical equivalent of the 'astonishing absence – the utter and complete absence – of depictions of natural landscape in Auden's poems placed in an American setting' (2002: 183). A view akin to Buell's, that Auden moved from socialist to social sympathies, is in essence propounded by Jacobs (1998), who sees a major effort of his post-England verse lying in its conscious construction of 'a community of friends and colleagues that he sustains and memorializes through his poetry'; noting the high number of poems dedicated to personal acquaintances, he asserts that 'a chief purpose of Auden's later poetry becomes the making of a permanent record of the nature and history of his friendships, that is to say, his community' (1998: 68). This is presumably different from the mutual dedications of the 1930s 'Auden gang', whose purpose was more to define an in-crowd or group of defiant outsiders. Jacobs defines as a key genre the menippean satire, whose 'carnivalesque spirit' informs Auden's light verse, 'neither nihilistic nor cynical, nor even necessarily skeptical' (1998: 111); and as in the title of Callan's book, in MacKinnon's theory of dandyism, in the 'comic self-mockery' Replogle finds, and in Hecht's noting Auden's 'lively and continuing interest in poetry as a linguistic "game" ' and his consistently held 'notion of the frivolity of art' (1993: 440, 442), there is a sense that, as Smith has put it, 'For Auden, silliness was part of the whole show' (*CCWHA*: 97).

Auden theorised

Smith goes on to observe that 'in recent years Auden has attracted wide critical attention for the hermeneutic indeterminacy, ludic iconoclasm and polymorphously deconstructive nature of writings, in the words of a late poem, "modern only in this – our lack of decorum" ' (*CCWHA*: 99). In 1968 Auden read Mikhail Bakhtin's *Rabelais and His World*, whose notions of 'carnivalesque' subsequently reverberated in the title of 'Work, Carnival and Prayer'; but as Boly points out in an essay on 'Auden and modern theory', the theoretical systems with which he principally engaged had been Marxian and Freudian – although he also observes that Auden's skills as analyser and decoder of a culture's dominants potentially align him with a continuity of ideas stretching before and after:

> The origins of Auden's cultural theory belong to an intellectual tradition that includes Kant's categories of the understanding, Marx's superstructure, Heidegger's *Dasein*, Gramsci's hegemony, Saussure and Lévi-Strauss's *langue*, Foucault's *epistème*, Raymond Williams's dominant discourse and Fredric Jameson's political unconscious.
>
> (*CCWHA*: 138)

Boly also notes that the prevailing literary-critical discourse in the America to which Auden translated himself was that of 'New Criticism'; and although he would have found congenial its emphasis on close reading, its tendency to regard the poem as a 'verbal icon' somehow elevated beyond historical contingency, and made to serve what Boly describes as 'patriarchal self-righteousness' (*CCWHA*: 142), was hostile to much that he affirmed. New Criticism typically addressed itself to well-wrought urns of lyric length, anathematising any ideological *parti pris* as artistic impurity; in this regard, the 'lack of decorum' of Auden's later poetry consisted in its length, discursiveness and Christian inflections – and in the persistent refusal of his shorter poems to be hermetically enclosed, self-consciously clever, or manifestly important utterances.

The majority of critical studies of Auden have been historically based expositions of his development, showing the evolution of his art and thought in the context of successive belief-systems with which he intersected; although Auden criticism, particularly since his death, has not been theoretically innocent, much of it has not taken a theoretical perspective as its starting-point. The most overtly theorised books about him have been written by Smith (1985), Boly (1991), Emig (1999) and, within the ambit of gender studies, Bozorth (2001). As seen earlier (see Works, **p. 96**), Boly is concerned to view poems as something other than a means whereby an author's meaning is delivered to 'the reader, a convenience at once indispensable and preposterous'; which 'historical being' he would prefer replaced by 'textual functions' such as 'effigy' or 'auditor' (2001: 76): the first is a compliant 'good recipient', the second is altogether less amenable, and inclined to resist routine dominance by any 'poetic voice' (2001: 158). If 'the poet' writes for an effigy who will receive 'an indubitable truth', 'the scriptor' by contrast authorises polysemy: 'from the standpoint of the scriptor, a good poem must break that trance of meaning and provoke inscriptive responses' (2001: 171). Auden's major effort Boly sees in a renunciation of any Prosperian or Romantic 'visionary/communicative role', in favour of a method 'dedicated to a play of contrasts rather than a serious expression of final truth' (2001: 47). This in turn strategically serves his perception that 'human freedom begins in an understanding of the discursive techniques through which well-entrenched social interests attempt to supervise meaning and truth' (2001: 45). The result is a 'ludic' writing whose social purpose is precisely to liberate its reader from subordination to such communicative intent, thereby subverting 'the culture of late capitalism' and its impatience with 'impractical activity', its ingrained belief that only instrumental communication can have value (2001: 49).

Emig, arguing that Auden 'paves the way for a poetics of postmodernism', is also concerned with indeterminacies, and offers a new perception of 'Auden country': 'the particularly new poetic territory exposed by Auden's writings is that which leads out of modernism into something uncharted, into a region where the only orientation is provided by images of borders, folds and ruptures' (1999: 3). With regard to the early verse, he contends that the 'absence of a definable meaning' operates as a 'calculated strategy' whereby 'Auden's poetic technique . . . puts into practice what Ferdinand de Saussure formulates theoretically as the arbitrariness of the sign' (1999: 15). This position is one which, however, later exposes the lack in Auden's poetry of what, after Lyotard, Emig terms 'underlying narratives of legitimation' (1999: 86); after his emigration, by which he evaded 'the Oedipal trap of Englishness' (1999: 128), a resolution is found, as 'the dialogic principle becomes dominant in Auden's poetry, a principle that develops interacting voices out of the dissenting and conflicting ones of his earlier poetry' (1999: 136), so that ultimately 'Auden's poems transform themselves into a writing of negotiation, openness, compromise, and dialogue' (1999: 204) – which tetradic formulation might, I suppose, equally describe Chamberlain's behaviour at Munich, although here presented as postmodernistic *desiderata*.

That the Auden whose work is the subject of critical interpretation is likely to be the creature of critical desiring is a fact directly confronted by Smith:

> The Auden we perceive as a historical figure is also the product of discourses which run through and beyond him. There was (no doubt about it) a poet called W.H. Auden. There is a general consensus that he did certain things, lived in certain places, and wrote certain texts. But the meaning of those events, like the meanings of those texts, is not perpetually fixed in history, unchangeably inscribed in the record. When we come to read Auden, we must be alert to the fact that we can, in reality, only *re*read him. The poems he produced have been rewritten by the historical process, as he himself acknowledged when he sought, with hindsight, to modify, censor and repress some of them. But Auden the historical subject has been rewritten too. . . . There is no original meaning we can recover, only the play of language in our own moment of history, interlocking with the play of language of texts which have a certain antiquity, but are nevertheless our contemporaries, waiting for their ideal reader – a perpetually deferred and imaginary subject.
>
> (1985: 5–6)

Such perceptions underlay Bryant's use of the phrase 'the signifier "Auden" '; for Smith, the work's indeterminacies are effectively rhetorical models of dissent from speciously unifying (and typically conservative) discursive practices seeking to instal the signifier 'England' as cultural dominant: 'The unitary subject and the unitary nation are alike mythical beasts, traversed by a class struggle that may abate from time to time, but never ceases' (1985: 216). His Auden is a poet of consistent political engagement whose alertness to such perceptions did not relax, and in respect of whose life and work – to allude to 'Address for a Prize-day' – the issue is, unavoidably, what it means to us here and now, rather than what it can have meant there and then.

Bozorth, by contrast, suggests that the real subject of Auden's 1930s poetry was 'his own inability to address politics meaningfully' (2001: 141); but, candidly, he too admits that 'like any other, this book's construction of Auden reflects my own needs and desires' (2001: 256), which involve situating Auden in the context of his homosexuality. Gregory Woods, in *Articulate Flesh: Male Homo-eroticism and Modern Poetry* (1987) had included a chapter on Auden that insisted on the importance of recognising this; Bozorth goes further in analysing ways in which it is the qualifying element from which his poetry emerged. This is despite the fact that whilst at first Auden was necessarily reticent, with age he became prudishly censorious and, unlike Isherwood – whose latterly unapologetic assertion of his homosexual identity made him an iconic figure for Gay Rights and gay writers

– considered his own sexual orientation to be wrong. Bozorth's title derives from Auden's definition of two theories of poetry in an essay written in 1947, 'Squares and Oblongs': one sees poetry as 'a magical means for inducing desirable emotions and repelling undesirable emotions', the second, as 'a game of knowledge, a bringing to consciousness, by naming them, of emotions and their hidden relationships' (*P II*: 345). This sense of the transactions between covert and overt kinds of knowing leads, Bozorth argues, to Auden's 'coded poetry', which offers 'a proto-Barthesian textual erotics – a sign system for exploring and representing homosexual desire. But while the secret agent embodies the seductive power of semiotic instability, Auden also portays the secret agent as victim of the duplicity in which he traffics' (1987: 20).

Bozorth opens his account referring to Auden's peripheral involvement in the scandal of British double-agent Guy Burgess's 1951 defection to Moscow; Firchow, too, explores the reality underlying images of espionage in Auden's work: not only was he acquainted with several persons who turned out to have been Soviet agents (Burgess, Blunt, Driberg), he knew people with connections to British Intelligence (Graham Greene, Malcolm Muggeridge), and his co-editor of the multi-volume *Poets of the English Language* (1950), Norman Holmes Pearson, then a Yale professor, had been wartime head of American counterintelligence in Britain (scathingly alluded to in 'Under Which Lyre'). Firchow shrewdly cites Auden's interrogator's atttitude to literary criticism: 'What kind of guy inhabits this poem? . . . What does he conceal from the reader? What does he conceal even from himself?' (*DH*: 50–1; the interinvolvement of culture and clandestine operations was later made embarrassingly public for Spender, in revelations that *Encounter*, the magazine he co-edited for a number of years, was actually bankrolled by the CIA in order to promote American values).

For Bozorth, if in the earlier work he created 'a textual arena in which the reader is forced to think like a spy because the poet is one himself' (1987: 30), later, 'Auden came to treat poetry itself as a kind of lovers' discourse: a site of intimate relation between poet and reader' (1987: 175). His sexual circumstances not only prefigured the ways in which he wrote about religious concerns ('Auden's games of knowledge use sexually coded tropes of angularity and crookedness to render the relation between the human and the divine', 1987: 14), they also preconfigured what became recognised as 'Auden country', for 'social forces of censorship and the closet come together in the characteristic topography of Auden's early work. Its source lay partly in the northern English landscape Auden knew as a child, and in later years he read his ideal landscape in more or less psychological and erotic terms' (1987: 25). Thus the response to and use of 'nature' in Auden's early work has radically unWordsworthian issue: 'In place of a redemptive drama of the recovery of psychic coherence and common humanity in Nature, Auden's landscape poems offer a revelation of alienation and social difference' (1987: 39). Auden's use of landscape has been most closely explored by Callan, when relating the action of 'Paid on Both Sides' to actual locations, and more recently a pamphlet (Myers and Forsythe 1999) has begun the work of exploring Auden's references to Pennine places, found in both early and later writing. Paola Marchetti (2001) has considered the symbolic aspects of Auden's 'landscapes of meaning'.

Poets' Auden

For Tom Paulin, however, one of Auden's significant achievements has been to enforce a perception that 'the admiration of landscape as significantly beautiful in itself is both boring and antisocial' ('*Letters from Iceland*: Going North', in Lucas 1978: 59). Including MacNeice, Paulin notes that 'the total effect of their work, and especially of *Letters from Iceland*, is to make it impossible to read a volume of nature or rural poetry (especially by any poet writing after the Second World War) without being affected by a peculiar feeling of emptiness' (1978: 75). Although he finds the social and political aspects of Auden's work congenial, his sense of that war's constituting a watershed of taste may also entail the view that it marked the point of no return for Auden's poetry: this seems to underlie the poem 'Somewhere to Get to' in Paulin's 2002 volume about the war, *The Invasion Handbook*, which turns Auden's imagery and vocabulary against him, closing with the oblique reproach of an airman shot down over the North Sea where now, a fallen Icarus, he bobs in a fragile life-raft. When bombing started you became, he tells Auden, 'eloquently dumb', 'quite an important failure', whose linguistic estrangement entails impoverishment and loss: 'the language you process now/ like chewing gum/has no kick no kick in it at all' (2002: 82).

Paulin is one of many contemporary poets who address Auden's work in criticism as well as in poems, following the pattern set in the 1930s by Spender, Day-Lewis, Empson and MacNeice; this attests to the continuing importance his writing has for fellow-practitioners. The kind of attention paid is sometimes pugnacious or prejudiced, and occasionally wrong; but it is usually lively, and productively unconstrained by scholarship's habitual cautiousness: I want to close with a brief survey. The roll-call of younger poets who have written about Auden is impressive and includes, as well as those already named, two Nobel laureates (Heaney and Joseph Brodsky), as well as successors to his Oxford chair (Peter Levi and James Fenton). As noted, influential voices on each side of the Atlantic have felt that somehow Auden's emigration entailed deterioration of his work, and Philip Larkin at the outset of the 1960s judged: 'At one stroke he lost his key subject and emotion – Europe and the fear of war – and abandoned his audience together with their common dialect and concerns. For a different sort of poet this might have been less important. For Auden it seems to have been irreparable' (Haffenden 1983: 416). Larkin has been taken to task by Fenton for writing a review calculated to demoralise its recipient, in a betrayal of poets' *esprit de corps* made worse by the fact of Larkin's being 'deeply indebted' to his senior (see his foreword to Clark's *Wystan and Chester* (1995)). Thom Gunn, himself a gay US-domiciled English poet with a stylistic debt to Auden, reviewed and disliked the same volume, but disagreed with any diagnosis of general decline; nevertheless, poets who write about Auden often prefer his earlier work. According to Firchow, this holds true for American as for British writers, for 'insofar as one can generalize usefully about Auden's influence on American poetry at all, that influence undoubtedly derives more immediately and noticeably from the work of the young or English Auden than it does from the older American one . . ., so that we are left with the rather odd and anticlimactic conclusion that the American Auden had relatively little impact on the work of the following generation of American poets. Only the English Auden did' (2002:

194). This is borne out, for example, by John Berryman's remembering, in his poem 'Shirley and Auden', that as a young man he 'recognized Auden at once as a new master', this early love surviving Auden's 'facile bodiless later books' (1971: 16).

Vivid testimony to the impact Auden could have in the USSR has been given by Brodsky in his 1983 memorial essay, where he recalled first reading the elegy for Yeats when exiled to 'a small village lost among swamps and forests, near the polar circle' (1986: 361): 'I remember sitting there in the small wooden shack, peering through the square porthole-sized window at the wet, muddy, dirt road with a few stray chickens on it, half believing what I'd just read, half wondering whether my grasp of English wasn't playing tricks on me. . . . I guess I was still refusing to believe that way back in 1939 an English poet had said, "Time . . . worships language", and yet the world around was still what it was' (1986: 363). Auden disliked being an object of veneration – he was embarrassed when Allen Ginsberg attempted to 'kiss the hem of his garment' – and so might have been discomfited to know that the young Russian poet whom he later met and helped would subsequently shower him with superlatives such as 'the most humble poet of the English language' (1986: 329) or 'the greatest mind of the twentieth century' (1986: 357); whilst it is true that Brodsky, here and in his preceding close analysis of 'September 1, 1939', is sometimes inaccurate (inventing a poem called 'The Ballad of St Barnaby', for example, or alleging that 'Letter to Lord Byron' employs *ottava rima*), there is a beguiling magnificence in his response – even if his answer to Auden's critical question 'What kind of guy inhabits this poem?' tends fulsomely to be (when the poem is by Auden): 'My hero'.

Many poets writing about Auden tend to recall, as Brodsky does, the first encounter; this is frequently represented as a *coup de foudre*, so that Jarrell in 1955 asked, 'has Auden ever again written quite so well as he was writing at the beginning of the 'thirties, in *Poems* and "Paid on Both Sides"? He wrote, then, some of the strongest, strangest, and most original poetry that anyone has written in this century; when old men, dying in their beds, mumble something unintelligible to the nurse, it is some of those lines that they will be repeating' (Haffenden 1983: 401). Poets naturally prefer to write poetry; like Auden's, their prose is often a matter of commissioned reviews, which militates against the extended critical treatise. Fuller and Hecht are two who have written at book-length about Auden (MacKinnon included Eliot and Lowell in his book); the helpfulness of Fuller's *Commentary* I have already attested (see Further reading, **p. 151**); Hecht's study is more personal and less disciplined in its approach, distinctly unmarked by Brodsky's venerative attitude and composed by one who, once Auden's junior, writes from a septuagenarian perspective Auden himself never attained. It is provokingly full of Hecht, as he deplores Auden's unhelpful punctuation, finds the second part of 'Memorial for the City' to be 'afflicted with a congestion of internal rhymes to a degree I find insupportable' (1993: 332), or proposes that 'Hunting Season' would be improved if its stanzas were in a different order. All this suggests impatience with conventionally academic approaches to poetry, that is signalled more acidly when he scornfully records the title of a paper given at a 1989 conference: ' "The Pea That Duty Locks": Clitoral Images and Masturbation in Emily Dickinson' (1993: 438; Auden, who once shared with MacNeice the absurdity of a symposium where some 'juggins' bored on about alienation, might have relished this). Discussing the 'vision of Agape' Auden implied had been experienced by himself and his colleagues in 'A Summer Night', Hecht strikes an untranscendental note: 'Having common concerns as they did, it is not difficult to imagine that a sense of deep mutual respect and liking would make itself felt, perhaps even quite suddenly, among them. The real test of being able to love one's neighbor would be to stand at the intersection of Broadway and Forty-second Street and undertake to love the first five, or twenty, or one hundred people who passed by' (1993: 55). He professes himself 'enormously grateful' for 'September 1, 1939' which he sees as a 'literary monument' (1993: 152), but finds that, here again, in evoking 'the Just' Auden offers a limiting vision of community: '[I]n addition to being either private persons or members of society, we may be, if fortunately endowed, members of an insulated elite, who view the historical calamity not quite with immunity, but with the dispassion that makes them "the Just". It is with this select group that Auden identifies himself' (1993: 169).

Judging that *Nones* and *The Shield of Achilles* contain some of Auden's best poetry, Hecht clearly does not align with the Jarrell–Larkin axis on what happened to Wystan; for him, 'In Praise of Limestone' is 'one of Auden's finest and most successful poems' (1993: 304). This view discriminates him from Levi, who in his Oxford lecture on his predecessor asserts that 'Auden's moment was the 1930s, the age of anxiety, but the climax of the 1930s was the war, and after the London Blitz what Auden has to say pales into insignificance' (1991: 234). That very closeness of association between poetry and age meant that when, as Levi sees it, Auden apostatised, history exacted her revenge: 'The peculiar inadequacy of ['New Year Letter'] is observable as falsity of tone, but more deeply it has to do with date. Auden's intellectual musings and his charm are not serious enough for 1940, because we know what happened then, and his poems demand to be read in their historical context' (1991: 239). This also recalls Jarrell's furious reproach that some remarks Auden made, reviewing an edition of Grimms' fairy-tales in 1944, showed how far he had lost touch with what the world consisted of during that terrible year (for this in particular and Jarrell's responses to Auden in general, see Ian Sansom's essay in *AS* III); Levi's position also resembles Larkin's view of early Auden that '[f]ew poets since Pope have been so committed to their period' (Haffenden 1983: 415). The story, thus, is one of diminution: 'When at last he turned to the attempt to write great poems on a social scale, "In Praise of Limestone" for instance, we feel an affection and admiration for the result, but they are not great poems any more than Clough's "Amours de Voyage". On almost all occasions, his art simply refuses to be monumental' (Levi 1991: 235).

Craig Raine, who collects prose pieces about Auden in both *Haydn and the Valve Trumpet* (1990) and *In Defence of T.S. Eliot* (2000), also believes that 'America seems to mark the turning point, the inauguration of the long change' (1990: 346); and like some others, he believes this change was for the worse: quoting the first twelve lines of 'New Year Letter' (Part II), he comments, '[w]hat inert stuff it is, this imitation Auden, rambling on until it finally bumps into the real thing' (embodied by the ensuing couplet). Unlike others, he is less inclined to see this deterioration as the consequence of Auden's desertion of England, but rather ascribes it to the religion he rediscovered, via Kierkegaard, whose explanatory force leaves the poetry 'curiously sapped' (1990: 353):

> Other once-potent properties reappear in the later poetry, sagging visibly. Satan, for instance, in Auden's early demonology was an unspecified personification – the Supreme Antagonist, the Adversary, the death-wish and defeatist in us all. After 1940, the Devil is still interior, but tricked out with traditional props, verging on a comfortably baroque caricature.
>
> (1990: 354)

So, too, when older Auden reinvokes his lead-mining landscapes, the spell no longer binds, because necessary elements of dread or uncertainty have been laid to rest: in Raine's view, whatever comforts Christianity brought the man, it was finally 'inimical to his poetic gifts' (1990: 355), and although his later poetry has its 'charm', 'it is markedly inferior' (1990: 354).

Raine's assessment of Auden is more measured than Brodsky's (whose work in English Raine comprehensively derides, in a piece in *In Defence of T. S. Eliot*). Heaney, who prints a memorial appreciation of Brodsky in *Finders Keepers: Selected Prose 1971–2001* (2002), also reprints with slight abridgements his 1986 lecture 'Sounding Auden', where the preference – implicit in his 1976 review of the *Collected Poems* (Haffenden 1983: 493–6) – for 'those entirely compelling, if estranged and estranging words of his famous earliest poems' continues to prevail: 'Even Eliot's openings, startling as they were, could not equal Auden's for defamiliarizing abruptness' (2002: 191). For the work of this first period Heaney has the highest praise, because like Raine he hears it fraught with a presentiment of the dreadful that turns out, in retrospect, to have struck a note of lasting truth:

> Yet the doom and omen which characterized the 'strange' poetry of the early 1930s, its bewildered and unsettling visions, brought native English poetry as near as it has ever been to the imaginative verge of the dreadful and offered an example of how insular experience and the universal shock suffered by mankind in the twentieth century could be sounded forth in the English language.
>
> (2002: 200)

Even work from the mid-1930s begins to lose that force; its increasing 'traditional formal obedience' suggests to Heaney 'a weakening of his original refusal of the conventional musics, and a consequent weakening of the newness and otherness of his contribution to the resources, if not to the supply, of poetry' (2002: 195). Although Heaney does his best to appreciate the virtues of what followed, his praise is fainter:

> Long before the parable poetry of post-war Europe, Auden arrived at a mode that was stricken with premonitions of an awful thing and was adequate to give expression to those premonitions by strictly poetic means. But this unified sensibility fissured when Auden was inevitably driven to extend himself beyond the transmission of intuited knowledge, beyond poetic indirection and implication, and began spelling out those intuitions in a more explicit, analytic and morally ratified rhetoric. In writing a poem like 'Spain', no matter how breathtaking its condensation

> of vistas or how decent its purpose, or a poem like 'A Summer Night', no matter how Mozartian its verbal equivalent of *agape*, Auden broke with his solitude and his oddity. His responsibility towards the human family became intensely and commendably strong and the magnificently sane, meditative, judicial poems of the 1940s, 1950s, and 1960s were the result.
>
> (2002: 199)

Wallace Stevens declared in a letter that 'the belief in poetry is a magnificent fury, or it is nothing' (1996: 446); Heaney audibly prefers the challengingly strange and discomfiting early Auden, whose later poetry embodying a magnificent sanity cannot command the same degree of admiration. Yet Stevens's formula precisely describes the kind of magniloquent Romantic frenzy against which Auden sternly and self-denyingly set his face; which Heaney recognises, in his speculation that 'it is perhaps because of Auden's susceptibility to this tremblingly delicious power of poetry that he constantly warns against it' (2002: 195). In 1963 Auden wrote to Spears that 'I cannot tell you how embarrassed and distressed I felt during those years in the Thirties when I was "in fashion". I knew the popularity had nothing to do with any real value my work might have and that I should, very justly, have to pay for it later' (quoted in Jacobs 1998: 133). This probably reflects 1960s rather than 1930s Auden; yet notwithstanding his assertion that poetry made nothing happen, Auden retained some concern for the ways in which it might actually prompt bad impulses and actions. This is implied by Fenton, who succeeded Levi in the Oxford Professorship, and in whose resulting volume, *The Strength of Poetry* (2001), Auden is a pervasive presence and subject of the last three lectures. 'Auden', writes Fenton, 'was a rhetorician. He knew himself to be a rhetorician of the highest powers, and, when he saw the power he had, he recoiled from it in deep horror' (2001: 218): this offers an explanation for his refusal to be 'monumental', in Levi's term. His career also valuably corrects any overestimate of an 'England' of diminishing returns: 'there was a forward impulse in Auden's life that involved renunciation. He had renounced in his poetry a certain kind of rhetoric. He had renounced political engagement. He had really renounced England, and that was not forgiven him' (2001: 240). Fenton repudiates as irrelevant any notion of Auden having betrayed England by his expatriation; but his final view of the poet interestingly suggests a recurrence, in the later life, of aspects of dread found and celebrated by others in the earlier work: 'perhaps that forward impulse of renunciation implied a gesture towards the terrible. This was where his gift had brought him, to this lean country and these caves of accusation' (2001: 249).

The Australian Peter Porter is untroubled by nationalist resentments; but in his essay 'Auden's English', he notes the astonishing derivative badness of much of Auden's juvenilia, and asks how nonetheless his voice emerged 'out of the Edward Thomas and Yeatsian imitations and the Hardy taciturnity into that Auden dawn' (*CCWHA*: 124). Sudden as the transformation was, however, Porter judges even early Auden inconsistent, finding 'Paid on Both Sides' overrated, compared to the brilliance of *The Orators*. This perhaps underlines my opening observation of the unlikelihood of achieving critical consensus; but what remains is the poetic consensus, that Auden repays attention; and this is where I want to come to rest. As well as those so far mentioned, Simon Armitage, Robert Crawford, Douglas Dunn, Glyn Maxwell and Paul Muldoon have all in one way or another addressed Auden in verse or prose, as have Iain Crichton Smith, Donald Davie and C.H. Sisson from an earlier generation; there will certainly be others (see also Sansom's essay 'Auden and influence', *CCWHA*). Why? One answer may be that, aside from the compelling if excluding solitude and oddity of the early work, there is a helpful quality of approachability to his *oeuvre*: Auden didn't mind being 'silly like us', embracing a kind of commonality, following that initial austere remoteness. Anne Ridler, who worked as Eliot's secretary during the 1940s and became a poet, recalled that whereas Eliot's example made her despair of ever succeeding, Auden's encouraged her to find it possible. For Fenton, who interestingly addresses Auden's criticism as well as his poetry, part of the older poet's value is his atttitude to poetry as a communal strength, rather than an individualised arena of struggle with contemporaries or precursors who might be discouragingly better than oneself. The title of his volume of lectures, *The Strength of Poetry*, derives from a comment Auden made in a 1942 letter to Spender, contrasting their respective attitudes to others' work; this articulates a relationship between the individual talent and tradition, and with contemporaries, different from Eliot's model: one which enabled Auden to be an enthusiastic anthologist as well as an embracer of light verse. It offers an appropriate note on which to end this section, and this book: 'You', he told Spender, 'can be jealous of someone else writing a good poem because it seems a rival strength. I'm not, because every good poem, of yours say, is a strength, which is put at my disposal' (*AS* I: 82).

Chronology

Bullet points denote events in Auden's life; asterisks denote historical and literary events. *(Volume titles given for Auden's poetry collections are as first published)*

1907

- Born at York, 21 February; family moves to Birmingham the following year

1914

- Auden's father enlists, does not return until war ends

* 'Great War' starts (August 1914 to November 1918)

1915

- Attends prep school in Surrey, where he meets Isherwood

1917

* 'February Revolution' in Russia leads to end of Romanov dynasty and installation of provisional government, itself overthrown by 'October Revolution' when Lenin and Bolsheviks seize power

1920

- Moves to Gresham's School, in Norfolk

1922

- March, discovers he wants to write poetry, at Robert Medley's prompting

* Publication of Joyce's *Ulysses* (in Paris) and Eliot's *The Waste Land*

1924

* January, death of Lenin; first Labour government (non-majority) in Britain under Ramsay Macdonald; November, Conservative government under Stanley Baldwin (huge majority)

1925

- Summer, takes the first of many trips abroad (to Salzburg, with his father); autumn, goes up to Christ Church, Oxford, with an Exhibition to read Natural Sciences, which he relinquishes on changing to English; during undergraduate years meets Spender, Day-Lewis, MacNeice, Rex Warner, Betjeman

* Start of Mussolini's dictatorship in Italy

1926

* May, General Strike lasts for nine days and, failing to achieve objectives, represents a setback for trade unionism generally and coal-miners in particular (Auden is untypical of his class in assisting the Trade Union Congress)

1928

• Graduates with a Third Class degree in Summer 1928; Spender publishes privately a pamphlet edition of Auden's poetry; becomes engaged to a nurse; August, apparently undergoes analysis in Belgium to 'cure' his homosexuality, but from October 1928 to July 1929 immerses himself in gay culture of Weimar Republic (mostly in Berlin, where he meets John Layard); brief visits back to England; breaks off engagement on his final return

* Stalin, established as Lenin's successor, announces centralised control of economy, collectivisation of agriculture, in first 'Five-Year Plan' for USSR (from October)

1929

* October, Wall Street 'crash' heralds economic collapse in USA and Europe

1930

• January, 'Paid on Both Sides' published by Eliot in *Criterion*; September, *Poems* published by Faber & Faber; from 1930 to 1932 Auden teaches at Larchfield Academy, Helensburgh

1931

* August, MacDonald resigns as Labour Prime Minister, returns heading a 'National Government' which in October General Election wins huge majority

1932

• May, *The Orators*, mostly written at Helensburgh; from 1932 to 1935 Auden teaches at the Downs School, Colwall, where he meets Michael Yates

1933

• November, *The Dance of Death*, Auden's play (privately performed by Group Theatre the following year, publicly in 1935 alongside Eliot's *Sweeney Agonistes*)

* January, Hitler elected Chancellor of Germany as Nazis decisively take power

1934

• Summer, drives through Germany and Central Europe with Yates and another friend; the trip is written up as 'In Search of Dracula' for the Downs School magazine

1935

- May, *The Dog Beneath the Skin*, end-product of an extended collaboration with Isherwood (performed by Group Theatre in the following year); July, leaves Downs School to work in London with GPO Film Unit on various projects, the best-known being the film *The Night Mail*; meets Britten

* June, Baldwin succeeds MacDonald, as leader of a 'National Government' Conservative in everything but name; September, Hitler addresses mass rally in Nuremberg, institutionalising Nazi policies of anti-Semitism; October, Fascist Italy invades Ethiopia, provoking ineffectual international outcry (Italy formally annexes Ethiopia in May 1936)

1936

- From May to September Auden visits Iceland, latterly in company of MacNeice and Yates; September, *The Ascent of F6* (with Isherwood; subsequently revised); October, *Look, Stranger!*

* January, Death of George V; accession – but not coronation – of Edward VIII, who abdicates in December and is succeeded by younger brother, George VI; July, Civil War breaks out in Spain; August, France proposes to Britain policy of non-intervention in Spain; October, 'Jarrow' march of unemployed from north-east to London – the best-known but not the first such demonstration

1937

- January–early March, visits Spain, mostly based in Valencia, intending but in his own view failing to make a significant contribution to Republican cause; writes the poem *Spain* on his return, published in May (royalties go to Spanish medical aid); August, *Letters from Iceland* (with MacNeice)

* April, destruction, by German bombers, of Basque city of Guernica

1938

- Mid-January to mid-July, travels with Isherwood to visit the Sino-Japanese conflict; Auden in Brussels during early autumn; October, *On the Frontier* (with Isherwood; performed November by Group Theatre)

* March, Austria is incorporated into Hitler's Germany (the '*Anschluss*'); September, 'Munich Crisis' – the threat of war posed by Hitler's aggressively expansionist policies is illusorily lifted, when Neville Chamberlain accedes to his demands for Czech territory in talks at Munich

1939

- January, Auden and Isherwood set sail for New York; March, *Journey to a War* (with Isherwood); April, meets Chester Kallman (18), with whom he travels across USA that summer

* January, Spanish Civil War ends with victory for right-wing Falangist forces, ushering in repressive Franco regime (until 1975); March, Hitler occupies Prague, breaking Munich agreement; September, Hitler's invasion of Poland triggers Second World War in Europe

1940

- February, *Another Time*, mostly containing poems written in Europe; during the war years and after Auden works in various teaching positions at school, adult education and university levels, returns to (an evolving version of) Christianity, and applies for US citizenship

* May, June, France collapses under German *blitzkrieg*, British and some French forces are evacuated from Dunkirk; USA rejects French plea to intervene

1941

- March, *The Double Man*, Auden's first wholly American collection; August, Auden learns of the death of his mother; this follows previous month's crisis in his relationship with Kallman

* June, Hitler invades Soviet Union, with which Germany had since August 1939 a mutual non-aggression pact – his new enemy becomes Britain's ally; December, Japanese attack on US fleet at Pearl Harbor brings USA into war as well and opens Asian theatre of conflict

1943

* July, Mussolini's rule ends; September, Italy surrenders to Allies (Mussolini is executed by Italian partisans in April 1945)

1944

- September, *For the Time Being*, including 'The Sea and the Mirror'

1945

- April, *Collected Poetry* published in USA; with the end of war in Europe, Auden undertakes his first trip back, as part of US military survey of effects of bombing on German civilian morale; he is away from April to August, and on returning takes up long-term residence in NYC

* 6 and 9 August, atomic bombs dropped on Hiroshima and Nagasaki compel immediate Japanese surrender; the aftermath of war reveals extent of Japanese brutality and German crimes against humanity; Stalin is the last monster left standing, already responsible for the deaths of millions of Soviet citizens, but soon to preside over client Communist states separated by an 'Iron Curtain' from capitalist West

1946

- For the next year or so, Auden has an intense heterosexual affair with Rhoda Jaffe; May, becomes citizen of USA

1947

- July, *The Age of Anxiety*, which wins Pulitzer prize

1948

- April–September, with Chester Kallman makes first extended visit back to Europe, staying in England on inward and outward legs, but spending the bulk of their time in Italy, where they decide to rent a house on Ischia for future summers; May, writes 'In Praise of Limestone' in Florence

- * Soviet land blockade of Berlin forces Western powers to organise airlift to provision their sectors of city (late July–end September; blockade officially ends May 1949)

1949

- • Delivers Page-Barbour Lectures at University of Virginia (published next year as *The Enchafèd Flood*); spends springs and summers at Forio, 1949–57
- * Communist armies establish control of mainland China; fears about Communist infiltration of USA and its allies increase

1950

- • *Collected Shorter Poems 1939–1944* published in UK
- * June, Communist-backed Northern forces attack South Korea, beginning Korean War (armistice finally signed in 1953), in first 'hot' emanation of cold war politics

1951

- • February, *Nones*; September, *The Rake's Progress* premiered in Venice, Auden and Kallman's libretto set to Stravinsky's music
- * Marginally involved in the controversial defection of Soviet double agent Guy Burgess, who had hoped to use Auden's villa *en route* to Moscow from London

1955

- • February, *The Shield of Achilles*
- * May, Austrian independence ends post-war period of allied supervision

1956

- • Auden elected Oxford Professor of Poetry (to 1961)
- * Kruschev denounces his predecessor Stalin, but any hopes of liberal tendency within Communist bloc are dashed by brutal crushing of attempted Hungarian uprising; Britain, France (with Israel) distract international attention by invading Egypt in ill-advised military venture, intended to secure control of Suez Canal and counter threat to shipping route posed by President Nasser; USA compels withdrawal

1958

- • Uses money from Italian literary prize to buy house at Kirchstetten, near Vienna in Austria, which now becomes European base for him and Kallman

1960

- • April, *Homage to Clio*

1961

- • May, *Elegy for Young Lovers*, music by Henze, libretto by Auden and Kallman

* August, erection of Berlin Wall actualises and symbolises division between political systems of East and West (dismantled November 1989)

1962
• *The Dyer's Hand* (based on Oxford lectures)
* October, 'Cuban Missile Crisis', in which President Kennedy uses atomic threat to force withdrawal of Soviet missiles from Cuba; the post-war nuclear 'arms race' intensifies over the next decade, alongside dread of its consequences

1963
* November, Kennedy assassinated in Dallas; US military involvement in Vietnam will escalate under ensuing administrations – as will the protest movement

1964
• October, Auden returns to Berlin for six-month stay sponsored by Ford Foundation
* October, in USSR Brezhnev and Kosygin supplant Kruschev

1965
• July, *About the House*

1966
• August, *The Bassarids*, music by Henze, libretto by Auden and Kallman; November, *Collected Shorter Poems*

1967
* June, 'Six Day War' between Israel and neighbouring Arab states ends in Israeli occupation of large areas of their territory

1968
• October, *Collected Longer Poems*; *Secondary Worlds* (T.S. Eliot Memorial Lectures)
* August, Soviet forces invade Czechoslovakia, to crush liberalising administration of Alexander Dubček and install repressive puppet regime (which lasts until 1989 when Dubček, briefly, returns to public life)

1969
• September, *City Without Walls*
* June, culmination of USA/USSR 'space race', as NASA succeeds in putting first human on the moon

1970
• *A Certain World* (Auden's 'Commonplace Book')

1971
• November, *Academic Graffiti*

1972

- September, *Epistle to a Godson*; September, leaves New York permanently, to take up residence in cottage in grounds of Christ Church, Oxford

1973

- February, *Love's Labours Lost*, music by Nicolas Nabokov, libretto with Kallman; *Forewords and Afterwords*, essays (edited by Mendelson in consultation with Auden); 29 September, Auden dies in a Vienna hotel; buried five days later at Kirchstetten

1974

- *Thank You, Fog*, Auden's final book of poetry (edited by Mendelson), is published posthumously

1975

- Death, in Athens, of Chester Kallman

Further reading

The Select Bibliography gives a fuller list, and Section Three offers more detailed accounts of a wider range of material; what follows, therefore, is a deliberately concise list of writing I have found particularly helpful (with emphasis falling on more recent work), most of whose items will be available in any good university library.

Biographical sources

Despite his stated aversion to biographical approaches in literary criticism, Auden habitually practised it in his assessment of other writers, and during the course of his life put ever more information about himself into the public domain, in prose as well as poetry. Sometimes this was indirectly done, as when he described the experience generating 'A Summer Night' in his foreword to Ann Fremantle's *Protestant Mystics*, or in the resonant allusiveness of *A Certain World*; sometimes it was more overt, as in early parts of *The Dyer's Hand*, his lecture to the Freud Association, or the essay 'As It Seemed to Us' gathered in *Forewords and Afterwords*.

Soon after his death, a commemorative volume of discreet but informative reminiscences was assembled under Spender's editorship, and later still there have been various personal memoirs penned by those who knew him, or believed they did. Auden's embargo on a biography was not, fortunately, long-lived: Charles Osborne made a useful first stab in 1980, but the following year Humphrey Carpenter set the standard with his biography, which benefited from wide research into unpublished material, and revealed many unknown aspects. Supplementing rather than competing with Carpenter, Richard Davenport-Hines's book was also thoroughly researched and profited from further discoveries; it was less bound by chronological exposition, and more sympathetic to the later work.

Carpenter, Humphrey (1981 and later revisions) *W.H. Auden: A Biography*, London: George Allen and Unwin.
Davenport-Hines, Richard (1995) *Auden*, London: Heinemann.
Spender, Stephen (1975) (ed.) *W.H. Auden: A Tribute*, London: Weidenfeld & Nicholson.

Alongside these, the most valuable sources for biographical detail are to be found in Mendelson's two monographs on Auden, and in his introductions to the volumes that have so far appeared, under his exemplary editorship of the *Complete Works*; in the monographs, especially, there is copious quotation from unpublished letters and notebooks. There is also a considerable quantity of information contained in the three volumes so far published in the *Auden Studies* series, which have included previously unpublished material, and sequences of letters to important correspondents such as Spender, the Doddses and the Sterns. The Auden Society publishes a useful if irregular *Newsletter*, sent to subscribers, but with earlier back-issues more generally accessible through the Society's website. Norman Page has written a helpful book about the Berlin years of Auden and Isherwood, which necessarily devotes more space to the latter, who spent more time there. Significant glimpses of Auden, from the perspective of lives with which he intersected, are to be found in Carpenter's later biography of Benjamin Britten, Jon Stallworthy's biography of MacNeice, Bevis Hillier's biography of Betjeman, John Sutherland's biography of Spender, Peter Parker's biography of Isherwood, and John Haffenden's ongoing biography of Empson.

Bibliographical

The standard Auden bibliography is the Bloomfield/Mendelson volume covering the years 1924 to 1969, updated by supplements published in *Auden Studies*. Auden's publishing history is very complicated, because of the different versions in which poems were published, and until a variorum edition has been issued it will remain difficult for readers to gauge precise effects. The 1991 reissue of *Collected Poems* represents Auden's final judgement on his work, but in doing so inevitably misrepresents what that work was as first published. *English Auden* and *Selected Poems* (ed. Mendelson) give earliest versions of the poetry they include.

Reviews of criticism

Haffenden, John (ed.) (1983) *W.H. Auden: The Critical Heritage* (London: Routledge & Kegan Paul).

This offers a very good selection from contemporary reviews of Auden's poetry and drama, from which it is possible to derive a sense of the changing graph of Auden's reputation during his lifetime; Haffenden provides a substantial and helpful Introduction, including a final glance at some of the books on Auden then in print.

Gingerich, Martin E. (1977) *W.H. Auden: A Reference Guide*, Boston, Mass.: G.K. Hall.

Secondary material relating to Auden up until 1976 has been well-described in this title; post-1976 material can most easily be sourced online, through MLA or BIDS databases.

Hendon, Paul (2000) *The Poetry of W.H. Auden: A Reader's Guide to Essential Criticism*, Cambridge: Icon Books.

This is a book-length review of twentieth-century criticism on Auden, providing long extracts from highlighted critical studies, plus bibliography.

Smith, Stan (ed.) (2004) *The Cambridge Companion to W.H. Auden*, Cambridge: Cambridge University Press.

This title includes an essay-length analysis of the reception of Auden's work and a 'Bibliographic essay and review of Auden studies', plus bibliography.

Critical studies

Two scholars are notable for the comprehensiveness of their treatments of Auden: Mendelson, whose *Early Auden* and *Later Auden* meticulously set the work in the context of its composition and its relation to Auden's evolving thought (helpfully rectifying some earlier commentators); and Fuller, whose *Commentary* updates and expands his earlier *Reader's Guide*, offering itself as a reference book which, poem by poem, assembles an enormous quantity of information within an easily retrievable format (*via* two good indexes). These are the fruits of decades-long engagement with Auden's writings, published and unpublished, and are indispensable for anyone wishing to acquire in-depth acquaintance with the entirety of his *oeuvre*.

Fuller, John (1998) *W.H. Auden: A Commentary*, Princeton, NJ: Princeton University Press.
Mendelson, Edward (1981) *Early Auden*, London: Faber & Faber.
—— (1999) *Later Auden*, London: Faber & Faber.

Auden and the 1930s

Hynes's study is focused around Auden, and remains the most helpful introductory overview of its subject; Cunningham and Montefiore focus more on the period. A reader looking to be well-informed about British writing in the 1930s should start with Hynes, progress to Cunningham, and then read Montefiore.

Cunningham, Valentine (1988) *British Writers of the Thirties*, Oxford: Oxford University Press.
Hynes, Samuel (1976) *The Auden Generation: Literature and Politics in England in the 1930s*, London: Bodley Head.

Montefiore, Janet (1996) *Men and Women Writers of the 1930s*, London: Routledge.

There is interesting commentary on work by three principal poets of this period in *Auden, MacNeice, Spender: The Thirties Poetry*, by Michael O'Neill and Gareth Reeves (Basingstoke: Macmillan, 1992).

Auden and religion

Several surveys of Auden's career address the issue of his return to religious belief (e.g., Spears, McDiarmid), which is also dealt with by his biographers. To date, only one book has devoted itself to the subject: Arthur Kirsch's *Auden and Christianity* (New Haven, Conn., and London: Yale University Press, 2005). This is a concise and sensible study attempting to present the centrality as well as the idiosyncrasy of Auden's faith; necessarily, its principal focus is on the later work.

Auden in the context of theory

Bozorth, Richard R. (2001) *Auden's Games of Knowledge: Poetry and the Meanings of Homosexuality*, New York: Columbia University Press.

This is a theoretically sophisticated account of the importance of Auden's homosexuality to the work, properly attentive to its serious playfulness.

Smith, Stan (1985) *W.H. Auden* (Rereading Literature), Oxford: Basil Blackwell.

Intended to bring Auden criticism up to date, this offers lively, disputatious readings of the poems; Smith has written copiously about Auden, and is the critic whose work I would recommend after Mendelson's and Fuller's.

Collections of critical essays

There have been numerous such collections, and any good library will offer more than one. A useful recent addition is the *Cambridge Companion to W.H. Auden* (Smith 2004), previously cited above.

Select bibliography

Note: editions of Auden's own works are listed under 'Abbreviations', **pp. xii–xiii**; the reader's attention is also drawn to the ongoing series of Princeton Critical Editions, under the General Editorship of Edward Mendelson.

Ansen, Alan (1991) *The Table Talk of W.H. Auden*, ed. Nicholas Jenkins, London: Faber & Faber.

Bahlke, George W. (1970) *The Later Auden: From* New Year Letter to About the House, New Brunswick, NJ: Rutgers University Press.

—— (ed.) (1991) *Critical Essays on W.H. Auden*, Boston, Mass.: G.K. Hall.

Bayley, John (1957) *The Romantic Survival*, London: Constable.

Beach, Joseph Warren (1957) *The Making of the Auden Canon*, Minneapolis, Minn.: University of Minnesota Press.

Bergonzi, Bernard (1978) *Reading the Thirties*, London: Macmillan.

Berryman, John (1971) *Love and Fame*, London: Faber & Faber.

Bloom, Harold (ed.) (1986) *W.H. Auden*, New York: Chelsea.

Bloomfield, B.C. and Mendelson, Edward (1972) *W.H. Auden: A Bibliography, 1924–1969*, 2nd edn, Charlottesville, Va.: University of Virginia Press.

Boly, John R. (1991) *Reading Auden: The Returns of Caliban*, Ithaca, NY: Cornell University Press.

Bozorth, Richard R. (2001) *Auden's Games of Knowledge: Poetry and the Meanings of Homosexuality*, New York: Columbia University Press.

Brodsky, Joseph (1986) *Less Than One: Selected Essays*, Harmondsworth: Penguin.

Bryant, Marsha (1997) *Auden and Documentary in the 1930s*, Charlottesville, Va.: University of Virginia Press.

Bucknell, Katherine (ed.) (2003) *W.H. Auden: Juvenilia*, 2nd edn, Princeton, NJ: Princeton University Press.

—— and Nicholas Jenkins (eds) (1990) *The Map of All My Youth: Early Works, Friends and Influences* (*Auden Studies I*), Oxford: Oxford University Press.

—— (1994) *The Language of Learning and the Language of Love: Uncollected Writing, New Interpretations* (*Auden Studies II*), Oxford: Oxford University Press.

—— (1996) *In Solitude, for Company: W.H. Auden After 1940: Unpublished*

Prose and Recent Criticism (*Auden Studies III*), Oxford: Oxford University Press.

Buell, Frederick (1973) *W.H. Auden as a Social Poet*, Ithaca, NY: Cornell University Press.

Caesar, Adrian (1991) *Dividing Lines: Poetry, Class, and Ideology in the 1930s*, Manchester: Manchester University Press.

Callan, Edward (1983) *Auden: A Carnival of Intellect*, New York: Oxford University Press.

Carpenter, Humphrey (1981) *W.H. Auden: A Biography*, London: George Allen and Unwin.

Carter, Ronald (1984) *Thirties Poets: 'The Auden Group'*, London: Macmillan.

Clark, Thekla (1995) *Wystan and Chester: A Personal Memoir of W.H. Auden and Chester Kallman*, London: Faber & Faber.

Collett, Anthony (1932) *The Changing Face of England*, 2nd edn, London: Nisbet & Co.

Cunningham, Valentine (1988) *British Writers of the Thirties*, Oxford: Oxford University Press.

Davenport-Hines, Richard (1995) *Auden*, London: Heinemann.

Day-Lewis, Sean (1980) *C. Day-Lewis: An English Literary Life*, London: Weidenfeld & Nicholson.

Duchêne, François (1972) *The Case of the Helmeted Airman: A Study of W.H. Auden's Poetry*, London: Chatto & Windus.

Ellis, Steve (1991) *The English Eliot: Design Language and Landscape in* Four Quartets, London: Routledge.

Emig, Reiner (1999) *W.H. Auden: Towards a Postmodern Poetics*, London: Macmillan.

Everett, Barbara (1964) *Auden*, Edinburgh: Oliver & Boyd.

—— (1986) *Poets in Their Time*, London: Faber & Faber.

Farnan, Dorothy J. (1985) *Auden in Love*, London: Faber & Faber.

Fenton, James (2001) *The Strength of Poetry*, Oxford: Oxford University Press.

Firchow, Peter E. (2002) *W.H. Auden: Contexts for Poetry*, Newark, Del.: University of Delaware Press.

Fuller, John (1998) *W.H. Auden: A Commentary*, Princeton, NJ: Princeton University Press.

Gingerich, Martin E. (1977) *W.H. Auden: A Reference Guide*, Boston, Mass.: G.K. Hall.

Gottlieb, Susannah Young-ah (2003) *Regions of Sorrow: Anxiety and Messianism in Hannah Arendt and W.H. Auden*, Stanford, Calif.: Stanford University Press.

Greenberg, Herbert (1968) *Quest for the Necessary: W.H. Auden and the Dilemmas of Divided Consciousness*, Cambridge, Mass.: Harvard University Press.

Haffenden, John (ed.) (1983) *W.H. Auden: The Critical Heritage*, London: Routledge & Kegan Paul.

Heaney, Seamus (2002) *Finders Keepers: Selected Prose 1971–2001*, London: Faber & Faber.

Hecht, Anthony (1993) *The Hidden Law: The Poetry of W.H. Auden*, Cambridge, Mass.: Harvard University Press.

Hendon, Paul (2000) *The Poetry of W.H. Auden: A Reader's Guide to Essential Criticism*, Cambridge: Icon Books.
Hillier, Bevis (2002) *John Betjeman: New Fame, New Love*, London: John Murray.
Hobsbawm, Eric (1994) *Age of Extremes: The Short Twentieth Century*, London: Michael Joseph.
Hoggart, Richard (1951) *Auden: An Introductory Essay*, London: Chatto & Windus.
Hynes, Samuel (1976) *The Auden Generation: Literature and Politics in England in the 1930s*, London: Bodley Head.
Isherwood, Christopher (1977) *Christopher and His Kind: 1929–1939*, London: Methuen.
Jacobs, Alan (1998) *What Became of Wystan: Change and Continuity in Auden's Poetry*, Fayetteville, Ark.: University of Arkansas Press.
Jenkins, Nicholas (forthcoming) *The Island: W.H. Auden and the Making of a Post-National Poetry*, Cambridge, Mass.: Harvard University Press.
Jones, Chris (2002) 'W.H. Auden and "the 'Barbaric' poetry of the North": unchaining one's daimon', *Review of English Studies*, 53 (210): 167–85.
Kermode, Frank (1988) *History and Value*, New York: Oxford University Press.
Kirsch, Arthur (2005) *Auden and Christianity*, New Haven, Conn., and London: Yale University Press.
Lawlor, Patrick T. (ed.) (1989) *W.H. Auden: Poems 1927–1929* 'A Photographic and Typographic Facsimile . . .', New York: New York Public Library.
Leavis, F.R. (1963) *Scrutiny: A Retrospect*, Cambridge: Cambridge University Press.
Levi, Peter (1991) *The Art of Poetry*, New Haven, Conn.: Yale University Press.
Lucas, John (ed.) (1978) *The 1930s: A Challenge to Orthodoxy*, Brighton: Harvester Press.
MacKinnon, Lachlan (1983) *Eliot, Auden, Lowell: Aspects of the Baudelairean Inheritance*, London: Macmillan.
Marchetti, Paola (2001) *Landscapes of Meaning: From Auden to Hughes*, Milan: Università Cattolica.
McDiarmid, Lucy (1978) 'W.H. Auden's "In the year of my youth . . ." ', *Review of English Studies*, XXIX (115): 267–312.
McDiarmid, Lucy (1984) *Saving Civilization: Yeats, Eliot, and Auden Between the Wars*, Cambridge: Cambridge University Press.
—— (1990) *Auden's Apologies for Poetry*, Princeton, NJ: Princeton University Press.
Mendelson, Edward (1981) *Early Auden*, London: Faber & Faber.
—— (1999) *Later Auden*, London: Faber & Faber.
Mitchell, Donald (1981) *Britten and Auden in the Thirties: The Year 1936*, London: Faber & Faber.
Montefiore, Janet (1996) *Men and Women Writers of the 1930s*, London: Routledge.
O'Neill, Michael and Reeves, Gareth (1992) *Auden, MacNeice, Spender: The Thirties Poetry*, Basingstoke: Macmillan.
Myers, Alan and Forsythe, Robert (1999) *W.H. Auden: Pennine Poet*, Nenthead: North Pennines Heritage Trust.

Orwell, George (1962 [1940]) *Inside the Whale and Other Essays*, Harmondsworth: Penguin.
Osborne, Charles (1980) *W.H. Auden: The Life of a Poet*, London: Methuen.
Page, Norman (1998) *Auden and Isherwood: The Berlin Years*, London: Macmillan.
Parker, Peter (2004) *Isherwood*, London: Picador.
Paulin, Tom (2002) *The Invasion Handbook*, London: Faber & Faber.
Pound, Ezra, (1971) *Selected Poems*, London: Faber & Faber.
Priestley, J.B. (1937 [1934]) *English Journey*, 'Cheap Edition', London: Heinemann (Gollancz).
—— (1960) *Literature and Western Man*, London: Heinemann.
Raine, Craig (1990) *Haydn and the Valve Trumpet*, London: Faber & Faber (Picador reissue, 2000).
—— (2000) *In Defence of T.S. Eliot*, London: Picador.
Replogle, Justin (1969) *Auden's Poetry*, Seattle, Wash.: University of Washington Press.
Rodway, Allan (1984) *A Preface to Auden*, London: Longman.
Rowse, A.L. (1987) *The Poet Auden: A Personal Memoir*, London: Methuen.
Scarfe, Francis (1942) *Auden and After: The Liberation of Poetry 1930–1941*, London: Routledge & Sons.
Sherry, Norman (1989) *The Life of Graham Greene*, vol. I, London: Jonathan Cape.
Sidnell, Michael. (1984) *Dances of Death: The Group Theatre of London in the Thirties*, London: Faber & Faber.
Smith, Stan. (1985) *W.H. Auden* (Rereading Literature), Oxford: Basil Blackwell.
—— (1987) 'Missing Dates: From *Spain 1937* to "September 1, 1939" ', *Literature and History* 13: 155–74.
—— (1994) 'Remembering Bryden's bill: Modernism from Eliot to Auden', *Critical Survey* 6 (3): 312–24.
—— (1997) *W.H. Auden* (British Council series), Plymouth: Northcote House.
—— (2004) (ed.) *The Cambridge Companion to W.H. Auden*, Cambridge: Cambridge University Press.
Spears, Monroe K. (1963) *The Poetry of W.H. Auden: The Disenchanted Island*, New York: Oxford University Press.
Spender, Stephen (1935) *The Destructive Element*, London: Jonathan Cape.
—— (1951) *World Within World*, London: Faber & Faber (1977 reissue).
—— (1975) (ed.) *W.H. Auden: A Tribute*, London: Weidenfeld & Nicholson.
—— (1985) *Journals 1939–1983*, London: Faber & Faber.
Stallworthy, Jon (1995) *Louis MacNeice*, London: Faber & Faber.
Stevens, Wallace (1996) *Letters of Wallace Stevens*, Berkeley, Calif.: University of California Press
Sutherland, John (2004) *Stephen Spender: The Authorized Biography*, London: Penguin.
Trotter, David (1984) *The Making of the Reader: Language and Subjectivity in Modern American, English and Irish Poetry*, Basingstoke: Macmillan.
Underhill, Hugh (1992) *The Problem of Consciousness in Modern Poetry*, Cambridge: Cambridge University Press.

Upward, Edward (1938) *Journey to the Border*, London: Enitharmon (1994 reissue).
—— and Isherwood, Christopher (1994) *The Mortmere Stories*, London: Enitharmon.
Woods, Gregory (1987) *Articulate Flesh: Male Homo-eroticism and Modern Poetry*, New Haven, Conn., and London: Yale University Press.

Index

Alston Moor (Cumberland) 3, 6, 19, 32, 40, 67, 72, 98
Andersen, Hans Christian 32, 75
Anderson, Lindsay 47
Ansen, Alan 60
Aristotle 13
Arnold, Matthew 36
Athens 8
Auden, Bernard (brother) 29
Auden, Constance (mother) 1, 2, 9, 28, 29–30, 59, 72, 74; death 5, 30, 59
Auden, George (father) 1, 2, 3, 6–7, 10, 16, 21, 28, 29, 31, 33, 43, 52, 68, 105; death 30
Auden, John (brother) 1, 4
Auden, Wystan Hugh: **Life and career:** as American 6, 12, 110, 136; collaborations 3, 4, 7, 12, 25, 39, 41, 52, 53, 54, 55, 122, 123; education 1–2; emigration 4, 27, 33, 36–7, 111, 123, 133–4, 136; homosexuality and heterosexual relationships 2, 3, 4, 5, 28, 30, 31, 42, 43, 46, 50, 72, 73, 84, 134–5; lead-mining interest 2, 3, 5, 31, 32, 58, 67, 71, 98, 139; lecturing 6, 7; literary attitudes 9, 10, 12, 13–14, 20, 23, 24, 38; 'nursery library' 8–9; political attitudes 5, 12, 13, 15, 17, 18–19, 20, 21, 23, 24, 25; religious attitudes 6, 35–6, 38, 57, 60, 62, 72, 79, 101, 104, 129–30, 139; schoolmastering 3, 24–5; scientific bent 33; travels abroad 4; wartime service 6, 28, 58; **Works:** *About the House* 7, 65, 113; 'Academic Graffiti' 64; *The Age of Anxiety* 6, 35, 59–61, 62, 63; 'Amor Loci' 66, 67, 98, 100–1; *Another Time* 4, 5, 55–6, 62, 84; 'Ascension Day, 1964' 65; *The Ascent of F6* 3, 49, 55, 105; 'As I Walked Out . . . ' 84; 'August for the People . . . ' 14, 15, 27, 50, 52, 90; 'Bucolics' 63, 101, 104–7; 'By the Gasworks, Solihull' 10; *A Certain World* 32, 71, 149; 'Certainly Our City . . . ' 50; 'The Chase' 54, 55; 'The Chimneys Are Smoking . . . ' 50; *City Without Walls* 7, 65–6, 112; *Collected Poetry* (1945) 6; *Collected Shorter Poems* (1966) 7, 61, 119; 'A Communist to Others' 13, 14, 51; 'The Composer' 56, 91; 'Consider this . . . ' 18, 76–8, 79; 'Control of the Passes . . . ' ('The Secret Agent') 71–2; *The Dance of Death* 3, 49, 54, 63; 'The Dark Years' 57; 'Dichtung und Wahrheit' 63, 64; *The Dog beneath the Skin* 3, 22, 49, 55, 79, 81, 82, 122; *The Double Man* (*New Year Letter*) 4, 56–8; *The Dyer's Hand* 7, 10, 67, 80, 95, 97, 103, 111, 135; 'Easily, My Dear, . . . ' 52; *The Enchafèd Flood* 7, 82; 'The Enemies of a Bishop' 41, 49, 54; *Epistle to a Godson* 7, 65, 113; 'First Things First' 64; 'Fleet Visit' 63, 92; 'For the Time Being' 35, 58, 59, 60, 95; *For the Time Being* 5–6, 58–9, 61; 'From Scars . . . ' 43, 72; 'From the Very First Coming Down' ('The Letter') 41, 69–70, 71, 75; 'The Garrison' 66; 'Get there if you can . . . ' 18, 34, 42, 77; 'Goodbye to the Mezzogiorno' 64, 65, 100; 'The Good Life' 34, 35, 38; 'The Group Movement and the Middle Classes' 35; 'Hammerfest' 65; 'Hearing of Harvests . . . ' 51; 'Here on the Cropped Grass . . . ' 51, 81; 'A Homage to Clio' 69; *Homage to Clio* 7, 63–5; 'Hongkong' 54; 'Horae Canonicae' 62, 63, 101–4, 129; 'A Household' 63; 'Hunting Season' 63, 137; 'I Chose this Lean Country' 10; 'In Memory of W.B. Yeats' 4, 11, 13, 38, 56, 61, 89, 94–5, 107, 111, 116, 137; 'In Praise of Limestone' 7, 62, 63, 98–100, 101, 138; 'In Search of Dracula' 25, 52, 68; 'In the Year of My Youth . . . ' 49, 78; 'In Time of War' 54, 58, 87–8, 91; 'It Was Easter As I Walked . . . '

('1929') 72–6, 78, 79; *Journey to a War* 3, 26, 53–4, 87, 121, 123; 'Journey to Iceland' 12; *Juvenilia* 9, 39, 69, 140; 'Lay Your Sleeping Head . . .' ('Lullaby') 4, 56, 67, 82–4; 'A Literary Transference' 9; 'Letter to Lord Byron' 9, 10, 16, 52, 58, 77, 84, 95, 105; *Letters from Iceland* 3, 11, 25, 52–3, 54, 123, 136; 'Look, Stranger . . .' ('On This Island') 50, 81–2; *Look, Stranger!* 4, 17, 40, 49–52, 56, 78; 'A Lullaby' 66; 'Macao' 54; 'Memorial for the City' 62, 93, 99, 137; 'Moon Landing' 66; 'A Moon Profaned' 65; 'Morality in an Age of Change' 37; 'Musée des Beaux Arts' 4, 56, 91–2, 94; 'A New Year Greeting' 66; 'New Year Letter' 4, 32, 57–8, 59, 63, 80, 92, 95, 98, 138; 'The Night Mail' 3, 122; 'Nones' 102–3; *Nones* 7, 61–3, 100, 138; 'Not in Baedeker' 62, 98; 'The Novelist' 56, 91; 'Now from My Window-sill . . . ' 51; 'O for Doors to Be Open . . . ' 51; 'O Love, the Interest Itself . . . ' 50, 79; 'Ode to Gaea' 63, 107; 'The Old Lead-Mine' 67; *On the Frontier* 3, 25, 55; *The Orators* 3, 12, 19, 20, 24, 43–9, 50, 51, 52, 57, 59, 60, 61, 71, 72, 78, 113, 121, 125, 132, 140; 'Out on the Lawn I Lie . . .' ('A Summer Night') 3, 24–5, 50, 51, 78–81, 93, 138, 140; 'Paid on Both Sides' 3, 20, 25, 140; *Paul Bunyan* 4; 'A Permanent Way' 63; *Poems* (1930) 3, 20, 40–3; *The Poet's Tongue* 12, 14, 24, 38, 125; 'The Prolific and the Devourer' 5, 13, 21, 31, 34, 35, 37, 38, 56, 57, 89; 'Prologue at Sixty' 10, 66; 'The Prophets' 5, 100; 'Psychology and Art Today' 33, 34, 38; 'The Quest' 57, 58; *The Rake's Progress* 7; 'River Profile' 66; 'The Sabbath' 63; *Secondary Worlds* 8; 'The Sea and the Mirror' 6, 58, 59, 61, 95–8, 131; 'September 1, 1939' 4, 11, 13, 14, 23, 27, 56, 58, 67, 84, 88–91, 96, 116, 137, 138; 'The Shield of Achilles' 92–3, 130; *The Shield of Achilles* 7, 62, 63, 64, 104, 138; 'Since' 25, 52, 66, 84; 'Sir, no man's enemy' 14, 41, 42; 'Spain' 3, 14, 15, 26, 84–7, 89, 91, 92, 116, 121, 122; 'Spain 1937' 55, 64, 84, 104; 'Squares and Oblongs' 17, 38, 135; 'The Strings' Excitement . . . ' 42; 'Talking to Myself' 66; 'Thanksgiving for a Habitat' 64, 65, 107–9; 'Thank You, Fog' 66; *Thank You, Fog* 7, 65; 'That Night When Joy Began' 50, 79; 'To Settle in This Village . . . ' 51; 'The Truest Poetry Is the Most Feigning' 63; 'A Walk after Dark' 62; 'Watch Any Day His Nonchalant Pauses' 41, 42; 'Which of You Waking Early' 41, 43; 'Whitsunday in Kirchstetten' 65; 'Who stands, . . . ' ('The Watershed') 2, 39, 43, 67–9, 70, 71, 101, 113; 'Who Will Endure' 106; 'Will You Turn a Deaf Ear' 41, 42; 'Woods in Rain' 39; 'Work, Carnival, and Prayer' 129 132

Auschwitz (concentration camp) 92, 93
Austria 7, 17, 22, 26, 53, 64, 65, 66, 69, 88, 108

Baldwin, Stanley 21, 22
Benjamin, Walter 93
Bergonzi, Bernard 16
Berlin 2, 3, 34, 40, 42, 43, 72, 73, 75, 76
Berlin, Isaiah 105
Berkeley, Lennox 50
Betjeman, John 2, 6, 12, 13, 30
Birmingham 1, 29; Harborne 2, 29, 67; Solihull 1, 10
Birmingham University 1, 29
Blake, William 34, 58, 129
Blea Tarn (Lake District) 10, 13
Blunt, Anthony 52, 53, 135
Boly, John 66, 68, 78, 96, 114, 115, 116, 132, 133
Bozorth, Richard 72, 76, 84, 115, 128, 129, 133, 134, 135
Brecht, Berthold 55, 108
Brezhnev, Leonid (and Kosygin) 66
Britten, Benjamin 3, 4, 5, 6, 24, 26, 50, 53, 59, 82, 84, 122
Brodsky, Joseph 67, 136, 137, 139
Brontë, Emily 96
Brussels 4, 54, 56, 91
Bryanston School 25, 50, 52
Buchan, John 71
Bucknell, Katherine 9, 10, 39, 69, 75
Burgess, Guy 28, 135
Burrows, Trigant 73
Butler, Samuel 57
Byron, George Gordon, Lord 11, 26, 52, 53

Callan, Edward 108, 125, 128, 132, 135
Campbell, Sir Malcolm 22
Campbell, Roy 119
Carpenter, Humphrey 11, 29, 34, 36, 50, 110, 112, 113, 128, 149, 150
Carritt, Gabriel 19, 69, 72
Carroll, Lewis 106
Cauldron Snout 71
Chamberlain, Neville 22, 134
Chaplin, Sid 69
Chekhov, Anton 74
Cheltenham 3, 21
China 20, 22, 25, 26, 28, 39, 53, 54, 91; Manchuria 22

CIA 92, 135
Claudel, Paul 94
Coghill, Neville 11
Coleridge, Samuel Taylor 69
Collett, Anthony 19, 79, 81, 98
Columbia University 4
Colwall 3, 50, 51, 80
Communist Party 15, 19
Connolly, Cyril 84, 114
Conrad, Joseph 71
Cowley, Malcolm 57
Cranston, Maurice 70
Criterion, The 3, 9, 10, 40, 44, 45, 89, 110
Cunningham, Valentine 11, 17, 19, 74, 79, 117, 119, 121, 122, 124, 151
Czechoslovakia 4, 22, 66, 92

Dachau (concentration camp) 80, 88, 90
Dante, Alighieri 17, 49, 53, 58, 125
Davenport-Hines, Richard 20, 21, 25, 29, 34, 149
Davie, Donald 63, 100, 141
Davies, W.H. 10
Day-Lewis, Cecil 2, 3, 19, 20, 21, 84, 114, 122, 136; *The Magnetic Mountain* 19, 20
De la Mare, Walter 10
Denmark 4
Derbyshire 2
Dickinson, Emily 9, 42, 126, 137
Dodds, E.R. 29, 84, 90; Mrs E.A. 29, 37, 64
Doone, Rupert 3, 75, 122
Dover 56, 82
Downs School 3, 25, 26, 50, 51, 52, 79, 121
Drayton, Michael 83
Dubcek, Alexander 66
Dunne, J.W. 74
Durer, Albrecht 6

Egypt 4, 26, 29
Eliot, T.S. 2, 3, 4, 9, 10, 11, 12, 14–15, 20, 27, 36, 39 40, 41, 42, 44, 45, 46, 51, 53, 75, 85, 89, 104, 110, 114; *Sweeney Agonistes* 3; *The Waste Land* 9, 12, 14, 15, 19, 40, 44, 45, 46, 48
Emerson, Ralph Waldo 37
Empson, William 40, 55, 136
Engels, Friedrich 95
Ethiopia 14, 22

Faber & Faber 3, 7, 9, 40, 41, 45, 49, 52, 56, 61, 84

Fenton, James 136
Fisher, A.S.T. 72
Florence 7, 98, 99
Forio (Isle of Ischia) 7, 28, 99, 101
Forster, E.M. 54, 67, 91
France 4, 23, 27, 53, 94, 120
Franco, Francisco 3, 22, 53, 86
Fraser, G.S. 62
Freud, Sigmund 23, 30, 33, 34, 35, 36, 56, 98, 100, 129, 130, 131
Frost, Robert 10, 105, 111
Fuller, John 44, 47, 48, 54, 56, 60, 65, 69, 71, 72, 74, 75, 77, 78, 79, 80, 81, 85, 87, 90, 91, 95, 99, 102, 103, 104, 106, 137, 151, 152
Fussell, Paul 16

Gardiner, Margaret 36
Garrett, John 12
General Strike 17
Germany 2, 4, 6, 14, 15, 17, 18, 21, 22, 23, 26, 28, 30, 34, 43, 52, 58, 60, 62, 73, 75, 88, 89; Nuremberg 6, 14; Weimar Republic 2, 21
George VI, King 4
Gide, André 75
Glasgow 2, 3, 25
Goering, Herman 25
Goethe, Johann Wolfgang von 13, 64, 91, 97
GPO Film Unit 3, 25, 121, 122
Graves, Robert 122
Great War 1, 16, 18, 29, 34, 44, 47, 90, 93
Greene, Graham 18, 27, 47, 135
Greenhurth (Teesdale) 71
Gresham's School (Holt) 2, 31, 33, 75
Grierson, John 122, 123
Grigson, Geoffrey 25, 38, 44, 53, 117, 126
Groddeck, Georg 34, 131
Groote, Kurt 73
Group Theatre 3, 25, 53, 122
Gunn, Thom 63, 71, 136

Hadrian's Wall 19
Haffenden, John 40, 44, 50, 54, 57, 62, 63, 84, 112, 113, 114, 136, 137, 138, 139, 150
Hall, Donald 63
Hammett, Dashiell 89
Hardy, Thomas 10, 24, 77, 140
Harrison, Tom 24
Hayward, John 44
Heaney, Seamus 66, 136, 139, 140
Hecht, Anthony 86, 99, 115, 127, 137, 138
Helensburgh 3, 12, 43, 44, 45, 47, 50
Hitler, Adolf 14, 21, 22, 23, 27, 36, 52, 53, 80, 89, 99, 107
Hobsbawm, Eric 16, 18, 26
Hopkins, Gerard Manley 42, 104
Hough, Graham 63, 117

Housman, A.E. 56, 91
Hughes, Ted 66, 112
Hunger Marches 18, 25, 80
Hungary 4, 22
Hynes, Samuel 14, 119–20, 121, 122, 124, 151

Ibsen, Henrik 55
Iceland 9, 11, 25, 52, 53, 64
Isherwood, Christopher 2, 3, 4, 5, 11, 14, 15, 17, 20, 25, 26, 27, 35, 36, 39, 41, 48, 49, 50, 53, 54, 55, 67, 72, 73, 82, 94, 95, 108, 110, 114, 122, 124, 134
Isle of Man 14
Isle of Wight 50, 81
Italy 7, 17, 18, 22, 23, 62, 98, 99, 100, 103

Jaffe, Rhoda 30, 61
Japan 4, 26, 60
James, Clive 65, 113–14
James, Henry 12, 15, 95, 96
Jarrell, Randall 57, 63, 111, 112, 114, 137, 138
Jenkins, Nicholas 116, 127
Joyce, James 14, 15, 114, 120
Jung, Carl 35, 60, 80 97

Kallman, Chester 5, 6, 7, 8, 30, 33, 37, 56, 58, 59, 64, 67, 95, 98, 101, 108, 123
Keats, John 10, 92
Kierkegaard, Søren 36, 57, 61, 97, 101, 129, 130, 131, 138
Kipling, Rudyard 94
Kirchstetten 7, 8, 64, 65, 101, 107
Köhler, Wolfgang 45

Lake District 7, 10, 28, 68, 69, 105, 106
Lane, Homer 34, 36, 41, 73, 132
Langland, John 49, 107
Larchfield Academy 3, 43, 46, 49
Larkin, Philip 63, 112, 128, 136, 138
Lawrence, D.H. 5, 34, 47, 73, 77, 129, 131
Lawrence, T.E. 34
Layard, John 34, 41, 45, 73, 97, 132
Lear, Edward 56
Leavis, F.R. 44, 111
Lee, Gypsy Rose 4
Levi, Peter 136, 140
Levi, Primo 93
Lipking, Lawrence 99
Listener, The 79
London 2, 3, 4, 7, 25, 26, 41, 45, 72, 80
Lowell, Robert 95, 112, 137

MacDonald, Ramsay 21–2, 46
MacNeice, Louis 2, 3, 5, 13, 25, 29, 39, 43, 52, 53, 64, 107, 114, 117, 122, 128, 136, 137
McCullers, Carson 4
McDiarmid, Lucy 49, 87, 93, 125, 130, 131
McDougall, William 78
McElwee, Bill 40, 69, 72, 73, 75; Patrick 40
Madge, Charles 24, 119
Malvern Hills 3, 51
Mann, Erika 30, 50, 56
Mann, Elizabeth 56
Marlborough School 52
Marvell, Andrew 57
Marx, Karl 15, 33, 34, 35, 36, 92, 120, 123, 129, 130, 131, 132
Mass Observation 24, 25, 120, 123
Mayer, Elizabeth 4, 5, 57, 98, 99
Medley, Robert 9, 31, 75
Melville, Herman 56, 84
Mendelson, Edward 4, 12, 27, 36, 37, 42, 45, 47, 48, 49, 51, 54, 57, 58, 59, 60, 61, 66, 73, 74, 82, 83, 87, 92, 96, 97, 99, 101, 102, 103, 105, 107, 110, 112, 115, 127, 128, 129, 150, 151
Meyer, Gerhart 73
Michelangelo 99
Milton, John 37
Mitchison, Naomi 43, 46, 47, 113
Montaigne, Michel de 56
Moore, Marianne 12
'Mortmere' 35, 48, 55, 72
Morton, H.V. 19
Mussolini, Benito 14, 15, 52
Myers, Alan (and Robert Forsythe) 69, 135

Nash, Ogden 89
Nash, Paul 93
Nation 37
Nenthead 68
New Mexico 5
New Republic 94
New Verse 25, 38
New York 4, 5, 6, 7, 8, 37, 60, 61, 62, 88, 89, 94, 116; Brooklyn 4; Fire Island 6, 62, 70; Long Island 4; Yorkville 35
Niebuhr, Reinhold 36, 62; Ursula 62

Orwell, George (Eric Blair) 26, 37, 84, 114
Owen, Wilfred 34
Oxford 2, 7, 8, 9, 14, 17, 18, 19, 20, 28, 30, 33, 39, 56, 69, 72, 73, 80, 106, 126, 136, 138, 140; Christ Church College 2, 8, 30, 72, 126
Oxford Book of Light Verse 11, 12

Page, Norman 34, 73, 150

Paris 2, 7, 27
Paris, Gaston 106
Parker, Peter 82, 110, 114, 150
Partisan Review 94, 114
Pascal, Blaise 56, 95
Pater, Walter 99
Paulin, Tom 136
Pears, Peter 4
Pearson, Norman Holmes 135
Pennines 7, 31, 58, 62, 67, 98
Perse, St John (Alexis St Leger) 105
Poland 22, 23, 35, 88
Pope, Alexander 57, 93, 128, 130
Porter, Peter 140
Portugal 4
Pound, Ezra 16, 19, 20, 125
Powell, Dilys 50
Priestley, J.B. 16, 19, 27; *English Journey* 19

Raine, Craig 138, 139
Random House 6, 7, 53, 56
Review of English Studies 49
Richards, I.A. 33, 36
Riding, Laura 9, 42, 122, 126
Rilke, Rainer Maria 87, 88, 90
Rimbaud, Arthur 56, 58, 91
Rivers, W.H.R. 34
Roberts, Michael 20, 117, 119
Robinson, John 108
Rookhope (Weardale) 32, 67, 100, 107
Rothermere, Lord 22

Sassoon, Siegfried 34
Schwartz, Delmore 59
Scrutiny 24, 62, 111, 112, 121
Second World War 5, 23
Sedbergh School 40, 69
Shakespeare, William 6, 17, 42, 61, 68, 80, 95, 96, 98; *Hamlet* 68, 97; *Macbeth* 103; *Midsummer Night's Dream* 80; *The Tempest* 6, 59, 95, 96, 97, 125
Shaw, George Bernard 18
Shelley, Percy Bysshe 38, 66, 128
Sherry, Norman 18, 27
'Slump, The' (Great Depression) 17, 18, 19, 21
Smart, Christopher 79
Smith, Stan 12, 22, 36, 44, 45, 46, 47, 54, 55, 57, 59, 62, 64, 76, 77, 87, 89, 91, 94, 101, 104, 107, 115, 120, 125, 127, 132, 133, 134, 152
Soviet Union 18, 23, 66
Spa (Belgium) 2
Spain 22, 25, 26, 28, 53, 82, 85, 88, 120; Barcelona 26, 35, 94; Civil War 3, 13, 22, 25, 26, 85, 94, 121; Guernica 22
Spender, Stephen 2, 6, 11, 16, 17, 20, 21, 23, 24, 35, 36, 39, 41, 43, 50, 58, 59, 63, 94, 114, 117, 118, 119, 127, 135, 136, 141; *The Destructive Element* 35; *World Within World* 17, 23
Stalin, Josef 18, 21, 23, 107, 111
Stein, Gertrude 9, 42, 73, 126
Stern, James (and Tania) 6, 8, 37
Stevens, Wallace 36, 99, 106, 115, 140
Stravinsky, Igor 7
Strong, Patience 17
Swarthmore College (Pennsylvania) 6, 59, 97

Tennyson, Alfred, Lord 9, 14, 42
Threlkeld 7, 69; Wescoe 29, 30, 69, 72, 74, 84, 105
Thomas, Edward 10, 140
Thucydides 89, 90
Tillich, Paul 35
TLS 44, 65
Toller, Ernst 56
Toynbee, Arnold 99
Treaty of Versailles 15, 22, 89
Trotter, David 85, 118, 127
TUC 18

Upward, Edward 2, 20, 21, 35, 48, 72
USA 4, 12, 26, 53, 56, 62

Venice 7
Vienna 8
Virginia, University of 7
Voltaire 56

Warner, Rex 20, 23, 24
Warrington 17
Waugh, Evelyn 53, 54
Whitman, Walt 11
Wigan 17
Williams, Charles 36, 57
Williams, William Carlos 12, 108
Wilson, Edmund 40
Wittgenstein, Ludwig 106
Wordsworth, William 10, 12, 13, 33, 53, 68, 82
Workers' Educational Association (WEA) 13
Wulf and Eadwacer 71

Yates, Michael 25, 50, 52, 56, 64, 66, 84
Yeats, W.B. 4, 10, 11, 40, 42, 48, 51, 56, 74, 75, 88, 89, 94, 99, 114, 125
Yugoslavia 4, 29, 43, 68, 116